Tribal Development and Inclusive Policy

About the Author

Dr. Nupur Tiwari is currently working as Associate Professor, Rural Administration and Panchayati Raj at The Indian Institute of Public Administration, (IIPA), New Delhi. She is also the Coordinator for Centre for Public Policy, Planning and Development.

Her current research interests include Decentralization and Local Governance (Panchayati Raj), Gender Issues in Public Policy and Tribal Self-Governance.

She has thirty eight research papers/articles published in National and International journals. She has authored four books and three monographs and has contributed chapters in eleven in this volumes.

She has headed four major projects, commissioned by Government of India, in the capacity of the Project Director on—1. PESA and Left Wing Extremism (LWE): A Study of Extremist Affected Areas of Jharkhand, Chhattisgarh and Odisha; 2. Impact of MGNREGA in narrowing Gender-gap in the Informal Workforce: A Comparative Study of Women participation in Uttar Pradesh; 3. Independent Evaluation of SHGs under ICDS; and 4. Independent Evaluation of "The Extent of Customers Satisfaction with the Quality of the Kendriya Bhandar".

She has also worked on five major projects funded by IDRC, Irish Aid, Union Ministry of Panchayati Raj, Ministry of Rural Development and UNDP. She has prepared several Reports for Government of India.

She has lectured vastly in India and Abroad. Earlier, she served as Senior Consultant to the former Union Minister of Panchayati Raj, providing inputs on Local government. She was a faculty member at LBSNAA, Mussoorie, and was involved in training the Civil Servants.

She is a Member of Research Committee of Ministry of Human Resource Development, Government of India. She is also a Member of Expert Committee of Women Study Centre of Mizoram University. She was a Member of Thematic Group on Panchayati Raj and Local-self Government set-up by Ministry of DoNER. She was involved in the Expert Committee for Leveraging Panchayati Raj, set-up by Ministry of Panchayati Raj, Government of India. She was recently nominated as the Domain Expert for the spot study for Prime Minister's award for excellence in Public Administration.

Tribal Development and Inclusive Policy

Edited by

Nupur Tiwari
Associate Professor
Rural Adminstration & Panchyati Raj
Indian Institute of Public Administration, New Delhi

CONCEPT PUBLISHING COMPANY PVT. LTD.
NEW DELHI-110059

ISBN-13: 978-93-86682-20-8

First Published 2018

Published and Printed by

Concept
Since 1974

Concept Publishing Company Pvt. Ltd.

Regd. Office:

A/15-16, Commercial Block, Mohan Garden,
New Delhi-110059 (INDIA)
T: +91 11 25351460, +91 11 25351794
E : publishing@conceptpub.com, *W* : www.conceptpub.com

Cataloging in Publication Data--Courtesy: D.K. Agencies (P) Ltd. <docinfo@dkagencies.com>

National Consultation on "Repositioning Tribal Question for Public Policy" (2014 : New Delhi, India)

Tribal development and inclusive policy / edited by Nupur Tiwari.

pages cm

"This book is an outcome of a two day National Consultation on "Repositioning Tribal Question for Public Policy" organized at the Indian Institute of Public Administration, New Delhi on 19-20th March, 2014. It was held in collaboration with the Indian Council of Social Science Research (ICSR)"—Preface.

Includes bibliographical references and index.

ISBN 9789386682208

1. Tribes—Government policy—India—Congresses. 2. Tribes—India—Economic conditions—Congresses. 3. Tribes—India—Social conditions—Congresses. I. Tiwari, Nupur, editor. II. Indian Institute of Public Administration, organizer. III. Indian Council of Social Science Research, organizer. IV. Title.

LCC GN635.I4N38 2014 DDC 305.800954 23

नन्द कुमार साय
अध्यक्ष
NAND KUMAR SAI
CHAIRPERSON

सत्यमेव जयते

भारत सरकार
राष्ट्रीय अनुसूचित जनजाति आयोग
छठी मंजिल, लोकनायक भवन,
खान मार्किट, नई दिल्ली–110003
GOVERNMENT OF INDIA
National Commission for Scheduled Tribes
6th Floor, Loknayak Bhawan,
Khan Market, New Delhi -110003
Tel. : 011-24635721, Fax : 011-24624628

Foreword

It is of vital importance to bring clarity to the discourse on tribal rights, which is often overshadowed by confusing rhetoric. The persistence of socio-economic backwardness of the Tribals, in spite of the development efforts, warrants a special and focused strategy, to enable them to share the benefits of overall economic growth in a more equitable manner.

A fairly well established fact today is that the institutions set up under the provisions of the Constitution of India for the protection of the *adivasis* have not functioned properly and the various laws and policies enacted from time to time for this purpose have not been implemented primarily due to the wrong development policies adopted by the state which have tended to strengthen rather than weaken the political and economic power of the non-*adivasis vis-à-vis* the *adivasis*.

Pressures from business interests, left wing extremism and ecological crises make it imperative to engage ever more urgently with the tribal scenario. A sustained grievance has been about consistent ignoring by the development-drivers, of empirical evidence on injustice and policy-failure gathering since independence. Unfortunately, community response has been emergence of identity politics which is antithetical to the tribal ethos, while official responses were mostly limited at updating the vocabulary.

I extend my heartiest congratulations on the coming of this book, which is an attempt to bring forward the issues and the challenges of Tribal Development. It is an effort to reach out to the wider public with the ideas that call for action and to generate deliberations and discussions.

I hope this book would be one of his kinds and be helpful to facilitate Tribal development. The book would prove to be a meaningful contribution to the academic world and would be quite helpful for research and consultation.

Please accept my best wishes to carry such deliberations and many more beyond seminars and conferences.

(Nand Kumar Sai)

5th July, 2017
New Delhi

Preface and Acknowledgements

The book is an outcome of a two day National Consultation on "Repositioning Tribal Question for Public Policy" organized at the Indian Institute of Public Administration, New Delhi on 19-20th March, 2014. It was held in collaboration with the Indian Council of Social Science Research (ICSSR). This Consultation was called to holistically reassess the issues pertaining to tribal rights and bring to light the issues and concerns of the Tribal areas to be able to shape a vibrant policy paper for future action.

Of all the views expressed by the speakers in the seminar the book tries to bring some of them, for the consultation of policy-makers, academicians, students, NGOs etc. This work would not have been possible without the contributions and involvement of a host of participants.

I take this opportunity to express a deep sense of gratitude to Shri T.N. Chaturvedi, Chairman, IIPA and Dr. Tishyarakshit Chatterjee, Director, IIPA for extending their valuable guidance, encouragement and support, which helped me in completing this task through various stages.

The support of the IIPA faculty, administration, and my research team are deeply acknowledged.

Thanks are due to Kapil Sikka, Research Scholar, Jamia Millia Islamia University and Jaya Kumari, University of Delhi for their Research assistance.

Finally, I would like to acknowledge the support and love of my family. They all kept me going and this book would not have been possible without them.

Editor

Contents

List of Contributors

Ashima Srivastava, Research Scholar, Department of Education, Allahabad University, Allahabad (U.P.), Email: ashimasri@yamail.com

Prof. B.N. Kamble, Professor, Centre for Educational Studies, Indian Institute of Education, J. P. Naik Path, Kothrud, Pune, Maharashtra, Email: bnkamble@hotmail.com, Ph.: 25436980, Extn-215

Dr. Gunajit Sarma, Assistant Professor in Economics, Department of Humanities and Social Sciences, Central Institute of Technology, Kokrajhar, BTAD, (Assam)-783370. Email: gsecit.2009@redoffmail.com

Minashree Horo, Research Scholar, Jawaharlal Nehru University, New Delhi, Email: minashree20@yahoo.co.in, Mob.: 09711940346

Dr. Nupur Tiwari, Faculty, Associative Professor, Indian Institute of Public Administration, New Delhi, Email: Nupur.tiwary@gmail.com, Ph.: 011-23468340

Dr. (Mrs) Prabha Shastri Ranade, Senior Fellow (ICSSR), M. S. University, Baroda (Gujarat), Email: ranadeprabha@gmial.com

Rahul Banerjee, Social Activist, Dhas Gramins Vikas Kendra, 74, Krishnodayanagar, Khandwa Naka, Indore (Madhya Pradesh), Email: rahul.indauri@gmail.com, www.dhasgraminvikaskendra.com

Dr. Ramya Ranjan Patel, Assistant Professor in Economics, Dayal Singh (E) College, New Delhi, Email: visionramya7@gmail.com, Mob.: 8800779221

Dr. S.C. Roy, Associate Professor, Chanakya National Law University, Patna (Bihar), Email: scroy2010@gmail.com, Mob.: 9431619749

Satyam Sunkari, Post-Doctoral Fellow, Council Social Development, Hyderabad (Telengana)-500030, Email: satyamnaani@yahoo.co.in, Mob.: 91-9912564877

Shankar Tadwal, Social Activist, Dhas Gramins Vikas Kendra, 74, Krishnodayanagar, Khandwa Naka, Indore (Madhya Pradesh), Email: rahul.indauri@gmail.com

Sthitapragyan Ray, Assistant Professor, National Institute of Rural Development and Panchyati Raj, Hyderabad (Telengana), Email: mail4sthita@yahoo.co.in

Introduction

The impasse in preparation of any policy for the Scheduled Tribes in India is of attaining the right balance between preservation of tribal identity, culture and values, protecting the tribes from being swamped by mainstream lifestyles, while increasing and ensuring their access to mainstream education, health care and income generation so that the quality of their life is improved.[1] The number of individual tribes scheduled under the Constitution is quite large (standing today at nearly 700 State specific Scheduled Tribes), and also the heterogeneity is immense. Each tribe is quite distinct from the other with, usually, separate languages and dialects, customs, cultural practices and life styles. To preserve this immense diversity is an enormously difficult task, particularly since, in bringing the benefits of development to them in education, health and income generation, a significant amount of mainstreaming, and consequent loss of diversity, is inevitable.[2]

Despite all the diversities, similarities do exists, though in broad generic contours. Their dwelling patterns, communitarian living, harmony with nature, the uniqueness of culture, distinctive customs, traditions and beliefs which are simple, direct and non-acquisitive by nature.[3] Some of these broadly similar characteristics like primitive traits, distinctive culture, geographical isolation, shyness of contact and backwardness have been used as criteria to identify and declare a particular community as a Scheduled Tribe, which in today's context are pejorative and hence needs to replace with terms that are not derogatory.

"The Constitution of India contains several provisions for ensuring a better quality of life for the weaker sections of society and STs, in particular, based on a policy of positive discrimination and affirmative action on the developmental and regulatory fronts. The architects of the Constitution being conscious of the separate identity of the tribal communities and their habitat provided certain articles exclusively devoted to the cause of the STs. These include Articles 244, 244A, 275(1), 342, 338(A) and 339".[4]

The Fifth Schedule of the Constitution provides for administration and control of Scheduled Areas and Scheduled Tribes and gives powers to the Governors to make regulations for the peace and good governance of the Scheduled Areas. Similarly, the Sixth Schedule also contains specific provisions for the administration of tribal areas in the States of Assam, Meghalaya, Tripura and Mizoram. Deriving force from these enabling provisions in the Constitution aimed at ensuring social, economic, and political equity, several specific legislations have further been enacted by the Central and the State Governments for the welfare and protection of STs and their tribal domain.[5]

Notwithstanding the Constitutional safeguards, the tribals particularly in the Fifth Schedule areas and Central India continue to remain deprived, exploited and alienated in various forms, be it the issue of forest right, land, water etc. In fact, the development paradigm of the Indian state in the post-independence period has only worsened the condition of the tribals rather than creating enabling conditions for them. Being rich in mineral and natural resources, the areas inhabited by the tribes became the target of the developmental agenda of the new Indian state. The rampant extraction of natural resources and building of dams to fuel the 'national growth' invariably rendered the tribals displaced, impoverished and alienated. The developmental strategy of the state not only excluded the tribals, but also left them utterly destitute and vulnerable. The much-vaunted popular support enjoyed by the Maoist party can be then discerned in the experience of exploitation and alienation suffered by the tribal population.

It is in recognition of the need to address the tribal discontent that Bhuria Committee was constituted in 1994. The Committee sought to explore and make recommendations on the matter of extending the provisions of Part XI of the Indian Constitution to the Scheduled Areas. Based on the report of the Bhuria Committee, the PESA (Panchayat Extension to Scheduled Areas) Act was enacted by Parliament in December 1996. The PESA Act covers the Fifth Scheduled Areas of nine States, namely—Chhattisgarh, Jharkhand, Orissa (Odisha), Gujarat, Himachal Pradesh, Maharashtra, Madhya

Pradesh, Andhra Pradesh and Telangana. The reasoning behind the enactment of PESA Act was that, through the qualified extension of the provisions of self-governance enumerated in the Part IX of the Constitution to the Scheduled Areas, the problems faced by the tribals could be addressed and mitigated.

The threat of Naxalism has loomed large on the Indian state for a little over four decades now. It has transformed itself from its humble revolutionary beginnings to what is now one of the biggest internal security threats in independent India. The link between left-wing extremism and tribal discontent is attested by the entrenchment of the Maoist or Naxalite (as they are interchangeably referred to as) activities in the Dandakaranya[6] forest region of Central India, which is predominantly inhabited by various tribal communities. Riding on the popular support of the *adivasis*, the Maoist party has managed to spread its influence and activities across. In fact, the violence has escalated in the recent years so much so that Naxalism has been termed by the Prime Minister of the time as "the biggest internal security challenge".[7] Conversely, the response of the government to Naxalism has, at most times, betrayed the absence of a cohesive policy to address the spiraling extremism as well as the lack of a deeper understanding of the structural problems that have generated a 'nexus' between the *adivasis* and the Maoists.

The book through various case studies questions the various Constitutional provisions, welfare programmes etc. focusing on the upliftment of the tribal population along with development.

The first chapter on **"Development Challenges in Tribal Areas: LWE and PESA"** by Dr. Nupur Tiwari starts with the history of tribal exploitation and alienation. The genesis and growth of the Naxalite movement and the infliction of considerable human suffering is illustrated and guerilla warfare as irregular warfare is dealt with. Most of the political commentators refer to the Naxalite operation as unconventional warfare. The difference between conventional combat and unconventional warfare is that in the former the objective is to gain control over a state by defeating the military force of the opponent. In the latter form however, the strategy is to first gain control over the civil population of the state and then proceed to gain total control over the state.

Naxalites present themselves as defenders of the poor and

marginalized, they and their ideology also attract several intellectuals. one needs to take note of the historical trajectory of the rights of the indigenous population of the country ever since the days of the independence. It involves several movements that were syncretic to the emergence of tribal resistance in the heartland of India. It is in recognition of the need to address the problem of tribal discontent that Bhuria Committee was constituted in 1994. The Committee sought to explore and make recommendations on the matter of extending the provisions pf Part XI of the Indian Constitution to the Scheduled Areas. Based on the report of the Bhuia Committee, the PESA (Panchayat Extention to Scheduled Areas) Act was enacted by Parliament in December 1996. The PESA Act covers the Fifth Scheduled Areas of nine States The main objective of the Act is to protect tribal communities from exploitative practices by creating a bigger role for the Gram Sabha. The optimism infused by the PESA Act has however failed to take a substantive root. Among the various problems, the biggest stumbling block has been the failure or rather the reluctance on the part of the states to implement the Act in letter and spirit. At present the Central Governemnt is already working with a four pronged approach to peace and development in the Naxal affected districts. One also has to note that as a long term solution, the effective functioning of the Gram Sabha is crucial.

The second chapter **Food Processing Industry and Its Impact on Socio-Economic Upliftment of BTAD Area in Assam** by Gunajit Sarma tries to frame a vision for proper utilization of agricultural products in the greater interest of the socio-economic development of the BTAD area of Assam. According to the autho., in spite of having ample prospect of raw-material, manpower and other element for development of food processing industries in BTAD area, no such satisfactory development has taken place in this area. Consequently, unemployment problem, rate of poverty, underutilization of natural resources and under use of human resources has been rapidly increasing. The author believes that all of these serious problems can be removed-up to a satisfactory mark by well-established food processing industry in BTAD area.

The third chapter **Tribal Sub-Plans and Implementation in India** by Ashima Srivastava focuses on the socio-economic conditions of the tribal population in India. The author believes that the Scheduled

Tribes (STs) have been among the most disadvantaged sections of our society due to their socio-economic exploitation and isolation over a long period of time. They lag behind the rest of the population in terms of both human development as well as economic indicators. The Twelfth Five Year Plan noted that the incidence of poverty is most pronounced among the STs across all social groups. Though efforts have been made for bringing them at par with the rest of the population, gaps still exist. Therefore, the chapter argues that the general welfare schemes and programmes can be quite helpful in addressing the problems.

The fourth chapter **Economic Empowerment of the Tribal Communities through Traditional Knowledge: Problems and Prospects** by S.C. Roy seeks to study the way to empower the tribal communities through the protection of their traditional knowledge. But there is no documentation of their knowledge. It is not limited to the medicinal herbs rather their cultural heritage, tribal system of medicine, folklore and dances which are being copied by the film industries. The Constitutional protection and PESA provision are also the subject of investigation in this chapter.

The fifth chapter **Effectiveness of Developmental Programmes for Scheduled Tribes in Maharashtra** by B. N. Kamble study the effectiveness of developmental programmes for Scheduled Tribes in Maharashtra. The study utilised data, both at secondary as well as primary levels. The secondary level data used in order to understand the trends in plan efforts of the developmental programmes for the Scheduled Tribes. The study is based on micro-level primary data of 375 sample households families belonging to Scheduled Tribes of Maharashtra, three divisions and three districts namely—Pune, Ahmednagar and Thane and three development blocks namely—Junnar (127 sample households), Akole (123 households) and Murbad (125 sample households) respectively.

The analysis of effectiveness of the programmes is broadly organised into four groups according to the spirit of the programmes, namely—socio-economic condition, poverty, educational development, and the impact of developmental programmes.

The sixth chapter **Impacting Development: Thought and Practice through Bhili Cultural Rejuvenation** by Shankar Tadwal & Rahul Banerjee study the federation of Bhil Adivasi mass organisations in Western India, the Adivasi Ekta Parishad (AEP), which has over the past two decades or so developed an innovative new tool of development in the form of cultural rejuvenation. The Bhil Adivasis under the aegis of the AEP have conserved and rejuvenated their traditionally rich cultural heritage to forge a new assertive identity for themselves to help them negotiate the complex social, economic and political milieu of a modern liberal democracy and have in the process developed an alternative framework of equitable and sustainable development. This chapter details this brave new world of the Bhil Adivasis of Western India.

The seventh chapter **Sustainable Agricultural Development and Poverty Reduction among the Tribal: A Case of Odisha** by Ramya Ranjan Patel studies the environmental degradation as an inherent part of economic development. The author believes that to achieve high economic growth, it is inevitable to destroy environment. Hence, comes the concept of sustainable development. World Commission on Environment and Development (1987) defines, Sustainable development as "a process of change in which the exploitation of resources, the direction of investments, the orientation of technological development, and institutional change are all in harmony and enhance both current and future potential to meet human needs and aspirations". But, no development activities could take place without the damage to the environment. The concept of sustainable development also has a component of damage to the environment, though it is minimum.

The chapter strongly proposes the case of tribal agriculture technology and practice that has the potential of promoting development (and poverty reduction) with the true spirit of the idea of sustainability, without any damage to environment. It is in this context the study seeks to answer the questions of development and environmental degradation.

The eighth chapter **Policy of Forest Development and Participation of Forest Dependent Tribal People: A Study in Andhra Pradesh** by Satyam Sunkari is an attempt made to understand the forest policies and evolution of people oriented community forestry and its effectiveness with relation to ongoing programmes of forest and forest development in the state. Hence, the study conducted in four prominent forest divisions of the districts of Adilabad, Mahabubnagar, Kurnool and Nellore covering 100 villages by bringing nearly 1646 Adivasis' voice through conducting Group Discussions in all the villages.

The nineth chapter **Tribals and Protected Areas: Protest Dynamics in a Conservation Project in Odisha** by Sthitapragyan Ray studies the dialectical interface between tribals and protected areas mediated through a number of key intervening factors including composition of affected population, historicity and geography of the project, political ideology of actors involved, articulation and mobilization of interest and response of the state. The movement in Nilgiri, located at the trijunction of Balasore, Mayurbhanj and Keonjhar districts in Odisha and part of a mega-habitat belonging to Mahanadian bio-geographical region (a transition zone between the eastern ghats and north-east India bio-geographical zone) derived strength from the local tradition of popular protest and an expedient utilization of tribal identity by a pro-poor political party. To fight for their rights, the affected population of the area consisting primarily of tribals had come together under the banner of the *Bhita-mati Jivan Jivika Surkhya Manch* (BJSM) (Homestead, Life and Livelihood Protection Front). The battle was being fought on two related yet different fronts, i.e., legal and political. The popular approaches, i.e., the Sons of the Soil model, the perversity model or the internal colonialism thesis are found inadequate in dealing with the BJSM-led movement. As a red-green movement, BJSM was trying to balance wildlife conservation and development in the context of Kuldiha sanctuary by recognizing their dialectical complementarity. The political ecology approach combined with the perspectives of populism seems to provide a more nuanced interpretation of the kind of localized environmental politics represented by the BJSM. Thus, the tribal protest discourse here represents the deployment of an acceptable "grammar" embedded within the system to voice doubts about the system itself. That is, it constitutes a discourse that is critical of state power and policies, albeit in a necessarily coded form, one that is permitted within the current climate of opinion.

The tenth chapter **Infrastructure Development and Population Growth in Tribal Belt: Gujarat Experience** by Prabha Shastri

Ranade discusses the population growth in the tribal belt of Gujarat, its infrastructure development and urbanization as Gujarat is one of the developed states in the country known for its high rate of economic development especially during the last decade. It highlights the issues of diversion of forest land for infrastructure development and consequences of urbanization. The chapter takes into consideration public health infrastructure, facilities of drinking water, electricity and development of roads in tribal areas.

Forests play a significant role in tribal economy and in the life of tribal population. Forests are exposed to various pressures including diversion of forest land for infrastructure development. The 2011 assessment of India's forest cover reveals a decrease of forest cover in all the tribal districts of the country. The extent of dense forest in Gujarat has also depleted.

Urbanization is considered as an index of development. Gujarat has emerged as the fastest growing urbanizing State of India. Census of India's 2011 figures reveals that 42.6 per cent of Gujarat's total population lives in urban areas, which is much higher than the national average of 31.16 per cent. The state's high-speed urbanization (an increase in urban population by 35.83 per cent in the last one decade) is the highest in the country and much ahead of the national average of 31.8 per cent. Number of towns in tribal districts have increased from 85 in 2001 to 163 in 2011. Gujarat has increased. On the criteria of urbanization, tribal districts of Gujarat are developing fast. A phenomenal increase in urban population by over 50 per cent has been registered in tribal districts of Sabarkantha, Banaskantha, Valsad and Surat districts. An average per cent of urban population to total population in 12 tribal districts has increased from 31 per cent in 2001 to 37.5 per cent in 2011. This is a pointer to the fact that the tribal belt of Gujarat is attracting population from outside due to development.

The eleventh chapter **Translating Communitization in Health: A Case of Village Health and Sanitation Committees (VHSCs) within National Rural Health Mission (NRHM) in Jharkhand** by Minashree Horo discusses the idea of Communitization Approach based on the underlying principles of community participation for achieving "Health for All". Here the government trust the community and allow them to participate in their health development. In this process community is seen as partners with the government where they handle the management parts of the health institutions and resources set-up for their use and the government looks after the skill development part of enhancing their knowledge and confidence in taking care of the institutions. And in ensuring this the governance system was approached by devolving the powers to the community to get their full involvement of the local people starting from the planning to its implementation. The NRHM accentuates this Communitization of the rural health institutions through strong community participation as an integral element of the functionaries and institutions providing primary health care. And so, VHSC was seen as important modes of allowing local village level planning for health care, ideally, an informed body that includes groups who are otherwise marginalized such as Tribal and especially, the women.

The chapter explores the Communitization process through the VHSCs in Jharkhand a newly formed Tribal dominated state emerged in adverse initial conditions with the little social development including health. A qualitative study of the VHSCs was conducted in the intervention (NGOs) and non-intervention (Governemnt only) area purposively selected from the two Tribal dominated districts namely Gumla and Khunti of Jharkhand by using different techniques like In-depth interviews, Key informant interviews, questionnaires, semi-structured schedules and observations of the 74 respondents of different categorized stakeholders of VHSCs.

Notes

1. See, Draft Report on "National Tribal Policy" (A Policy for Scheduled Tribes in India), http://www.indiaenvironmentportal.org.in/files/tribal.pdf (accessed January 18, 2017).
2. *Ibid.*
3. *Ibid.*
4. *Ibid.*
5. See, https://jobs.undp.org/cj_view_job.cfm?cur_job_id=43348 (January 18, 2017)
6. Dandakaranya region is a stretch of forest area that expanses across the intersecting parts of Chhattisgarh, Andhra Pradesh and Orissa.
7. The Naxal violence has been on the spiral increase since the People's War Group and Maoist Communist Centre merged to form Community Party of India (Maoist) in 2004. It prompted Prime Minister Manmohan Singh to make the statement in 2006.

1

Development Challenges in Tribal Areas
LWE and PESA

Nupur Tiwari

The history of tribal exploitation and alienation goes back to the colonial period when the British enacted legislations to control and manage the forests for commercial purpose.[1] The arrival of colonial administration into the tribal region engendered the introduction of the market economy into the region. This was further accompanied by the influx of moneylenders, landlords and other plainsmen who began to exercise their dominance and control over the tribal population. The double experience of subjugation and exploitation under the colonial administration and the plainsmen locally known as 'dikus' gave rise to numerous tribal rebellions.[2]

The tribal insurrection undoubtedly testified to the resistance of the tribals against the encroachment and violation of their autonomy and way of life. It also led the British to evolve a policy on how to administer the restive tribal areas perceived as distinct from the other parts of India. Accordingly, a policy entailing exclusion of the tribal areas from the standard colonial administration was envisaged, notably ensconced in the Government of India Act, 1919 and Government of India Act, 1935.[3] However, the question over which policy should be adopted *vis-à-vis* the tribes continued to be intensely debated among the colonial administrators and anthropologists.

The onset of the Independence only brought forth the urgency to frame a concrete policy. Consequently, the Fifth Schedule and Sixth Schedule were introduced in the Indian Constitution with the former pertaining to the tribal areas in Central India region and Sixth Schedule to tribal areas in the North East.[4] The Sixth Schedule envisaged a creation of Autonomous District Council while the Fifth Schedule stipulated for the formation of Tribes Advisory Council. The rationale behind the Schedules, in spite of the qualitative difference between the two, was to involve the tribals in the governing of the affairs and matters bearing upon their (own) well-being.

Notwithstanding the Constitutional safeguards, the tribals particularly in the Fifth Schedule areas and Central India continued to remain deprived and alienated in various forms, be it the issue of forest right, land, water etc. In fact, the development paradigm of the Indian state in the post-Independence period has only worsened the condition of the tribals rather than creating enabling conditions for them. Being rich in mineral and natural resources, the areas inhabited by the tribes became the target of the developmental agenda of the new Indian state. The rampant extraction of natural resources and building of dams to fuel the 'national growth' invariably rendered the tribals displaced, impoverished and alienated. The developmental strategy of the state not only excluded the tribals but also left them utterly destitute and vulnerable. The arrival of multi-national/private companies and manufacturing industries resulted in large-scale displacement, exploitation of the tribals not to mention about the spread of diseases and the deaths due to contamination and pollution caused by dumping of industrial wastes.

The tribals also have to face the increasing alienation of their lands to the demand of urbanization to accommodate the outsiders who came to share the spoils of the neo-liberal development. What has added to the misery of the *adivasis* is the complicity of the administration in the rampant onslaught of the private companies and industries. The flipside of this scheme of exploitation is the helplessness and powerlessness of the victims—the tribal people. The much-vaunted popular support enjoyed by the Maoist party can be then discerned in the experience of exploitation and alienation suffered by the tribal population. Given the injustices meted out to them, what more could be appealing to the *adivasis* than the promise of dismantling the structures of oppression, domination, and exploitation?

In fact, the Maoist violence has escalated in the recent years so much so that Naxalism has been termed by the Prime Minister of the time as "the biggest internal security challenge."[5] Conversely, the response of the government to Naxalism has, at most times, betrayed the absence of a cohesive policy to address the spiraling extremism as well as the lack of a deeper understanding of the structural problems that have generated a 'nexus' between the *adivasis* and the Maoists. This has often facilitated the emergence of unwarranted and inhumane campaigns such as 'Salwa Judum'[6] which rather than addressing the root of the problem, ended up exacerbating the predicament of the *adivasis*.

The threat of Naxalism has loomed large on the Indian State for a little over four decades now. It has transformed itself from its humble revolutionary beginnings to what is now one of the biggest internal security threats in independent India. The struggle of the people of the land to fight for what is their right in every sense of the word—the right to life, the right to livelihood, and the right to their property, etc. has resulted in the direct the confrontation with the Indian State. The Naxalite problem for the Indian State is severe and challenging because it has grown and evolved right in the heartland of the country." *The Naxalite movement calls for a total transformation of the political system".[7] They reject parliamentary democracy and attempt to overthrow the state, as to create a new social order ending the exploitation of marginalized and vulnerable communities*

"On April 21, 2010 Indian Prime Minister Manmohan Singh repeated his message that estimated Left-wing Extremism as the gravest internal security threat for the country."[8] This was said two weeks after the worst Maoist attack, where 76 security men were killed in an ambush in the Dantewada District of Chhattisgarh. This recent event is the culminating point of a long persistent escalation process.[9]

The armed group that is challenging the Indian State follows Maoist ideology and calls them self-Naxalites. The genesis of the Naxalite movement can be traced back to a small village in West Bengal known as Naxalbari. In 1967, Bimal Kissan, a young tribal man obtained an order from the court which gave him permission to plough his land. The powerful local landlords had him attacked. This incident caused an outrage among the tribal people and led to a violent movement by them to reclaim their land. This event was the starting point of an organized armed struggle and a movement that spread across other regions in West Bengal, Bihar, Tamil Nadu and Andhra Pradesh.[10] In West Bengal, the government aggressively attempted to clamp down the rebellion using repressive and violent measures. This led to more discontent and anger among the participants of the rebellion and ultimately led to the formation of the All India Coordination Committee of Communist Revolutionaries (AICCR) in 1968. ***"Allegiance to armed struggle and non-participation in the elections"*** formed the cornerstone of the AICCR.[11]

At present, the geographical spread of Naxalism is from the Nepal border to the northern part of Kerala. The Ministry of Home Affairs has stated that there are 223 districts in 20 states which have been impacted. Out of these seven states are severely affected and together, the districts in these states form what is termed as 'the Red Corridor'. These regions comprise mainly of tribal groups and Dalits who form the two most vulnerable communities in the country. The Maoist leadership mobilizes the poor, exploited and discontented. That is why some parts of these affected territories are under the firm control of Maoists and they receive huge support from the inhabited population.[12] Any observer who has taken a glance at the *Red Corridor* will immediately come to the conclusion that the affected areas are those, which are extremely rich in natural resources.[13] These regions are considered geographically to be rich in minerals like natural gases, iron ore, bauxite, nitrates and the like along with other natural resources like timber, tendu leaves, etc.

What is of particular significance is the fact that the advent of neo-liberalism has escalated tensions in the region. On the one hand, the government has been forced to scout for mineral rich lands to be auctioned off to the highest bidder in order to bring in foreign exchange into the country. Hence, it has started targeting the lands of the poor tribals who have occupied these lands from time immemorial. The activities of the Naxalites have also started to become stronger. The reason for the above is the fact these people now have access to information and technology in this era of globalization and have learned to channel resources, including money and other resources from different parts of the world to the desirous locations. They often receive arms and ammunition from various regions of the world, transfer money around the world at the click of a mouse and are more able to effectively keep a tab on the activities of the security personnel using newer and effective technology apparatuses.[14] The government has critically focussed on maintaining law and order in the affected areas as most of these areas which are under Naxal occupation believe in running the parallel administration in the region along with kangaroo courts (*Janta adalats*) to dispel justice. The situation has worsened after the general elections in 2009 and especially after the elected government launched a massive counter operation known as Operation Green Hunt, whereby 70,000 paramilitary troops were deployed in Naxal dominated areas.[15]

Over the last decades or so there has been an increasing awareness on the part of various entities, whether state or non-state actors concerning the use of technology in professing aggression against their enemies. This comes as no surprise to most commentators who have analyzed the evolution of warfare over the last couple of decades. The tremendous technological advancements in the field of arms and ammunitions manufacture have created a scenario resulting in the world arena becoming a highly vulnerable place. This development has been further coupled with the more troubled development of not following any code or mandate with regard to warfare as was previously the case a couple of centuries ago. Both the above-stated developments have resulted in a catastrophic series of wars resulting in huge technological advancements in the field of warfare coupled with heightened levels of profits for firms manufacturing arms and ammunitions. It is recognized and emphasized that military-conflict models do not (and possibly cannot) adequately reflect the full spectrum of terroristic, political, and sociological factors that can be associated with the insurgency. They are, therefore, not sufficient for making predictions about the overall outcome of such conflicts. With the advent of globalization, the boundaries of the world have been increasingly shrunk to advance the interests of mankind. This shrinking of the world has also made easy the availability of technology, the transfer of funds, and the delivery of supplies to non-state actors situated in any part of the world.[16] Seeing that war is waged (in order) to defeat the enemy such object can rarely be accomplished without the infliction of considerable human suffering. Nevertheless, it is (generally) held that the method and scale of destruction are not a matter of arbitrary caprice or mere expediency, but one, which must be kept within well defined limits.

Some commentators like Joseph Kutger refer to guerilla warfare as irregular warfare because they consider it as an aberration to the more conventional forms of warfare as have existed and taken place in history between nations. He states that, *"Irregular warfare comprises all those types of warfare alien to the conventional warfare of the period involved. It is usually employed against an adversary as a means of minimizing his relative advantages, either in numerical strength or in the technology of his weaponry."*[17] The use of irregular warfare has been observed in rebellions against the state, as aid to allies who may be engaged in conflict with an enemy, as an addition to conventional warfare techniques and also as a last resort when regular armed forces are defeated by a superior opponent. It has been observed that once guerilla forces overcome their limitations and weak points, by either raiding enemy supplies or by gaining civil support, they ultimately abandon guerilla tactics since such actions alone cannot be used to defeat the enemy completely. Such ultimate transition of guerrilla campaigns was seen in Tito's triumph in Yugoslavia, Mao Tsetung's in China, Ho Chi Minh's in northern Vietnam, and Fidel Castro's in Cuba.

Most of the political commentators refer to the Naxalite operation as unconventional warfare. The difference between conventional combat and unconventional warfare is that in the former the objective is to gain control over a state by defeating the military force of the opponent. In the latter form however, the strategy is to first gain control over the civil population of the state and then proceed to gain total control over the state.

Naxalite movement in the country draws its genesis from the movements in Asian countries as well as the historic defeat of the Americans in Vietnam. The Naxalites call themselves revolutionaries and draw serious inspiration from the above-stated movements. With the advent of globalization these outfits are able to transfer funds to arms dealers more often than not located outside the international borders of India and receive their consignments wherever they deem fit. The government points to their links with the ISI of Pakistan and the LTTE of Sri Lanka, the LeT and other banned organizations.

Naxalites believe in building physical bases, which are usually located in rural, remote areas. These areas are developed and converted in what they term as 'guerilla zones' and then into 'liberated areas'. In India, Naxal groups operate in central India in the Dandakaranya region, which stretches over parts of Andhra Pradesh, Telangana, Maharashtra, Odisha, Madhya Pradesh and Chhattisgarh. The Government of India has not surveyed this area till date. The Naxalites consider it as a totally liberated area. The concept of guerilla warfare has been closely followed by the Naxalites because it is a very useful way to evade the security personnel who are not familiar with the terrain of the forests. Often the armed struggles between these two groups take place in the jungles as the Naxalites rely on pitched battles and fading into the thick forest growth after the attack.

It would be worthwhile to turn our attention towards some of the social and political causes for the growing sympathy towards the cause of the extremists in the countryside of India. The persistent land revenue policies of the government have also resulted in innumerable losses suffered by the *adivasi* population of the country (Kaur, 2010). With the advent of globalization, a number of Indian and multinational private companies began to operate in Chhattisgarh, Andhra Pradesh, Jharkhand and Odisha to exploit the natural resources in these states with the help of MOU's worth millions. While these companies enter with the promise of development to the inhabitants, it is a known fact that the local people do not get any benefits from such projects. Apart from the problem of extensive mining, the creation of Special Economic Zones and the construction of dams have also led to the displacement of thousands of people and often it is the tribals and Dalits who are affected the most. Nor do the affected receive adequate compensation. Such conditions have led to tribal discontent and have furthered the objective of Naxal groups.

Unfortunately, in our country, the records of resettlement and rehabilitation and payment of compensation for lands and assets acquired from the people for various purposes have been very poor. For certain poor families, it has meant generations of resettlement without being given any compensation. This has led to deprivation and marginalization of the people.[18] Although industrialization did take place in the country, the tribals were deprived of the basic benefits of education and training. Therefore, they could not avail of new opportunities in the industries and remained marginalized.

Being very poor and unmonitored, these areas were developed but had poor connectivity. Even post-independence, the agrarian reforms did not reach these areas. Cosmetic solutions like *Bhoodan* and *Gramdan* were not effective. Corruption, vote bank politics, and atrocities against the Scheduled Castes played havoc with the economic and social fabric of the society. Considering the fact that the Naxalites present themselves as defenders of the poor and marginalized, they and their ideology attract also several intellectuals and students. "*The Naxal movement always had well educated leaders and numerous recent research papers by the Maoists imply an intellectual background by some of their cadres.*"[19]

The major factor behind the creation of a vacuum for Maoists to fill in was the poor functioning of administrative machinery, corruption and inefficiency. Since successive governments had failed to address the needs and aspirations of the people, a sense of disillusionment came over the masses which provided fertile ground for the resurgence of left wing extremism. Naxal leaders have taken advantage of government apathy, reached out to the people and earned goodwill among the tribal people. The absence of a functioning civil administration has given a free hand to Naxal forces to run their own government in these areas. Evidence of such parallel systems can be seen in the holding of *Jan Adalats*, construction of irrigation facilities and collection of tax by Maoist cadres.

The factors of this development resulting in the upsurge of Naxalism in the country are numerous. However, one can state that some reasons are far too apparent in the development of Naxalism in the country. The then President of the National Congress Party, Shri Sharad Pawar in an interview had stated that 'poverty' is one of the primary factors responsible for the spread of Naxalism in the country. The same has been echoed by the then Finance Minister of the country, Mr. P. Chidambaram who said at a recent gathering of the Home Ministry that the only way to curb Naxalism would be to reduce the levels of poverty in the regions affected by the violence and ensure that the government sponsored schemes and programmes are easily available to the people of the region. The government post-1990s has the era of neo-liberal reforms initiated one of the reasons for the unmitigated growth of poverty.

The policies enacted by the government have led several

commentators to allege that the rich-poor gap has extensively increased post the adoption of the opening of the economy. Another interesting factor that can be stated is the fact that the adoption of governmental policies adversely affected the farming community and in a majority of cases, the growth of Naxalism has coincided with those regions where there has been a steady decline in agriculture. Agricultural production expanded all over India in the early years of independence. The reasons were quite a few. The stranglehold of semi-feudal relations of production on the agrarian structure was loosened because of the first phase of land reforms. Pre-independence inflation caused by the Second World War had reduced the burden of land revenue and to some extent, of debt. This resulted in some private investment in the agrarian economy. With the end of colonial rule, some public funds also flowed into agricultural sector in the context of planning for development. All these resulted in a spurt in agricultural production. But this did not last long. The big industrial bourgeoisie gradually acquired dominance among the ruling classes were averse to large public fund flowing into agriculture.

PESA: The Struggle for Self-Governance

One needs to take note of the historical trajectory of the rights of the indigenous population of the country ever since the days of the independence. It involves several movements that were syncretic to the emergence of tribal resistance in the heartland of India. The Bharat Jan Andolan, The National Front for Tribal Self Rule, *Adivasi* Sangaman and the Indigenous and Tribal People's Initiative are some of the prominent movements that in many ways led to an assimilation of cultural identity *vis-à-vis* state intervention. The above coupled with the sensitive intentions shown by administrators like B.D. Sharma prompted the administration to set up the Bhuria Committee, which released its report in 1995. The Report vociferously argued for the control of the productive elements should be handed over to the local population and that state interference in their affairs should be relegated to a minimum. However, as many of the well-intentioned reports deserve, the government too conveniently ignored this.

It is in recognition of the need to address the problem of tribal discontent that Bhuria Committee was constituted in 1994. The Committee sought to explore and make recommendations on the matter of extending the provisions of Part XI of the Indian Constitution to the Scheduled Areas. Based on the report of the Bhuria Committee, the PESA (Panchayat Extension to Scheduled Areas) Act was enacted by Parliament in December 1996. The PESA Act covers the Fifth Scheduled Areas of nine States, namely Chhattisgarh, Jharkhand, Orissa (Odisha), Gujarat, Himachal Pradesh, Maharashtra, Madhya Pradesh, Andhra Pradesh and Telangana. The reasoning behind the enactment of PESA Act was that, through the qualified extension of the provisions of self-governance enumerated in the Part IX of the Constitution to the Scheduled Areas, the problems faced by the tribals could be addressed and mitigated.[20]

The main objective of the Act is to protect tribal communities from exploitative practices by creating a bigger role for the *Gram Sabha*. Since the *Gram Sabha* is a body that is constituted of the people of the village, it would be built with a sense of responsibility and accountability. Panchayats are closer to the people, and therefore, the people of the area have greater confidence in them. According to the provisions of PESA, the *Gram Sabha* is assigned with the power to approve plans and programmes for development and the rehabilitation of persons affected by land acquisition. The tribal communities have also been given control over land, forest and water through the authority of the *Gram Sabha*.[21] The Act entrusts the *Gram Sabha* with the following as paraphrased:

- **Section 4.d:** *Gram Sabha* shall safeguard and preserve the traditions and customs of the people, their cultural identity, community resources and the customary mode of dispute resolution.
- **Section 4.e (i):** *Gram Sabha* shall be responsible for approval of plans, programmes and projects for social and economic development.
- **Section 4.e (ii):** responsible for the identification or selection of persons as beneficiaries under the development programmes.
- **Section 4.(i):** Consultation with Panchayat prior to land acquisition and Rehabilitation and Resettlement activities in the scheduled areas.
- **Section 4.m (ii):** Endows ownership of minor forest produces to *Panchayats*.

- **Section 4.m (iii):** endows power to prevent alienation of land in Scheduled areas and to take appropriate action to restore any unlawfully alienated land of STs.[22]

In particular section (4) (i) of the PESA Act, 1996 which states:

"*The Gram Sabha or the Panchayats at the appropriate level should be consulted before making the acquisition of land in the scheduled Areas for development projects and before re-settling or rehabilitating persons affected by such projects in the Scheduled Areas*".[23] Upadhyay, Sanjay (2004), "Tribal Self-Rule Law and Common Property Resources in Scheduled Areas of India—A New Paradigm Shift or Another Ineefective Sop?" Presented Paper, Tenth Biennial Conference of the International Association for the. This very clearly shows that in case of acquisition in the schedule V areas the provisions of PESA should be strictly adhered to which was enacted to safeguard and preserve traditions and customs of tribal communities and prevent alienation from their homelands.[24]

As tribal societies are mostly homogeneous and monolithic, a participatory democracy constitutionally provided through *Gram Sabhas* is very appropriate for them. Keeping this in view, the Bhuria Committee has recommended making *Gram Sabhas* fulcrum of the entire scheme of Decentralized governance, planning and development in tribal areas. The State legislatures of the states of the fifth scheduled areas were required to amend their respective *panchayat* Acts in conformity with the Extension Act before the expiry of one year. All the States except Bihar and Rajasthan have amended their *panchayat* Acts in consonance with the Extension Act before the deadline. The Odisha Panchayat Act has also made a provision that the customary mode of dispute resolution should be consistent with the "relevant law in force and in harmony with the tenets of the Constitution and human rights."

It may be stated that the provisions of the different State Panchayat Acts have largely been influenced by the biases and mindsets of the State Governments. The meetings of the State Ministers of Panchayati Raj and Tribal Welfare held on September 8, 1997 at New Delhi to discuss the implementation of PESA is a testimony to these biases and mindsets.[25] Most of the Bureaucrats and Ministers from States like Andhra Pradesh and Gujarat raised various questions with the intention to delay the implementation of the act. And States like Rajasthan felt that there was absolutely no need for a Central legislation like this. N.C. Saxena, Secretary, Rural Development was quoted as saying, "...it was unfortunate that certain elements in bureaucracy still had anti tribal and anti-poor bias. When it comes to helping the rich, laws and policies are flouted easily, whereas meaningless objections were being raised when a pro-poor legislation is sought to be implemented." He continued and stated, " in Odisha, control over bamboo forests have been given to the paper mills. Tribal women are not even permitted to process, store or sell hillbrooms."

Devolution, understood as any political Act in which a Central Government formally devolves powers to actors and institutions at lower levels in a political-administrative-territorial hierarchy and which involves the creation of a realm of decision-making in which a variety of lower-level actors exercise a certain degree of autonomy. The belief in greater responsiveness is based on the assumption that local authorities have better access to information about their constituents and that they are more easily held accountable by local populations.

According to the stipulations of the provisions of PESA, the exceptions and modifications consist of the following:[26] *A State legislature on the Panchayats that may be made shall be in consonance with the customary law, social and religious practices and traditional management practices of community resources; a village shall ordinarily consist of a habitation or a group of habitants or a hamlet or a group of hamlets comprising a community and managing its affairs in accordance with traditions and customs; every village shall have a* Gram Sabha *consisting of persons whose names are included in the electoral rolls for the* Panchayat *at the village level*[27]*; every* Gram Sabha *shall be competent to safeguard and preserve the traditions and customs of the people, their cultural identity, community resources and the customary mode of dispute resolution; every* Gram Sabha *shall—(i) approve the plans, programmes and projects for social and economic development before such plans, programmes and projects are taken up for implementation by the Panchayat at the village level; (ii) be responsible for the identification or selection of persons as beneficiaries under the poverty alleviation and other programmes; every* Panchayat *at the* *village level shall be required to obtain from the* Gram Sabha *a certification of utilisation of fund by the* Panchayat *for the plans, programmes and projects referred to in clause; the reservation of seats in the Scheduled Areas at every* Panchayat *shall be in proportion to the population of the communities in that* Panchayat *for whom reservation is sought to be given under Part IX of the Constitution: Provided that the reservation for the Scheduled Tribes shall not be less than one-half of the total number of seats; Provided further that all seats of Chairpersons of Panchayats at all levels shall be reserved for the Scheduled Tribes; the State Government may nominate persons belonging to such Scheduled Tribes as have no representation in the Panchayat at the intermediate level or the Panchayat at the district level: Provided that such nomination shall not exceed one-tenth of the total members to be elected in that Panchayat; the* Gram Sabha *or the* Panchayat *at the appropriate level shall be consulted before making the acquisition of land in the Scheduled Areas for development projects and before re-settling or rehabilitating persons affected by such projects in the Scheduled Areas; the actual planning and implementation of the projects in the Scheduled Areas shall be coordinated at the State level; Planning and management of minor water bodies in the Scheduled Areas shall be entrusted to* Panchayats *at the appropriate level; the recommendations of the* Gram Sabha *or the* Panchayats *at the appropriate level shall be made mandatory prior to grant of prospecting licence or mining lease for minor minerals in the Scheduled Areas; the prior recommendation of the* Gram Sabha *or the* Panchayats *at the appropriate level shall be made mandatory for grant of concession for the exploitation of minor minerals by auction;*

While endowing *Panchayats* in the Scheduled Areas with such powers and authority as may be necessary to enable them to function as institutions of self-government, a State Legislature shall ensure that the *Panchayats* at the appropriate level and the *Gram Sabha* are endowed specifically with—(i) the power to enforce prohibition or to regulate or restrict that sale and consumption of an intoxicants; (ii) the ownership of minor forest produce; (iii) the power to prevent alienation of land in the Scheduled Areas and to take appropriate action to restore any unlawfully alienated land of a Scheduled Tribe; (iv) the power to manage village markets by whatever name called;

(v) the power to exercise control over money lending to the Scheduled Tribes; (vi) the power to exercise control over institutions and functionaries in all social sectors; (vii) the power to control over local plans and resources for such plans including tribal sub-plans; (viii) the State Legislature that may endow *Panchayats* with powers and authority as may be necessary to enable them to function as institutions of self-government shall contain safeguards to ensure that *Panchayat* at the highest level do not assume the powers and authority of any *Panchayat* at the lower level or of the *Gram Sabha*; (ix) the State Legislature shall endeavour to follow the pattern of the Sixth Schedule to the Constitution while designing the administrative arrangements in the Panchayats at district levels in the Scheduled Areas.[28]

Yet, the implementation of PESA has been fraught with problems and difficulties right from its very inception.[29] *All states have amended their state laws and incorporated the provisions of PESA but gaps and inconsistencies. The subject laws realted to mining, forests and money lending have also not been duly amended.*[30] *Such laws continue even after being declared invalid and are followed as they have not been replaced with alternative guidelines. Vital issues highlighted under PESA such as the recognition of tribal rights, management of minor water bodies, land alienation and minor forest produce continue to remain neglected.*[31] While powers have been devolved to the *Gram Sabha* and the *Panchayats*, this legislative step has not been supplemented with the transfer of functionaries and funds.

The optimism infused by the PESA Act has however failed to take a substantive root. Among the various problems, the biggest stumbling block has been the failure or rather the reluctance on the part of the states to implement the Act in letter and spirit.[32] The lackadaisical attitude towards the implementation of the Act means that the tribal population continues to remain wretched and alienated.

The provisions of the PESA enacted in 1996 attempted to restore pride and dignity in the affairs of the tribal population. It recognized their right to effectively govern themselves according to their own cultural and traditional practices.[33] The healthy provisions also helped restore some confidence of the tribal population *vis-à-vis* the Indian state. The lack of execution of the powers of the *Gram Sabha* by the State administration is the crucial point of disjuncture. There are two aspects with concerning the execution of PESA in the Fifth Schedule/Extremist affected areas—the issue of governance, and the issue of commitment. The lackadaisical attitude of the administration coupled with the insensitivity and the pre-dispositions towards the cause of the tribal is an alarming characteristic that has been plaguing our administration for decades.

At present the Central Government is already working with a four pronged approach to peace and development in the Naxal affected districts. This includes security, development, entitlement of tribal rights and perception management and dissemination of information.

One also has to note that as a long term solution, the effective functioning of the *Gram Sabha* is crucial to meet the basic services like health, eduction, drinking water, sanitation, Village markets etc. of the tribals and to wean them away from Naxal influence, also the Naxals survival rests on the exploitation of the tribals in the name of *Jal*, *Jameen*, and *Jangle*. But the *Gram Sabha* can function only when there is a minimal level of peace. Therefore, the requirement of State security cannot be done away with completely.

However, a phased approach whereby different areas are prioritized according to the degree of insecurity and lack of development can be applied. Security alone will not achieve long term peace and development and will have to be immediately followed by emphasis on strong development goals and a commitment to social justice.

The concept of an integrated approach that brings together security and development therefore requires greater interaction and coordination among different levels of administration and law implementation. The administration must be able to understand and appreciate the role of law enforcement while units concerned with security and order must understand the nuances of development and entitlement of rights. Therefore, a joint initiative could be conducted at Central, State and District Levels wherein the administrative as well as law enforcement units are provided with a platform to review the situation jointly and create a joint action plan for each level. Such an integrated plan would not simply deal with the allocation of funds, but chalk out operational and doable actions with outcomes as well as pros and cons.

While the emphasis is kept high on development, what needs to be ensured is that the concept of development should not be an alien imposition on the community since it has its own unique set of customs, traditions and means of livelihood. It is essential to understand and acknowledge what the tribal people themselves understand by the term 'development', as they say that they donot want state imposed development. In the name of development, tribal people have had to face decades of land alienation and have been losing access to forests, land and water, while private groups have reaped profits. Therefore, the requirement is for proper implementation of PESA in letter and spirit, in phased manner, especially on land acquisition and prevention of land alienation. Apart from enforcement of such laws, concrete steps need to be taken to enhance communication between the people and the state. A viable initiative could be to organize special '*Sabhas*' between members of the *Gram Sabha*, and Central and State Officials.GPDP under PESA is a good initiative on similar lines. These could be annual special meetings to discuss development agendas, projects and schemes and their impact on the local population.

Notes

1. Ramachandran Guha and Madhav Gadgil, (1989). "State Forestry and Social Conflict in British India," *Past and Present*, no. 123 (May, 1989).
2. Ranajit Guha, (1999). *Elementary Aspects of Peasant Insurgency in Colonial India* (Duke University Press).
3. The Government of India Act, 1919 declared the tribal areas as "Backward Tracts" and stipulated against application of any Act of Indian Legislature without being directed so by the Governor-General. Following on this, the Government of India Act, 1935 declared the tribal areas as "Excluded Areas" and 'Partially Excluded Areas' and prohibited the extension of legislation functioning in other parts of India to these areas.
4. Savyasaachi, (1998). Tribal Forest-Dwellers and Self-Rule: The Constituent Assembly Debates on the Fifth and Sixth Schedules (New Delhi: Indian Social Institute).
5. The Naxal violence has been on the spiral increase since the People's War Group and Maoist Communist Centre merged to form Community Party of

India (Maoist) in 2004. It prompted Prime Minister Manmohan Singh to make the statement in 2006.

6. Salwa Judum, also known as "Purification Hunt", was orchestrated as a "People's reisistant movement" against the Maoists in the State of Chhattisgarh roughly from the year 2005 onwards. However, it soon became clear that the *adivasis* were the hapless victims caught between the State-sponsored violent campaign and the counter-violence unleashed by the Maoists. For detailed report on the Salwa Judum campaign, see, People's Union of Civil Liberties (PUCL), When the State Makes War on its Own People: A report on violations of people's rights during the Salwa Judum Campaign in Dantewada, Chhattisgarh (2006) and Ramachandra Guha *et al.*, *War in the Heart of India: An Enquiry into the Ground Situation in the Dantewara District*, Chhattisgarh (Independent Citizens' Initiative, 2006). In 2011, the Supreme Court disbanded 'Salwa Judum' branding it illegal and unconstitutional.
7. Kujur, R. (2008). "*Naxal Movement in India: A profile*", New Delhi: IPCS Research Paper "Communist Party of India—Maoist (CPI-M) document", South Asia Terrorism Portal.
8. See, Bendfeldt, Lennart (2010) "Naxalism: The Maoist Challenge to the Indian State", Heinrich Boll Stiftung, India, p. 2.
9. *Ibid.*
10. Banerjee, Sumanta, 2010: The Pathology of India's Security Forces; in: *Economic & Political Weekly*, June 19.
11. "Problems and Tasks before the Party", a review by the extended Central committee meeting of CPI(ML) of the period from November 1971 to June 1974.
12. *Ibid.*
13. Choudhary, C. & Dandekar, A. (2010), "*PESA, Left-Wing Extremism and Governance: Concerns and Challenges in India*'s Tribal Districts", IRMA Ahmedabad: Ministry of Panchayati Raj, Government of India.
14. See, Bendfeldt, Lennart (2010) "*Naxalism: The Maoist Challenge to the Indian State*", Heinrich Boll Stiftung, India, p. 2.
15. FICCI 2009: *Task Force Report on National Security and Terrorism*, New Delhi.
16. Dunbar, N.C.W. (1954), "The legal Regulation of Modern Warfare," British Institute of International and Comparative Law, Vol. 40.
17. Kutger, P. Joseph (1960), "Irregular Warfare in Transition," *Military Affairs: Irregular Warfare Issue*, Vol. 24, No. 3, pp. 113-123.
18. Balagopal, K. (2007): "Land Unrest in Andhra Pradesh Ceiling Surpluses and Public Land", *Economic & Political Weekly*, September 22-28.
19. Bendfeldt, Lennart (2010). "Naxalism: The Maoist Challenge to the Indian State", Heinrich Boll Stiftung, India, p. 21. Quoted from Mehra, Ajay K.; 2008: India's Experiment with Revolution; Heidelberg Papers in South Asia and Comparative Politics, Working Paper 40, 7/24/2010; http://

archiv.ub.uniheidelberg.de/volltextserver/volltexte/2008/8710/pdf/Heidelberg_Paper_Mehra.pdf

20. See, Land acquisition FRA AND PESA, http://www.slideshare.net/pkachare/land-acquisition-frapesa (accessed January 19, 2017).
21. See the provisions of the Panchayat (Extension to Schedule Areas) Act, 1999 [PESA].
22. See the provisions of the Panchayat (Extension to Scheduled Areas) Act of 1999, URL: htt://lawmin.nic.in/Id/p-ACT/1996/The%20 Provisions%20 the%20 Panchayatas%20((accessed January 19, 2017).
23. Upadhyay, Sanjay (2004), "Tribal Self-Rule Law and Common Property Resources in Scheduled Areas of India—A New Paradigm Shift or Another Ineffective Sop?" Presented Paper, Tenth Biennial Conference of the International Association for the Study of Common Property (IASCP) "The Commons in an Age of Global Transition Challenges, Risks and Opportunities". Hosted by the Instituto de Investigaciones Sociales, Universidad Nacional Autónoma de México Oaxaca, México, 9-13 August 2004, URL: http://unpan1.un.org/intradoc/groups/public/documents/APCITY/UNPAN021306.pdf
24. See, "PRI Key to Land Acquisition, Relief and Rehabilitation", Inclusion, July-September, 2008 [Online Web], URL: http://inclusion.skoch.in/story/613/pris-key-to-land-acquisition-relief-&-rehabilitation-913.html
25. See, Ojha, Nabaghana (2004), "The Scheduled V Areas: Rights over MFP Still a Far Cry," *Community Forestry*, Vol. 3, Issue.3. http://www.anthrobase.com/Txt/O/Ojha_N_01.htm (accessed January 19, 2017).
26. Ministry of Law and Justice, The provisions of the Panchayats (Extension to the Scheduled Areas) Act, 1996 (24 December, 1996). http://www.panchayat.gov.in/documents/10198/348968/PESA%20Act%2C%201996.pdf
27. See, ST & SC Development, Monorities & Backward Classes Welfare Department, "Provisions of the Panchayats", http://www.stscodisha.gov.in/Provisions.asp?GL=citizen&PL=1 (accessed January 19, 2017).
28. See, THE PROVISIONS OF THE PANCHAYATS (EXTENSION TO THE SCHEDULED AREAS, http://lawmin.nic.in/ld/P-ACT/1996/The%20Provisions%20of%20The%20Panchayatas%20((accessed January 19, 2017).
29. See, "The Report on Status of Panchayat Extension to Scheduled Areas Act of 1996 in the States of Andhra Pradesh, Odisha, Jharkhand, Gurajat and Chhattisgarh", A Report submitted by P.R. Memorial Foundation to the Planning Commission of India, New Delhi.
30. Ramachandran Guha and Madhav Gadgil, (1989). "State Forestry and Social Conflict in British India," *Past and Present*, No. 123 (May).
31. Ranajit Guha, (1999). *Elementary Aspects of Peasant Insurgency in Colonial India*, (Duke University Press).

32. This has been underscored in the report on each state submitted by Enviro Legal Defence Firm to the Ministry of Panchayati Raj. A damning assessment of PESA implementation in the states has been made by Ajay Dandekar and Chitrangada Choudhury in PESA, Left-Wing Extremism: Concerns and Challenges in India's Tribal's Districts. http://www.downtoearth.org.in/dte/userfiles/images/PESAchapter.pdf
33. Ministry of Law and Justice, The provisions of the Panchayats (Extension to the Scheduled Areas) Act, 1996 (24 December, 1996). http://www.panchayat.gov.in/documents/10198/348968/PESA%20Act%2C%201996.pd

References

Balagopal, K. (2007): "Land Unrest in Andhra Pradesh Ceiling Surpluses and Public Land", *Economic & Political Weekly*, September 22-28.

Bandyopadhyay, D. (2006): "Is Land Reform Still Relevant?" *Yojana,* August. (2007): "*Land, Labour and Governance*", Kolkata: World View.

Banerjee, Sumanta, 2010: The Pathology of India's Security Forces; in: *Economic & Political Weekly*, June 19.

Choudhary, C. & Dandekar, A. (2010), "*PESA, Left-Wing Extremism and Governance: Concerns and Challenges in India's Tribal Districts*", IRMA Ahmedabad: Ministry of Panchayati Raj, Government of India.

Dunbar, N.C.W. (1954), "The legal Regulation of Modern Warfare," *British Institute of International and Comparative Law,* Vol. 40.

Guha, Ramachandra and Madhav Gadgil, (1989). "State Forestry and Social Conflict in British India," *Past and Present*, No. 123 (May).

Guha, Ranajit, (1999). *Elementary Aspects of Peasant Insurgency in Colonial India* (Duke University Press).

Kraemer S. Joseph, (1971). "Revolutionary Guerilla Warfare and the Decolonization Movement", Palgharve MacMillan Journals, *Polity,* Vol. 4, No. 2, pp. 137-158.

Kujur, R. (2008). "*Naxal Movement in India: A profile*", New Delhi: IPCS Research Paper "*Communist Party of India – Maoist (CPI-M) document*", South Asia Terrorism Portal.

Kutger, P. Joseph (1960), "Irregular Warfare in Transition," *Military Affairs,* Vol. 24, No. 3.

Ramesh Chand, S.S. Raju, L.M. Pandey (2007): "Growth Crisis in Agriculture: Severity and Options at National and State Lands", *Economic & Politicai Weekly*, June 30-July 6.

Savyasaachi, (1998). *Tribal Forest-Dwellers and Self-Rule: The Constituent Assembly Debates on the Fifth and Sixth Schedules*, New Delhi: Indian Social Institute.

2

Food Processing Industry and Its Impact on Socio-Economic Upliftment of BTAD Area in Assam

Gunajit Sarma

Introduction

The progress of a country is mainly depends upon its industrial development. To be a strong power in the world, a country needs to be industrially advanced too. Although agriculture has its own importance and provides the basic necessaries of life, but it alone cannot take a country forward. Even to modernize and improve agriculture, industrialization is necessary. Without industries our country cannot make progress. Assam is situated at the North-Eastern Himalayan Sub-region of India. In spite of having huge development potential, the economy of Assam remained underdeveloped as it is characterized by poverty, underutilized man power and untapped natural resources. Assam is one of the industrially backward States of the country. In spite of being blessed with a high potential for development of resource-based and demand-based industries in the State, the pace of industrialization in Assam had not been satisfactory. Bodoland Territorial Area Districts (BTAD) is the latest regional tribal development area constituted under a special enactment of the Constitution of India. Bodo Territorial Council is the outcome of an Agreement reached at among the Government of India and Government of Assam and the Bodo Liberation Tigers on February 10, 2003. Bodos are a traditional tribal ethnic group in Assam primarily concentrated in the Bodoland area. With the formation of the BTC (Bodo Territorial Council) a new vistas of development has begun in BTAD (Bodoland Territorial Area District) area. BTC is now preparing the Bodo Territorial Area Development Plan and the Central Government sanctioned funds for the development of the area. BTC is a para–state administrative body with its separate Executive Council and Administrative staffs. The total area of BTAD is approximately, stands at 8300 sq. km. comprising 3110 villages. There are four Districts in BTAD *viz.* Kokrajhar, Chirang, Baska and Udalguri. The BTAD was created under the Sixth Schedule of the Constitution of India. At present Kokrajhar town serve as the headquarters of Bodoland. Industries are generally classified into four categories Agro-based industry, Mineral-based industry, Forest-based industry and other industries. Food processing Industry is under the category of Agro-based industry. The industries which draw the raw- material from agriculture are called agro-based industry.

This study suggests that there is a need to develop the processed food processing industries throughout the country specially in BTAD area of Assam in order to provide more employment opportunities and to reduce regional imbalances and to improve the socio-economic situation of the people of that area.

The basic logic of the study is to frame a vision for proper utilization of agricultural products in the greater interest of the socio-economic development of the BTAD area of Assam. Because in spite of having ample prospect of raw-material, manpower and other element for development of food processing industries in BTAD area, still no such satisfactory development can take place in this area. Consequently, unemployment problem, rate of poverty, underutilization of natural resources and under-use of human resources has been rapidly increasing. All of these serious problems can be removed up to a satisfactory mark by well-established food processing industry in BTAD area. Considering all of the above fact and circumstances, there is a need of careful study on this topic.

Unemployment is a chronic economic problem almost common to each and every economies of the world. The problem of growing unemployment continued to be a matter of great concern for North-East. In spite of having huge natural resources, the State economy still largely remains backward and underdeveloped as these natural resources have not yet been thoroughly exploited. Therefore, we can say that on the basis of the locally available agricultural product the North-Eastern Region has greater scope to develop the food processing industry. It will create lots of employment opportunity as well as it helps to proper utilization of the local agricultural products. That is why, I think that there is a great significance to study the opportunity-*cum*-employment prospect of Food Processing Industry in BTAD area of Assam. Because, I think that this will help in proper utilization of agricultural raw-material of this area as well as it will help to create employment opportunity of the local people and improve the socio-economic situation of the people.

Objective of the Study

The basic objective of the study is to examine the role of Food Processing Industries in BTAD area and study the prospect of this industry as how can this industry help in the overall development of the socio-economic situation of the area. In doing so we have try to identify the employment opportunity of this sector as well as try to identify the various types of processing industry which have great scope to develop on locally available agricultural raw-material in BTAD area.

Methodology

In methodology I have collected data both from primary sources and secondary sources. In Primary sources I have collected the data from the offices of Gram Panchyat, local DIC oifice, NGO, Self-help Groups (SHG), State Government and Central Government offices, Block Offices, Agricultural Department etc. Apart of these some of the primary data can be collected from the field using sample survey method, personal interview and questionnaires and try to collect some of the data from visiting various Food Processing Industry outside of Assam. In case of secondary sources I have collected the data from published research paper, journals, books, annual reports of research organizations and institutions, various website like Ministry of Food Processing, Government of India, Indian Institute of Entrepreneurship etc. The database such as Google Search, Google Scholar, and

Wikipedia may be used to search for food processing industry research by using various keywords like packaging, processing, hygienic, etc.

Food Processing Industry

The industry concerned with processing, preparing, distributing and serving of foods and beverages is called food processing industry. In India, North-East is the state where large varieties of foods are produced. This region has achieved the potential of having the food and agriculture sectors. Indian food industry is considered to be occupying about two thirds of the total Indian retail market. India is one of the largest food producers in the world. The food sector contributes about 28 per cent of India's GDP. Therefore, this industry sector has greater potentiality to develop in urbanized sector because urban people are always ready to spend more money to buying the readymade food items as well as food processing items. The growth experience of the sector in the past two decades seems to justify this optimism and future expectations on its growth and probable increased contribution of the sector to overall growth of the economy are also high. Much of this is based on factors like increasing per-capita income in the country, favourable demographic structure, rapid urbanization, changing consumption patterns, rising share of organized food retail etc. in the same order. That is why, these factors have created a great demand for this industry sector. The processed food products have high income elasticity of demand and increases with income. Therefore, the proportion of processed food is likely to increase in India also and necessitate higher production of processed food products to cater to the changing consumption needs of the people with quickly rising per capita incomes. In India now the population at 1.1 billion and is expected to overtake China in the coming decades and it is going to be the largest populated country in the world. In India relatively young population is boon for the processing sector in the world. Another factor, which is likely to encourage the growth of food processing sector, is the rapid urbanization in the country. The pace of urbanization in Asia expected to be very high in the coming decades and this is very encouraging factor for growth of this industry sector. In India, in the last few decades the consumption pattern of food has been undergoing marked changes. There has been diversification of the Indian diets away from foodgrains to high value products like milk, meat products, package food, beverages, bakery products etc. In North-Eastern part of India this sector has a greater potentiality because this industry mainly depends upon the agricultural products. Out of the Indian market Assam has the greater potentiality because in Assam climate is more suitable for producing Food Processing Industry. In Assam BTAD is an area which is constituted under the Sixth Schedule of Assam. BTAD area is truly blessed with vast agro-*cum*-Food industrial potentialities. There are tremendous scope for development of food processing industry in based on locally available raw-matérials and skills. Agriculture and forestry being the backbone of this region, therefore, food processing industry has great scope for growth and development in this area. BTAD area possesses vast natural resources such as agricultural products, oilseeds, ginger, chillies, turmeric, potatoes, tomatoes, horticulture products, fruits and vegetables etc. for industrial inputs. The seasonal fruits found in this reason include orange, star-fruits, mango, guava, pineapple, jackfruit, coconut etc. will help in emergence of jelly and juice and other processing industries. There is large number of fisheries, poultry firm and cattle rearing farms that can be utilized as a small scale meat, poultry and dairy processing industries. Fruits, vegetables, spices, meat products and poultry are some of the prospective processing products. Fruits and vegetables like pineapple, bamboo shoot and jack fruit have good marketing scope in this region if properly harvested, processed and packaged. The region has also good source of cattle and broilers for setting-up of meat processing or slaughter house. Even though the region have abundance of resources, but trade is approximately 0.5 per cent and that is mainly because of low yield levels per hectare. Less than 1 per cent of the products are commercially processed. But in spite of having vast natural and human resources the entire Assam is quite dependent on supplies from other parts of the country even for food items. Therefore, there is an utmost importance for development of such industry in this area. Food and food processing technologies are developing gradually. The various types of food industry which have greater potentiality to develop in BTAD area of Assam are discussed below:

1. Fruits and Vegetables Processing Industry: North-East is the agricultural-based state. Among the sub-sectors of Indian Food industry, fruits and vegetable industry has greater potentiality in this region. Vegetables such as potato, tomato, cabbage, cauliflower etc., and fruits like banana, mango, orange etc. have been reported to be around 20 per cent of the total production in the country. On the basis of these products, the state has greater potentiality to set-up lots of industry like juice industry, chips (banana, potato) industry, biscuits industry, pickle industry etc. These fruits and vegetables industries manufacture health food as well as health food supplements are rapidly improving segments of this industry, which is gaining vast popularity amongst the health conscious population of the country. Therefore, this industry has greater potentiality to develop in urban areas and it created lots of employment opportunity for the people of BTAD area.

2. Meat, Poultry and Fishery Industry: It is one of the fastest growing segments of the agricultural related food industry under informal sector in urban areas at present. In this industry the production of eggs and broilers has been rising at a rate 8 to 10 per cent per annum in India. Therefore, this industry has greater potentiality in BTAD areas, which will help to solve the unemployment problem in this region. Fisheries also have gained popularity as a major Indian food industry. India is the third largest producer of fish in the world. In Assam more than 30 per cent land are wetland, therefore, the state has greater potentiality to be develop such type of industry. In Assam BTAD area district has also great scope to develop such type of industry because here maximum area is wetland.

3. Bakery Products: Bakery goods are almost common in every culture. In fact they have formed a specific part of diet, as cereals and grains occupies a special part in the regular diet. Bakery products like cake, biscuits, bread etc. are famous world-wide and consumed by many people. Bakery foods come in large variety of flavour and constitute mixture of different ingredients like wheat, cornflower, sugar, water etc. Children are fond of cakes of different flavours, pasties and cookies which may even constitute a specific daily food item. Bakery item like cake and sweet flavour in many occasions and function like birthday, ceremony, anniversaries etc. Bakery products are one of the essential fast food item easily liked and adopted by the new generation not only in India, but also all-over the world. Human factors like tastes, fashion, styles, foods and beverages all help baked item a choice of every age. Hence, every commercial restaurants, bars, shopping malls, food bazaar, fast food corner and retail shop need to get regular and bulk supplies of confectionary and bakery goods. Therefore, we can say that this sector has greater potentiality to develop in BTAD area. In Assam BTAD area district has also urbanization is increasing day-by-day therefore; demand for such industry has also great scope to develop in this area.

4. Dairy Industry: Dairy is a place where handling of milk and milk product is done and technology refers to the application of scientific knowledge for practical purpose. The dairy sector in India has shown remarkable development in the past decade and India has now become one of the largest producer of milk and value added milk products in the world. In India both the production and consumption of milk and its derivatives are traditionally high in the country. Infant milk food, milk powder, butter, cheese, ice-cream and ghee are the major value added products from the dairy sector. In North-East also greater scope to develop such type of industry is necessary. If we are able to develop such type of industry than it has bring a rapid change in the Economy. We have seen that in urban areas these sectors have greater potentiality because such type of products has lots of demand among the all sections of the people.

5. Alcohol Industry and Alcoholic Beverages: Another important food industry is liquor industry. In Assam as well as BTAD has produced large varieties of fruits. So, the basis of this fruits we have greater potentiality to set-up liquor industry as well as the beverages industry. On the basis of the locally available fruits in BTAD area, there is a greater scope to develop such type of industry and it will help to proper utilization of locally available raw-material as well as help to solve the unemployment problem in this region.

6. Chocolates and Confectionary Industry: Confectionary is the set of food items that are rich in sugar, any one type of which is called a confection. Confectionary item include sweets, lollipops, candy bars, chocolate and other sweet items of snack food. We have seen that such type of industry has lots of demand in urban areas and demands are increasing day-by-day. In Assam also this industry has great scope to develop because this industry is mainly depends upon the agricultural raw-material.

7. Packaged and Convenience Food: Convenience food is commercially prepared food designed for ease of consumption. Products designed as convenience food are often prepared foodstuffs that can be sold as hot, ready to eat dishes or as refrigerated or frozen products that require minimal preparation. These products are often sold in portion controlled, single serve packaging designed for portability for "on the go" eating. Convenience food can include products such as candy, beverages such as soft drinks, juices and milk, fast food, nuts, fruits and vegetables in fresh or preserved states, processed meat and cheeses and canned products such as soups and pasta dishes etc. These types of industry are growing mainly under informal sector in urban areas. Therefore, we can say that this type of industry will create large number of employment in the local people in urban areas.

Therefore, the Indian food industry sector covers fruits and vegetables, meat and poultry, milk and milk products, alcoholic beverages, fisheries, plantation, grain processing and other consumers product groups like confectionary, chocolates and cocoa products, soya-based products, high protein foods etc. In this sector cover an exhaustive database of an array of suppliers, manufactures, exporters and importers widely dealing in sectors like the food industry, dairy processing, Indian beverage industry etc. In this sector covers like dairy plants, canning, bottling plants, packaging industries, process machinery etc. The most promising sub-sectors includes soft-drink bottling, fishing, aquaculture, grain milling and grain-based products, meat and poultry processing, milk processing, tomato paste, fast food, ready to eat breakfast cereals, food additives, flavours etc. If we are able to properly develop such type of industry and Government will take the necessary action than it will play a dominant role for growth of this region.

Future Prospect of Food Processing Industry in BTAD Area of Assam

The future prospect of food processing industry in BTAD area is very bright. Rapid change in the lifestyles of peoples, mainly those living in urban area has led to dramatic increase in the demand of processed foods. As it offers further convenience to cooking because, they do not need to spend long period in cooking to get delicious food. Furthermore, the increase in travels abroad and presence of foreign media in the country has resulted in more Indians opting for processed foods. All these factors create an encouraging picture on the future of food processing industries in Assam as well as BTAD area. Food processing industry has great significance in BTAD area growth because of the vital linkages that it promotes between two pillars of Indian economy, they are industry and agriculture. Food processing includes a group of products from sub-sector compromising agriculture, horticulture, plantation, animal husbandry and fisheries.

Economic liberalization and rising consumer prosperity is opening-up new opportunities for diversification in Food processing sector. Liberalization of world trade will open-up new vistas for growth. With the advent of liberalization process of economy, there is a rapid change in the processed food industries in India. Now we discussed how it is possible to improve food industry with the advent of liberalization. Liberalization brought through entry of large multinational and transitional corporations, foreign investment in this sector. This resulted in competition, technological up-gradation and market expansion. In the face of the competition, domestic industries are gradually losing market share and thus selling their business to the new entrants MNCs well before the value of the brand and businesses drops further due to ongoing attack multinational brands. Food processing industry in India has undergone a total transformation over the last six to seven years, in terms of types, variety, quality and presentation which is a result of liberalization leading to foreign direct investment in frontiers of processed food sectors.

With the emergence of market liberalization, food processing industry development has been identified as one of the most important factors for economic development. The North-East India is known for its unexploited natural and human resources, which are the basic factors for economic development. Therefore, the growth of Food Processing Industry is necessary for development of BTAD area. In this regard the Government should also take the necessary action for development of the Food Processing Industry. In addition, very recently with the emergence of Look East Policy trade and commerce has become an important tool in linking this region with the South-East Asian countries. It is apparent that NE India as a whole needs a big push or a kick starts to launch the economy on the development path. Look East policy provides an opportunity to overcome the problem of distance from big markets and it will help to dynamic growth of BTAD area.

Conclusion

The problem of unemployment cannot be tackled by creating more jobs in the public sector and other various Government departments; there must be development of micro, small and medium enterprises for self-employment and expansion of job opportunities. The food processing industry sector can play an important role in this regard. For this, the Government should take proper policy for development of the region through setting-up food processing industry and try to improve the growth of this region. Thus, the growth of food processing industry sector implies usually the development of agriculture as well as other sub-sectors like agriculture, horticulture, plantation, animal husbandry, fisheries etc. and it has a significant role in the economic development of the backward region like BTAD area of Assam. The World Bank defines inclusive growth as that growth which equals economic growth, while sharing the benefits of growth to reduce poverty. Inclusive growth refers to distribution of economic benefits among a larger section of people, particularly those who have not yet received the benefits of development. Therefore, to achieve the inclusive growth Government should give the emphasis on development of agriculture as well as development of Agriculture-based industry like Food Processing Industry.

To solve the growing unemployment and the resultant social unrest problems in Assam needs new avenues and vistas to be opened-up through the medium, micro and small scale industries, so that, the million dreams can be fulfilled through setting-up such type of industry. Food Processing Industry is one such type of industry. North-Eastern Region, by virtue of its diverse agro-climatic conditions, varied soil type and abundant rainfall has the promise of becoming an excellent sourcing point for high value horticulture produce and value added products unique to the region, for onwards marketing both within the country and abroad. Employment and economic opportunity are key factors driving urbanization, attracting people from rural to urban areas. In many developing countries, the formal employment sector has not been able to provide adequate jobs for rapidly growing urban populations, leading to more than half of those economically active being employed in informal sector. Food processing industry sector generate significant employment both formal as well as informal sector. The multiplier effect of investment in food processing industry on employment generation is 2.5 times higher than in any other industrial sector. Even within the food processing industry the employment intensity is significantly higher in the informal sector as compared to the formal sector for the same level of investment. Expansion of food processing activity in both formal and informal sectors would give benefit in two ways. Creating new employment opportunities in quantitative terms. Improving the quality of employment so that traditional low quality, low income, employment opportunities is gradually replaced by higher income better quality employments. Therefore, we can say that this sector has greater scope to create employment opportunity in Assam especially in BTAD area as well as it will help to increase the inclusive growth of that area. Inclusive growth refers to a growth process which yield broad-based benefits, and ensure equality of opportunity for all. Inclusiveness stands for equitable growth for justice and development. The continuing food inflation in the country has brought in sharp focus "supply side" constraints, especially in case of perishables. There is thus an increasing realization about the need to increase agricultural production in the country and a strategy to usher in second green revolution is under preparation. At the same time, it needs to be understood that it will not be enough only to produce more, but it is equally important to save each grain produced by reducing wastages. This would improve farmers' income and economic viability of agricultural operations. Such a strategy would also be essential to meet the twin national objectives of "inclusive growth" and "food Security". The growth of food processing sector would need to be a significant component of this strategy, considering its possible role in achieving increased agricultural production by ensuring better remuneration for farmers. The food processing sector makes it possible by not only ensuring better market access to farmers, but also reducing high level of wastages, ensure value addition, generate additional employment opportunities as well as export earnings and thus lead to better socio-economic condition of millions of farmer families. In BTAD area also Food Processing Industry sector plays a major role in inclusive growth of that area through proper utilization of agricultural raw-material as well as creating employment opportunity for the mass people and it will increase the socio-economic situation of the people of BTAD area.

References

Dhar, P.K. (2013). *Urbanisation: Its Challenges and Environmental Degradation*, Guwahati: EBH Publisher.

Amalesh Chandra Banarjee and Sourabh Singh Roy (2010), *Problems and Prospects of Bodoland*, New Delhi: Mittal Publications.

B.M. Desai, V.K. Gupta and N.V. Namboodiri—*Food Processing Industries Development and Financial Performance*—Calcutta: OXFORD and IBH Publishing Co. Pvt. Ltd.

Bhatnagar, B. and Budhiraja, A., (2009), *Entrepreneurship Development and Small Business Management*, New Delhi: Vayu Education of India.

Dhar, P.K., (1998). *The Economy of Assam*, Ludhiana: Kalyani Publishers.

Dhar, P.K., (2005). *Indian Economy*, Ludhiana: Kalyani Publishers.

Dhiman, P.K. and Rani, A. (2011) Problem and Prospect of Agro-based Industries: An Analysis of Patila District—*International Journal of Multidisciplinary Research*, Volume 1, Issue 4, August.

Farm Mechanization in India—www.agrievolution.com/atti/ficci.pdf

Food Processing in Andhra Pradesh Opportunities and Challenges—Working Paper No. 57, June-2004, Centre For Economic and Social Studies, Hyderabad-50016.

Kachru, R.P. Agro-Processing Industries in India—Growth, Status and Prospects—www.npkv.academia.edu/...Papers.

Kulkarni, S.D.—Mechanization of Agriculture—Indian Scenario—www.unapcaem.org/Activities/20 Files/A09105th TC/ppt/in-doc pdf.

Mandal, Ram Krishna, (2011), *Entrepreneurship and Rural Development in North-East India*, DVS Publishers, H.B. Road, Panbazar, Guwahati-781001.

N. Chandrasekhara Rao (2009), *Enhancing Growth and Productive Employment Linkages in the Food Processing Sector*—Published by, Centre For Economic and Social Studies, Begumpet, Hyderabad—50016, September.

Padberg, D.I., Ritson C., Albisu, L.M. (2002)—*Agro-Food Marketing*, New York: CABI Publishing.

Prasad, C.S., Mathur, V. and Chatterjee, A., (2007), *Sixty Years of Indian Economy-1947 to 2007*, New Delhi: New Century Publications.

Roy, Anuradha, (2010). *Food Processing*, Jaipur: Yking Books.

S. Barghouti, E. Cromwell and A.J. Pritchard—Agricultural Technologies For Market Led Development Opportunities in the 1990's—Working paper, *Centre for Economic and Social Studies*, Hyderabad-50016.

Sudershan, R.V., Rao Pratima and Polasa Kalpagam (2009), Food Safety Research in India: A review—*Asian Journal of Food and Agro-Industry*, 2 (03), 412-433.

White Paper on Food Processing Industry in India—www.dessence consulting.com/...White_paper_Food_pdf

3

Tribal Sub-Plans and Implementation in India

Ashima Srivastava

Introduction

The persistence of socio-economic backwardness of the STs, in spite of the development efforts, warranted a special and focused strategy, to enable them to share the benefits of overall economic growth in a more equitable manner. In order to ensure direct policy-driven benefits for STs through specific interventions, the Planning Commission during the 1970s introduced plan strategies—The Special Component Plan for the Tribal Sub-Plan (TSP). The TSP for STs was later renamed as Scheduled Tribal Plan (TSP). The main objective of TSP is to channel Plan funds for the development of STs in accordance with the proportion of these communities in the total population which was 8.2 per cent respectively at the national level as per the 2011 Census. Under these strategies, Plan funds are to be earmarked for STs (through TSP) under separate budget heads (TSP with budget head 796) for each Ministry implementing TSP. These strategies could include allocations for area-oriented programmes benefitting ST hamlets or designing new appropriate developmental programmes for the development of this group. The TSP funds should be non-divertible and non-lapsable.

Table 3.1: Socio-Economic Indicators for Scheduled Tribes

Indicators	*Year*	*STs*	*Other Groups*
Literacy Rate (Rural) %	2007-08	58.8	76.9
Literacy Rate (Urban) %		78	89.9
Unemployment Rate by Current Daily Status (Rural)	2007-08	7.5	8.4
Women with BMI < 18.5 (%)	2005-06	46.6	29.3
Women with Anemia (%)	2005-06	68.5	51.2
Infant Mortality Rate (per 1000)	2005-06	62.1	48.9
Households with Pucca houses (%)	2008-09	39.5	66.1
Households with Electricity (%)	2008-10	18.8	75

Source: India Human Development Report 2011, Towards Social Inclusion, Institute of Applied Manpower Research, Planning Commission, GoI [Computed from NFHS, NSS various years).

Allocations under TSP the sub-plans statements show the allocations reported by various Ministries/departments for welfare of STs.

Annexure 1

Assessment of Fund Allocation Through Statement 21 in Union Budget 2013-14

(in Rs. Crore)

Sl. No.	*Ministry/Department*	*2010-11 RE*	*2011-12 RE*	*2012-13 RE*	*2013-14 BE*
1.	Department of Animal Husbandry, Dairying and Fisheries	0	160.11	291.59	328.05
2.	Department of Agriculture and Cooperation	–	1401.98	1533.71	1888.11
3.	Department of Commerce	–	90	94	100
4.	Ministry of Civil Aviation	0.1	–	–	–
5.	Police	2.66	–	–	–
6.	Ministry of Labour and Employment	9.8	210.6	352.59	408.89
7.	Ministry of New and Renewable Energy	0	42	40.25	53.23
8.	Department of Science and Technology	3	31.52	25.97	69.43
9.	Department of Biotechnology	3.5	–	–	–
10.	Ministry of Social Justice and Empowerment	3434.76	4019.1	3888.93	4755.8

(Contd.)

Sl. No.	Ministry/Department	2010-11 RE	2011-12 RE	2012-13 RE	2013-14 BE
11.	UT of Chandigarh	10.41	–	–	–
12.	UT of Daman & Diu	0.56	–	–	–
13.	Ministry of Agriculture	272.5	–	–	
14.	Department of Industrial Policy and Promotion	30.73	30.01	5.8	42
15.	Department of Information Technology	53.2	45.08	51.74	60
16.	Ministry of Environment and Forest	0	51	43.36	53.46
17.	Department of Health and Family Welfare	2163	3137.61	3712.88	4433.08
18.	Department of AYUSH	–	32.5	33.5	53.45
19.	Department of AIDS Control	0	228	267.45	271.32
20.	Ministry of HUPA	0	234.91	162.5	328.5
21.	Department of School Education and Literacy	5881.83	7791.4	8545.8	9931.8
22.	Department of Higher Education	2175.67	1922.85	2076.91	2431.51
23.	Ministry of Micro, Small and Medium Enterprises	276.26	186.09	309.69	357.24
24.	Ministry of Panchayati Raj	11	14.01	23.78	75.49
25.	Ministry of Power	–	502.23	390.76	800
26.	Department of Rural Development	7492	4375.06	3819.74	6358.37
27.	Department of Land Resources	0	279.75	491.69	933.85
28.	Department of Drinking Water and Sanitation	0	2200	2860	3358
29.	Ministry of Textiles	139.2	265.16	225	231.55
30.	Ministry of Women and Child Development	2349	2530	3700	4070
31.	Ministry of Youth Affairs and Sports	204.98	136.55	137.4	168
	Total Allocation	**24514.16**	**29917.52**	**33085.04**	**41561.13**

Annexure 2

Assessment of Fund Allocation through Statement 21A in Union Budget-2013-14

(in Rs. Crore)

Sl. No.	Department/Ministry	2010-11 RE	2011-12 RE	2012-13 RE	2013-14 BE
1.	Ministry of Agriculture	139.3	692.33	–	–
2.	Dept. of Agricultural Research and Education	–	100.8	86.4	123
3.	Dept. of Agriculture and Cooperation	–	–	757.3	932.5
4.	Ministry of Coal	–	27	31.01	31.6
5.	Dept. of Telecommunications	0	5.02	5.99	14.5

(Contd.)

Sl. No.	Department/Ministry	2010-11 RE	2011-12 RE	2012-13 RE	2013-14 BE
6.	Dept. of Information Technology	0	196.2	138.46	201
7.	Dept. of Food and Public Distribution	0	1.96	3.44	6.28
8.	Ministry of Culture	7.4	16.1	17.28	28.7
9.	Ministry of Environment and Forests	–	15	14.51	16
10.	Dept. of Health and Family Welfare	1167	1683.7	1804	2391.53
11.	Dept. of AYUSH	8.21	13	13.4	21.38
12.	Dept. of AIDS Control	0	123	144.28	146.37
13.	Ministry of Housing and Urban Poverty Alleviation	0	25.06	17.32	35.04
14.	Dept. of School Education and Literacy	3441.06	4168.4	4572	5313.52
15.	Dept. of Higher Education	621.29	961.33	1021.53	1219.59
16.	Ministry of Labour and Employment	0	106.6	169.01	206.95
17.	Ministry of Micro, Small and Medium Enterprises	147.32	133.96	211.11	244.21
18.	Ministry of Mines	–	8.12	8.72	9.72
19.	Ministry of Panchayati Raj	11	7.08	12.27	37.55
20.	Ministry of Road Transport and Highways	–	375	500	800
21.	Ministry of Rural Development	0	3081.94	2778.87	4452.03
22.	Dept. of Land Resources	0	246.42	302.4	576.45
23.	Dept. of Drinking Water and Sanitation	0	1000	1300	1526
24.	Dept. of Science and Technology	3	32.75	21.86	69.43
25.	Ministry of Social Justice and Empowerment	–	–	0	46
26.	Ministry of Textiles	27.6	63.63	54.75	55.57
27.	Ministry of Tourism	0	27.5	23.75	32.05
28.	Ministry of Tribal Affairs	3203.3	3723.01	3100	4279
29.	Union Territories (Andaman and Nicobar Islands)	–	2.71	2.94	2.94
30.	Union Territories (D&D)	0	1.16	1	1
31.	Ministry of Water Resources	0	10.4	17.5	19.5
32.	Ministry of Women and Child Development	0	1037.3	1517	1668.7
33.	Ministry of Youth Affairs and Sports	75.9	72.55	73.23	90.28
34.	Ministry of Civil Aviation	0.05	–	–	–
35.	Department of Biotechnology	1.75	–	–	–
36.	UTs of Andaman & Nicobar Islands, Dadra & Nagar Haveli, Daman & Diu and Lakshadweep	367.13	–	–	–
	Total Allocation	**9221.31**	**17959.03**	**18721.33**	**24598.39**

Source: Compiled from Statements 1, 21 and 21A, Expenditure Budget in with Vol. I, Union Budget (various years).

Allocations for SCs reached an all-time high at 10.43 per cent of the total plan allocation of Union Budget 2012-13 (RE). The increase in outlay was mainly due to a substantial fall in the total plan allocation of the Union Government from Rs. 321405.55 crore to Rs. 317184.62 crore, which increased the proportionate share of TSP in the total allocations. However, the share of TSP in the total plan allocations of Union Budget (Excluding Central Assistance to States and Union Territories) has dipped to 9.92 per cent in 2013-14 BE. Similarly, it is interesting to see from Graph 2 that in no year have the allocations under the TSP reached. The stipulated 8 per cent mark, remaining below 6 per cent in all the years under analysis. As has been the case with the proportionate allocations under TSP have remained almost stagnant in the last few years.

Problems

Reporting is not being undertaken by all the Ministries/departments, and some of these are the ones which are liable to allocate funds under TSP. Further, a few Departments and Union Territories (UTs) have discontinued reporting under the statement. Annexure 1 shows allocations under this Statement by various Ministries/departments. As per Statement 21 of Union Budget 2013-14, the Government's allocation under TSP has gone-up to Rs. 41561 crore from Rs. 33085.04 crore in 2012-13 (RE). This marks an increase of Rs. 8476.09 crore over the year. Even so, several Ministries and departments still remain out of the ambit of the TSP. As the case with even in TSP, not all the Ministries/departments are allocating funds under this Statement (see Annexure 2). The Ministry of Agriculture which had been reporting funds till 2012-13 BE, has stopped reporting under Statement 21A from 2012-13 RE. Similar is the case with the Ministry of Civil Aviation and Department of Biotechnology which reported allocations for just one year (2010-11 RE). There has not been any increase in the number of Ministries/departments reporting under it from last year. Annexure 2 shows allocations by various Ministries/departments for TSP, over the years. As per Statement 21A of Union Budget 2013-14, the Government's allocation under the Tribal Sub-Plan (TSP) has increased to Rs. 24598.39 crore from Rs. 18721.33 crore in 2012-13 (RE), marking an increase of Rs. 5877.57 crore. On the positive side, the Statements (21 and 21A) have, for the first time reported figures of Actual in the Union Budget 2013-14, which could be seen as a step towards greater transparency. Moreover, the Finance Minister in his budget speech this year, emphasized that the funds allocated to the Sub-Plans cannot be diverted and must be spent for the specified purposes. However, much remains to be done with regard to the reporting under these statements. Some concerns that continue to affect the proper implementation of these plan strategies have been highlighted in the following section.

Concerns in the Implementation of TSP

As noted above, the implementation of these two strategies has been fraught with three major problems: allocations not meeting the stipulated earmarking of 8.3 per cent; many Ministries remaining out of the ambit of these statements and several Ministries not having the required budget heads for TSP in their detailed budget books (Detailed Demands for Grants). Additionally, there also remain issues regarding the overall approach of these plan strategies. Another key issue that has adversely affected these plans is the approach taken by the Narendra Jadhav Task Force. The Narendra Jadhav Committee's roadmap for implementation of TSP has not addressed the core issue pertaining to misplaced rationale underlying the interventions being reported. In several schemes, the nodal Ministries are reporting a part of their Plan allocations as a proportion of funds meant for benefiting STs even though the schemes/component(s) may not target the specific needs and challenges of STs. Reporting under TSP over the years has been more in the nature of "retrospective Budgeting" where allocations for STs are earmarked after the Plan budgets of the Ministries are finalized in the process of formulation of the Union Budget, without any special measure taken for formulating TSP during the budget preparation phase. Secondly, a scrutiny of the programmes/ schemes across several such Ministries also indicates that they are merely 'assuming' that a certain proportion of funds in a certain scheme would benefit STs based on the share of ST population in the country's total population, giving rise to the debate on 'notional' allocation of funds under the TSP. Moreover, in some cases the interventions reported under the statements are not ST specific; they are more in the nature of general interventions that cannot be perceived as meant largely for the benefit of STs. There are some glaring examples of how the TSP funds, particularly the TSP funds, are being used for very general purposes that cannot be perceived as meant largely for the benefit of STs. This can be clearly seen from some state level examples. Example from Madhya Pradesh State Budget:

Madhya Pradesh State Budget reported interventions like purchase of furniture and equipment, constructions of channels and survey and mapping of projects, under TSPs. These interventions clearly do not promote empowerment of STs or address their specific developmental needs. Inclusion of such interventions under TSP does cast doubts over the reporting under TSP in the state.

Use of TSP Funds in Madhya Pradesh in 2010-11 (BE)

- In the Department of Medical Education, Rs. 22 lakh have been booked for purchase of furniture and equipment for establishing Homoeopathy and Ayurvedic clinics.
- Under Higher Education department, there is a provision of Rs. 1 crore for construction of staff room.
- Water Resources Department has allocated Rs. 6.4 crore for the construction of channels.
- For Narmada Valley Development Project, Rs. 40 lakh is allocated for survey and mapping of the detailed project for Narmada Valley Development.

Example from Odisha

Table 3.2: Excerpt from the Detailed Demand for Grant for Home Department in Odisha

(in Rs. Crore)

Schemes	2009-10 BE	2010-11 BE
Construction of Building for Jails	2.30	4.77
Construction of Building for Fire Services	3.32	4.11
Construction of Building for Police Welfare (37062-Construction of Office building through O.S.P.H.&W. Corporation)	7.49	1.70

Source: Data compiled by National Campaign on Dalit Human Rights (NCDHR), a Delhi-based NGO, from Detailed Demands for Grants in the State Budget of Madhya Pradesh for (2010-11).

State Budget: The Odisha State Budget for 2010-11 reported construction of Jail Buildings under TSP with an allocation of Rs. 4.77 crore (under the Head 4059-60-789). Clearly, construction of jails, building for police or fire stations does not lead to the development of STs or accrue any benefit to them.

Example from Gujarat State Budget: Similarly, Gujarat State Budget has reported certain interventions under TSP which do not have any specific provision for the development of the STs, as shown below. Reporting general schemes which do not have specific provisions for STs or reporting allocations on celebrating a birth anniversary cannot be seen as programmes addressing specific concerns of STs.

Use of Tribal Sub-Plan (TSP) Funds in Gujarat in 2012-13 (BE)

- *Under Minor Head 796, Sub-Head*: 07—Celebration of Swami Vivekanand's 150th Birth Anniversary for which an amount of Rs. 5 crore is allocated for the year 2012-13.
- *Under Minor Head 796, Sub-Head*: 08-UDP-Swarnim Jayanti Mukhya Mantri Shahari Vikas Yojana for which an amount of Rs. 170 crore is allocated for the year 2012-13. This scheme is meant to provide assistance for basic social infrastructure to ULBs, e.g. construction/re-strengthening school buildings, creating facilities in urban health centres, kindergartens, e-Libraries, play grounds, Solid and Liquid Waste Management, e-Governance, Parking and Public Toilets, facilities for vegetable and Seasonal venders Markets, etc.

(*Source:* State Budget Documents (2012-13), Government of Gujarat)

Such practices of use of funds for general purposes defy the purpose of initiating strategies like TSP. Projects meant for STs should have a beneficiary oriented approach as far as possible and cover ST dominated hamlets in projects related to infrastructure and basic amenities, ensuring development of these groups with planned interventions for addressing their specific concern. Thirdly, the Narendra Jadhav Task Force has exempted a number of Ministries/departments from reporting under these statements primarily on the grounds of 'indivisibility' of these sectors. But, it needs to be noted here that no sector is indivisible and the Ministries can identify some specific challenges confronting STs in their respective sectors and then formulate a new intervention/a new scheme to address such challenges, even if the allocations may be small as compared to the total budget of the Ministry. Such concerns do stress the need for rethinking the plan strategies of TSP on how to make them more responsive to the needs of the STs respectively.

Conclusion

The objective of TSP should not be to merely capture the assumptions/ perceptions of Ministries with regard to 'incidental' benefits accruing to STs from their general schemes, but to ensure availability of adequate budgetary resources with Ministries for providing direct 'policy-driven' benefits to STs in their respective sectors. The main objective of TSP should not be to just report/show that 8.3 per cent of the total plan budgets of all Ministries are for benefiting STs, because such an objective pushes several Ministries to focus merely on retrospective reporting. The main objective of the Sub-Plan should be to encourage all Ministries to—

(i) Identify what could be the additional difficulties/challenges confronting STs in their sectors of concern.
(ii) What kind of measures could be taken by them to address those special difficulties/challenges?
(iii) How much additional resources would be required for such special measures. These additional resources devoted for the special measures for STs should then be reported under TSP.

Clearly, it would be neither feasible nor necessary for all Ministries to meet the 8.3 per cent benchmark for TSP. But if the Ministries make serious efforts along these lines, the combined Plan allocations reported for all Ministries is quite likely to be higher than the benchmarks—if not in the first year itself, then over a span of a few years.

References

Anderson, Robert S., and Huber Walter (1988). The Hour of the Fox: Tropical Forests, the World Bank and Indigenous People in Central India (Vistar, New Delhi) (DELNET).

Antrolikar, K.B.: Antrolikar Committee Report, 1950 (Report of the Ex-Criminal Tribes Rehabilitation Committee, November 1950). (Central Government Press, Bombay, 1951).

Bhowmick, Prabodh Kumar (ed.) (2008). Tribal People of India: Society Culture and Development (R.N., Bhattacharya Kolkata).

Burman, B.K.R. (1994). Indigenous and tribal people: Gathering mist and new horizon. New Delhi: Mittal Publications (NHRC).

Chaudhuri, Kumar Sarit (2004). Constraints of tribal development. New Delhi: Mittal Publications (NHRC).

Gupta, P.K. (1991). Commentaries on the Scheduled Castes and the Scheduled Tribes Lucknow: Eastern Book Company (SCJL).

India. Ministry of Information and Broadcasting: Tribal People of India. (Publications Division, New Delhi, 1973) (DELNET).

Jain, Sandhya (2004). Adi deo arya devata: A panoramic view of Tribal-Hindu Cultural Interface. New Delhi: Rupa & Co., (NHRC).

Kumar, Suresh Singh (1982). *Tribal Movements in India*. New Delhi: Manohar.

Majumdar, D.N. (1944), *Fortunes of Primitive Tribes* (Lucknow: Universal Publishers, pp. 185-208).

Rath, Govind Chandra, (2006). *Tribal Development in India: Contemporary Debate*. (Sage).

Sharma, Anuradha (1998). *Castes and Tribes in India*. New Delhi: Commonwealth Publisher (NHRC).

Sharma, B.D. (1992). *Tribal affairs in India: The crucial transition*, New Delhi: Sahyog Pustak Kuteer Trust (NHRC).

Tiwari, Shiv Kumar (2002). *Tribal Roots of Hinduism*. New Delhi: Sarup & Sons.

Seventh Report of 2nd ARC.

PESA Act, 1996.

Fifth Schedule [Article-244(1)].

Sixth Schedule [Articles 244, 244(2), 275(1), 342, 338(A), 339]

4

Economic Empowerment of the Tribal Communities through Traditional Knowledge

Problems and Prospects

S.C. Roy

Introduction

Protecting the Traditional Knowledge (TK) of the local and indigenous communities seem to be one of the most contentious and complicated issue. The historical development of the protection of intellectual property in the wake of individual private property rights, pushed the traditional knowledge and the innovative practices outside the purview of the formal intellectual property protection regime. Millennium poses serious challenge to the legal community to set new legal standard for tackling the problem of protection of Traditional Knowledge for the economic empowerment of the Tribals. Traditional Knowledge was treated as Knowledge in the public demeans for free exploitation without showing any respect or concern for the effort taken by the communities to preserve and promote the same. The new technological developments, particularly in biotechnology, clearly demonstrate the significance and usefulness of traditional knowledge for the development of new product of commercial importance. Traditional Knowledge (TK) associated with the biological resources is the knowledge about a country's biodiversity; the applied uses and applications of biological resources and the prevalent practices. TK has direct correlation with the biodiversity of the country. It is an intangible component of the resource itself.

TK has the potential of being transformed into commercial opportunity, providing useful leads for development of products and processes. Hence, a share of benefits must accrue to creators and holders of TK. TK is valuable in global economy, important for biotechnology-based industries, and agriculture. Traditional societies depend on it for their food and healthcare needs, important for conservation and sustainable development of environment and management of biodiversity, food security of the country is linked to protection of TK. Need to enable tribal communities to harness TK for their economic uplift and growth Fast mobility of tribal societies. The TK is a knowledge developed by local and indigenous communities over time in response to the needs of their specific local environment. The World Intellectual Property Organization (WIPO) defines traditional knowledge as—indigenous cultural and intellectual property, indigenous heritage, and customary heritage rights. The need to protect the traditional knowledge captured the attention of the international community only recently, but the standard setting was left to the national governments. The absence of the international standards that causes serious negligence for the protection of the traditional knowledge and the benefits of new technology to the inhabitants of the locality, i.e. Tribals. It is the Tribals who have protected the herbs by protecting the forests and animals. But the traditional that is a community property at present is exploited by the corporates without compensating anything to the Tribals. Even the culture they have developed, is utilised by the movie industries as a source in the public domain. But the TK is a knowledge which is learnt, experimented, protected and carried over from generations to generations with all reverence creates rights in the community for its personal use and commercial exploitation for livelihood and economic progress. But the fact is quite different. The biotechnology industry depends on the herbs and shrubs, but the Tribals have no share in price of the raw-material nor in the profit of the product. Further, the electricity generated out of the hydel projects which use water of the springs does not supply the same to the Tribals. In this context, the mechanism Requires to be Developed for tribal economic empowerment.

Patenting of the Traditional Knowledge

It is a fact that there are around 100 million forest dwellers in India, most of them belong to tribal communities. They depend on the both timber and non-timber forest produce. In turn, the forest dwellers have over the centuries gathered knowledge from the natural environment around their community. This community has in one sense been thankfully insulated from the ways of modern man and has carried on the traditions of their ancestors. As a whole, the forests and its dwellers give to India an abundant knowledge about the traditional value of various forest products. The way intellectual property rights have been designed in modern commerce, traditional knowledge cannot be protected. For instance, traditional knowledge cannot be patented because such knowledge lacks inventive character, because of the inherent lack of novelty. Traditional knowledge is also often held collectively by communities, rather than by individual owners. This traditional knowledge is information that is transmitted from generation to generation generally within the community or within families within the community in an oral form without any adequate documentation. This has caused traditional knowledge to be undervalued and marginalized. In fact, one of the fears in these communities is that if the knowledge were to be documented it would have been lost to the community by expropriation. In India, the Forest Act itself acknowledges this fact and provides a framework for documentation of such knowledge and the nature of evidence required for recognition of the rights of these communities in the intellectual property in respect of such knowledge. The provisions of the Biological Diversity Act and Forest Rights Act of 2006 both provide a shield for tribal traditional knowledge, by, on the one hand, respecting and protecting the knowledge of the local communities related to biodiversity and on the other, declaring that the intellectual property rights, in such knowledge belongs primarily to members of the community collectively. In broad terms, patents can be defined as exclusive rights granted for an invention—either a product or a process—that offers a new technical solution to a specific problem. A patent implies the grant of a—monopoly to an inventor who has used his knowledge and skills to produce a product or process which is new, involves an inventive step and is capable of industrial application. The TRIPS Agreement also has some provisions having limited application to the protection of Traditional Knowledge. The obligation to protect geographical indications can be used to protect traditional knowledge if associated with the indication used for production and sale of goods. It is made clear that a given quality, reputation or other characteristics of the goods essentially attributable to its geographical origin are to be considered in identifying the geographical indications for protection. Thus, it may be possible for protection through geographical indication the traditional knowledge associated with goods. Disclosing traditional knowledge which forms part of an invention and of the state of the art or prior art will promote the progress of science by creating an incentive for the maintenance of traditional knowledge systems. This will happen by TK being widely and universally accepted within "western" or "modern" innovation protection systems and becoming a reference point within the regular operations of the international patent system. It will provide opportunities to the Tribals for economic exploitation along with the scientists. It will also stop the theft of the traditional knowledge. The biotechnological industry will be benefited.

National Knowledge Commission and Traditional Knowledge

The national knowledge commission in India has also showed its concern over the threat and danger on the TK. It has recommended to protect traditional knowledge and said—"Establish goals for conservation of natural resources: Natural populations of around 12 per cent of the 6000 species of potentially medicinal plants are currently estimated to be under threat due to degradation and loss of habitats alongside unsustainable ways of harvesting and lack of cultivation. The problem of growing scarcity also leads to the danger of more counterfeit material being marketed. It is therefore necessary to support conservation and sustainable harvesting efforts in the forestry sector and cultivation in the agricultural sector. Direct support for conservation and cultivation as well as indirect methods through incentive policies should be pursued for nurturing these plant resources. The wild gene pool of India's medicinal plants should be secured, *via* establishment of a nation-wide network of 300 'Forest Gene Banks' across the 10 bio-geographic regions of the country". "Support primary healthcare in rural areas: With 70 per cent of Indian population relying on traditional medicine for primary health care in the absence of adequate state primary health care, it becomes necessary to establish evidence-based guidelines for this informal-sector usage. A nation-wide network of Home Herbal Garden (HHG) and Community Herbal Gardens (CHG) can be created to support the primary health care needs of rural communities for those plants and medications established as efficacious by evidence-based research.

The knowledge commission has proposed that a major re-branding exercise of Indian traditional medicine can ensure health revolution in India. Better branding of Indian traditional medicines can prove to be effective in well-designed clinical trials and can increase safe and effective healthcare options. Such proven medications can be integrated with the national healthcare system. Such evidence-based, well-validated and uniquely Indian holistic healthcare system combinations must be marketed extensively globally. In order to achieve these goals as rapidly and efficiently as possible, the Government of India may consider establishing a National Mission on Traditional Health Knowledge (NMTHK), which would take-up these tasks in an organized way. It should be a relatively small body in terms of its own infrastructure with powers to enable it to recommend targeted funding in identified areas. It should support initiatives at many different levels, including state and local levels, and coordinate with Ministries of Health, Science and Technology, Forestry, Agriculture, and Commerce as well as with the NGOs and private sector. The Mission leader must be a person with high public credibility, have extensive knowledge and experience in the field with established managerial capabilities and experience of dealing with all the concerned stakeholders."

Biopiracy, TK and the Tribals

One of the biggest threats to biodiversity and related traditional knowledge is ever-increasingly bio-prospecting activities on behalf of enthobotonists, pharmaceutical companies and others who wish to profit from the rich biodiversity and traditional knowledge in indigenous territories. Current legal systems are inadequate, allowing for the bio-piracy of biodiversity and traditional knowledge. As demand for commercialization of biodiversity and traditional knowledge increases at a rapid pace and as the world globalizes, the indigenous societies are being encroached upon faster than traditional knowledge can be protected. Their cultures and knowledge are being lost. In many parts of the world, the very existence of indigenous societies is under threat. The reason lies in the Inadequacy of Legal System that address Traditional Knowledge. General issues relating to the protection of traditional knowledge and clash within systems all make traditional knowledge highly vulnerable to Bio-piracy.

Several traditional plants and related knowledge in Asia, specifically India, have also been allegedly falsely patented by the US patent office, including: *Neem, Haldi, Pepper, Harar*, Mustard, *Basmati* rice, Ginger, Castor, *Jaramla*, *Karela*, and *Jamun*. The African continent has too been plagued by bio-piracy—with the case of West Africa's sweet genes and one of the most recent cases involving—'Hoodi' still unresolved. Some cases have been resolved, but clearly demonstrate the problems with the intellectual property system. Traditional knowledge is generally associated with biological resources and is invariably an intangible component of such a biological resource. Traditional knowledge has the potential of being translated into commercial benefits by providing leads/clues for development of useful practices and processes for the benefit of mankind. The valuable leads/clues provided by TK save time, money and investment of modern biotech and other industries into any research and product development. Reasonably, we can say that a share of such benefits should accrue to the creators and/or holders of such Traditional Knowledge. Some countries have specific legislation protecting this kind of knowledge while some other countries feel their existing IPR regime protects such knowledge. As of now, India does not have a specific *sui generis* legislation to protect such TK and folklore, but is in the process of developing such legislation.

In the recent past, there have been several cases of bio-piracy of TK from India. First, it was the patent on wound-healing properties of *Haldi* (turmeric); now patents have been obtained in other countries on hypoglycaemic properties of *Karela* (bitter gourd), brinjal, etc. An important criticism in this context relates to foreigners obtaining patents-based on Indian biological materials without acknowledging the source of their Knowledge or sharing the benefits. There is also the view that the TRIPS Agreement is aiding the exploitation of biodiversity by privatizing biodiversity expressed in life forms and knowledge. The Neem, a legendary tree to India has been used as a bio-pesticide and medicine in India for centuries… The European Patent Office (EPO) revoke in its entirety patent number 436257 which had been granted to the United States of American and the multinational corporation W.R. Grace for a fungicide derived from seed of the *Neem* tree. Despite *Neem*'s ancient tradition, over 12 US patents were recently taken out *Neem*-based emulsions and solutions. Secondly, Turmeric, in 1993, the US PTO granted the University of

Mississippi Medical Centre patent rights over a—healing a wound by administering turmeric to a patient afflicted with a woundbut again, Turmeric has been used for centuries in India. Indians grow-up with a constant awareness of turmeric the tuber when dried keeps practically forever. The patent was eventually cancelled in 1998 after re-examination proceedings. But revealed to India and to indigenous societies around the world, again, how easy it was to falsely patent centuries-old traditional knowledge. Thirdly, Basmati Rice in 1997, the US patent office granted a patent in September 1997 to Rice Tec for a strain of Basmati rice, anaromatic rice grown in India and Pakistan for centuries. This case has not yet been resolved, but the Indian Government is actively pursuing the case, stating that it violates both TRIPS and the CBD. According the South Asia Commission on conomic and Social Policy, Rice Tec's patent also violated the CBD in not recognizing the sovereign rights of India and Pakistan over 'Basmati rice'. In *basmati* case demonstrates the problem as illustrated in TRIPS that patents are granted to bio-technological processes. Thus, even though *basmati* rice has been in South Asia for centuries, Rice Tec just altered it slightly through crossing with a Western strain of grain, and successfully claimed it was its own. Fourthly, 'Maca' in 2001 after the Viagra craze, two US companies patented extracts of the Andean plant,—Maca which has traditionally been used to enhance fertility and sexual function. The patents were granted on the basis of—unlocking mica's chemical secrets through advanced processes. It has become clear, though narrating these few cases that IP laws cannot or are not being effectively applied to prevent the bio-piracy of traditional knowledge. Traditional knowledge is being treated as a free input into research and commercial product development. When patents are falsely granted, equitable benefit sharing is not taking place either, while indigenous peoples remain subject to bio-piracy and become ever more marginalized in the process. Recently amended patent law of ours contains provisions for mandatory disclosure of source and geographical origin of the biological material used in the invention while applying for patents in India. Provisions have also been incorporated to include non-disclosure or wrongful disclosure of the same as grounds for opposition and for revocation of the patents, if granted. To protect Traditional knowledge from being patented, provisions have also been incorporated in the law to include anticipation of invention by available local knowledge including oral knowledge, as one of the grounds for opposition as also for revocation of patent. In order to further strengthen these provisions, a new provision has been added to exclude innovations which are basically traditional or aggregation or duplication of known properties of traditionally known component or components from being patented. Granting of patents in respect of traditional knowledge, concern that has been expressed in the discussion in the council for TRIPS is about the grant of patents or other IPRs covering traditional knowledge to persons other than the indigenous peoples or community who have originated the knowledge and legitimately controlled it. The view has been expressed that the granting to patents on traditional knowledge already in the public domain or without the consent of indigenous peoples and local communities amount to unauthorized appropriation of the knowledge. The Tribals are required to aware about the TK and train them for documentation so that they can be ensured for their livelihood.

Empowerment Mechanism for the Tribals

Traditional knowledge is being used without the authorization of the indigenous peoples or communities who have originated and legitimately controlled it and without proper sharing of the benefit that occurs from such use. It has been suggested that the starting point should be explored possibility for making more effective use of the exiting IPR system for protecting the traditional knowledge of indigenous peoples and local communities. It has been suggested that the best mechanism of protection of TK and provisions of livelihood to them would be through system-based on bilateral contract between holder of traditional knowledge and persons or companies wishing to access and use the knowledge. Secondly, the applicant for patent that use traditional knowledge associated with genetic resources should be required to disclose the course or the origin of the source of the traditional knowledge in their patent applications. Thirdly, only a system of protection of traditional knowledge which provides "proprietary rights" can insure that market forces will be operative to generate fairness and equity. The Indian legislation for the Protection of Plant Varieties and Farmers' Rights Act, 2001, also acknowledge that the conservation, exploration, collection, characterization, evaluation of plant genetic resources for food and agriculture are essential to meet the goals of national food and nutritional security as also for sustainable development of agriculture for the present and future generations. It also acknowledges that the plant genetic resources for food and agriculture are the raw-material indispensable for crop genetic improvement. The concept of effective benefit sharing arrangement between the provider and the recipient of the plant genetic resources forms an integral part of our Act. The protection provided to a plant variety bred by a breeder can be cancelled if there is an omission or wrongful disclosure of such information.

Indian Traditional Knowledge available to the USPTO—Patent examiners of the United States Patent and Trademark Office (USPTO) are now able to access the Database of Traditional Knowledge. Thanks to the Government of Indian according its permission in November 2009, India's Council of Scientific and Industrial Research, and the Department of Ayurveda, Yoga and Naturopathy, Unani, Siddha and Homoeopathy was credited with the development of the Traditional Knowledge Digital Library (TKDL), which is a 30 million page searchable database of traditional knowledge translated from numerous languages such as Hindi, Sanskrit, Arabic, Persian, Urdu and Tamil into English, Japanese, French, German and Spanish. The EPO was allowed the use of the TKDL in February 2009. The Indian Department of Industrial Policy and Promotion (DIPP) and USPTO announced on the 23rd of November, 2009 that they have entered into a MoU on comprehensive bilateral cooperation for IPR protection and enforcement. Under the terms of the MoU, the USPTO and DIPP will cooperate on a range of IPR issues, focusing on capacity-building, human resource development, and raising public awareness of the importance of IPR. *Protection of Traditional Knowledge in India by Patent: Legal Aspect.*

This UN Draft Declaration, in Article 29, specifically states that "Indigenous peoples are entitled to the recognition of the full ownership, control and protection of their cultural and intellectual property. They have the right to special measures to control, develop and protect their sciences, technologies and cultural manifestations, including human and other genetic resources, seeds, medicines, knowledge of the properties of fauna and flora, oral traditions, literatures, designs and visual and performing arts". A recent positive initiative is the drafting of a set of corporate guidelines for businesses that want to use native plants and traditional knowledge from indigenous communities to make commercial drugs. In April 2002 in The Hague, delegates of the UN Biodiversity Congress from 166 countries negotiated and adopted global guidelines during a two-week long U.N. sponsored CBD conference that was designed to encourage pharmaceutical companies to make responsible agreements with countries whose resources they use "The Cancun Declaration and Cusco Declaration on Access to Genetic Resources". In February 2002, Environmental Ministers from 12 countries met in Cancun, Mexico met to discuss issues related to biodiversity in their countries, identifying a need to establish terms governing the granting of patents.

It has also been suggested that a requirement on patent applications to disclose in their applications any traditional knowledge used in the invention in question could help in the assessment of novelty and also assist countries with possible claims to examine the application and oppose the patent in time. The Geographical Indication of Goods (Registration and Protection) Act, 1999 passed by Parliament is another step taken by India. The Act primarily intends to protect the valuable geographical indications of our country. The protection under the Act is available only to the geographical indication registered under the Act and to the authorized users. The Act permits any association of persons or producers or any organization or authority established by law representing the interest of the producers of goods to register a geographical indication. It may be possible to argue that the holders of the traditional knowledge in goods produced and sold using geographical indication can register and protect their traditional knowledge under this law.

Conclusion

The development and use of the traditional knowledge in the market economy can protect the rights of the Tribals, their exploitation, migration and dehumanisation due to joblessness. The exploitation of TK without their consent, may facilitate otherwise of exploitation of their knowledge without any rewards to them. It has been suggested that the development of database on traditional knowledge would help patent examiners discover relevant prior art so as to improve examination of patent application and prevent the grant of patents for subject matter that should not be patentable. Database would also help potential licensees in terms of searching for knowledge, innovations and parties various suggestions have been advanced in India to extend protection to knowledge, innovations and practices. These includes documentation of TK; Registration and innovation patent system; and development of a *sui generis* system. It is sometimes believed that proper documentation of associated TK could help in checking bio-piracy. Documentation could be a double-edged sword. It is assumed that if the material/knowledge are documented, it can be made available to patent examiners the world over so that prior art in the case of inventions based on such materials/knowledge are/is readily available to them. It is also hoped that such documentation would facilitate tracing of indigenous communities with whom benefits of commercialization of such materials/ knowledge has to be shared. The PESA Act, 1996 also confirms the rights of the Tribals for their economic sustainability. The Tribals who have been living in the natural environment from age have rights over entire ecosystem. They have rights because they been protecting these resources from ages emotionally. But because of illiteracy and innocence, the corporates are taking away their TK for their commercial gain. They are now bewildered. More so the coffer dams and hydel projects are forcing them, to migrate from their traditional home destroying their rich IP. Thus, the rehabilitation of the Tribals at their natural abode along with Commercial Exploitation with their consent, sharing the profits are the way to empower them.

References

Convention on biodiversity.
The Biodiversity Act, 2002
The Cancun Declaration.
The forest dwellers rights.
The Forest Rights Act, 2006.
The GI Act, 1999
The Patents Act, 1970 as Amended in 2005.
The PESA Act, 1996.
The Plant Variety and Farmers Rights Act, 2001
UN draft declaration on the Indigenous people u/Article 29.

5

Effectiveness of Developmental Programmes for Scheduled Tribes in Maharashtra

B.N. Kamble

Introduction

The society of Indian people is divided into various castes and tribes from ancient periods. Whereas, the other groups of the society had better access of the developmental opportunities as well as resources. After the Independence specific and general statutory safeguards were provided to the Scheduled Castes and Scheduled Tribes in the Constitution of India. From the First Five Year Plan, a policy of positive discrimination was adopted and emphasis was laid on growth with social justice. This was continued in all the successive Five Year Plans. Several developmental schemes were framed and implemented by the Central as well as State Governments and other agencies. These efforts indicate possibilities of substantial change in the living conditions of these groups as they are availing the benefits of several multi-objective programmes. However, the Scheduled Tribes did not notice expected changes, despite the plan efforts through expenditures on various programmes, Constitutional safeguards and strong emphasis on bringing these groups into the mainstream of socio-economic development. It was pointed out in the Report that the inequalities have increased and continued to increase. In the background of this, it become necessary to analyse the structure, direction emphasis and the impact of the developmental programmes being operated in the country for the Scheduled Castes and Scheduled

Tribes. The analysis of effectiveness of the programmes can be broadly organised into four groups according to the spirit of the programmes, namely—socio-economic condition, poverty, educational development, and the impact of developmental programmes.

The specific objectives of the study are:

1. To attempt a schematic review of the studies analysing the problems and programmes for the development of the Scheduled Tribes.
2. To analyse the emergence of the tribe system and important factors governing it.
3. To ascertain the growth and distribution of the Scheduled Tribes in the country as well as in the State of Maharashtra.
4. To attempt to analyse the strategies adopted towards amelioration of their conditions during various plan periods with respect to the philosophy and expenditure pattern.
5. To study the changes in different parameters and social conditions of Scheduled Tribes due to the operation of different programmes in the sample region at micro-level.
6. To analyse the effectiveness of the developmental programmes at micro-level, in terms of the determining factors for effectiveness represented by the economic parameters.

The study utilised data, both at secondary as well as primary levels. The secondary level data used in order to understand the trends in plan efforts of the developmental programmes for the Scheduled Tribes. For the collection of primary data, the field schedule prepared. It spread over the sub-components namely general information of sample households, employment situation, agriculture, participation in various developmental programmes, value of assets and consumption pattern, etc. for the purpose of micro-level study. The study, three stage systematic random sampling procedure followed with the first stage as the Talukas, second as villages and the third stage as the selection of the households. The present study is concerned with the socio-economic development of Scheduled Tribes of Maharashtra. The study focused on various infrastructural facilities available to the people in Maharashtra and selected districts of the study, i.e. Pune, Ahmednagar and Thane and their development blocks—Junnar, Akole and Murbad respectively.

The analysis is based on micro-level primary data of 375 sample households families belonging to Scheduled Tribes of Maharashtra, three districts namely—Pune, Ahmednagar and Thane and three development blocks namely—Junnar (127 sample households), Akole (123 households) and Murbad (125 sample households) respectively. To conduct the primary survey 27 villages were selected from three development blocks of three districts—Junnar (12 villages), Akole (9 villages) and Murbad (6 villages).

The methodology of analysis involved use of simple statistical techniques and Tables-based on the collected data. The study covered the period from 1951 to 2008. The scope of the present study is confined mainly to the effectiveness of the developmental programmes implemented by Central Government and State Government of Maharashtra for the upliftment of Scheduled Tribes.

The Present Status of Scheduled Tribes

Since, most of the tribal habitations are located in isolated villages and hamlets in undulating plateau lands coinciding with forest areas, they have limited access to critical infrastructure facilities such as roads, communication, health, education, electricity, drinking water, and so on. This widens the gap between the quality of their life and the people in the country. The STs are mainly landless poor forest dwellers and shifting cultivators, small farmers and pastoral and nomadic herders. The livelihood strategy would thus have to take into account the land structure, level of skills, socio-economic conditions, low level of HDI along with the physical infrastructure and natural resource base in the tribal areas.

The incidence of poverty amongst STs continues to be very high at 47.30 per cent in rural areas and 33.30 per cent in urban areas, compared to 28.30 per cent and 25.70 per cent, respectively in respect of total population in 2004-05. A large number of STs who are living below the poverty line are landless, with no productive assets and with no access to sustainable employment and minimum wages.

Between 1961 and 2001, the literacy rate of STs increased 5.32 times, while that of total population increased 2.69 times. However, the gap between the literacy rates of STs and of the general population continued during the three decades between 1971 and 2001 almost at the same level of 17.70 per cent and above, but with marginal variations.

The dropout rate is a critical indicator reflecting lack of educational development and inability of a given social group to complete a specific level of education. In the case of tribals, dropout rates are still very high–42.3 per cent in Classes I to V; 65.9 per cent in Classes I to VIII; and 79.0 per cent in Classes I to X in 2004-05. About 4.34 lakh ST students were studying at different levels of higher education as on 30 September, 2004.

81.56 per cent of the total ST workers, both rural and urban taken together, are engaged in the primary sector, of whom 44.71 per cent are cultivators and 36.85 per cent are agricultural labourers. The corresponding figures for all workers are 31.65 per cent (cultivators) and 26.55 per cent (agricultural labourers). This indicates that STs are essentially dependent on agriculture.

Development of Scheduled Tribes in Maharashtra

The study attempted to analyse social developmental programmes initiated by Central Government and State Government of Maharashtra and across the estates. The study covers changes in different parameters in policy for the development of Scheduled Tribes. The present study discussed the various issues related to the development programmes implemented for the Scheduled Tribes. The issues are: the status of Scheduled Tribes in Indian society, population profile, Scheduled Tribe population in India and Maharashtra, Census 2001 and 2011. Along with this distribution of Scheduled Tribes in Maharashtra their activities, literacy, health development programmes are covered in detailed in the study. The study observed on the basis of above analysis there is a gap between policy programme and implementation at grassroot level. Government introduced many programmes for the development of Scheduled Tribes. Apart for this the socio-economic condition of Scheduled Tribes is not reflecting even however micro-data analyse of sample households as family and also individuals. There is a need of a programme should be effective to reflect in standard of living of Scheduled Tribes in general and particularly in Maharashtra State.

To understand the various characteristics of the study area the study focuses on the population profile, male female sex-ratio, household size, workers house type, literacy, educational levels etc., and also study attempted to collect participation of Scheduled Tribes in self-help groups (SHG) and number of BPL families in districts. Moreover, the study attempted to review the vision development prospective plan of the districts. The analysis of the Thane district comparatively shows first position in characteristics followed by Pune and Ahmednagar.

The study shows a marked improvement in the representation of STs in various categories of services during 1994 and 2004, though they are yet not adequately represented in any of the four categories. The situation is especially unsatisfactory with respect to the A and B categories.

The village-wise profile-based on Census 2001 is presented in appendices. The primary data shows the socio-economic status of the sample household are very low in respect of asset, income, education and income generated activities. The sample households are engaged in daily labour activities in other blocks. The sample household adults are in search of daily agricultural employment needs to move from their villages to other places. However, some sample households benefited of various socio-economic development programmes in study area. The sample households are benefited educational programmes particularly hostels, ashram schools etc., landholders reported that partly benefited of agricultural development programmes. From the Thane district sample households benefited from the activities like self-help groups (SHG) than Pune and Ahmednagar districts. Most of the families from three development blocks benefited under Indira Awas Yojana, however, the beneficiaries of the scheme faced the problem of their own contribution in the scheme. The study observed that at the time of the survey visits the Indira Awas Yojana works were in progress in blocks. However, the beneficiaries reported that the fund was not sufficient to construct the house. The study discusses the food and non-food cosumption pattern in detailed in sample households.

Determinants of Effectiveness of the Developmental Programmes

The effectiveness of the developmental programmes can have multiple facets. First of all defining effectiveness would mean finding the positive changes in the intended parameters and standardising this change by expressing it in terms of the units of efforts taken. In other words, the change due to programme per unit of the efforts taken will indicate the effectiveness of the programmes. The implemented programme improve the economic well being of the Scheduled Tribes (reflected by income earned due to the programme), then the incremental income generated gives the impact of the programme. But such incremental income per unit of the efforts (represented by either the investment or total cost of the programme) will give a clear indicator of effectiveness. This will help in deciding the effectiveness not only across the programmes, but also across the sample households. Thus, effectiveness can be defined mathematically as follows:

$$EIH = \frac{\sum_{i=1}^{P}(IA - IE)}{\sum_{i=1}^{P} PIi} \times 100$$

Where,

EIH = Effectiveness Index of the Household
IA = Total Income after the programme participation
IE = Income before the programme participation (socio-economic condition before joining the programmes)
PI = Total Programme Investment (Loan + Subsidy)

The determinants of effectiveness could be analysed in two ways. Firstly, a look at the correlation matrix of the main sample characteristics offers important clues. These can be used in terms of broad indicators. The major parameters considered here can be grouped into some broad groups for the case of analysis. Secondly, after obtaining the broad clues from the correlation matrix (Appendix: 1 and 2), it becomes easy to fit regression models to certain chosen variables to locate their degree of influence on effectiveness.

For the purpose of analysis, with the help of correlation matrix (Appendix: 1 & 2), the variables are grouped into five broad groups, namely—

1. *Income*—Pre-assistance and ex-post income, income from wages, scheme income and other income;
2. *Agriculture related variables*—Size of landholding, fallow land and irrigated/dry land;
3. *Assets*—Livestock, family assets and household assets;

4. *Scheme related variables*—Scheme expenditure, loan amount, and subsidy; and
5. *Consumption*—Size of family, consumption expenditure on food and non-food items and per capita consumption.

The first group of variables indicate the earnings of the family after participating in the programmes as well as from different sources. Agriculture income and wage income are the dominant sources of income. Therefore, these have high and positive relationship with the total income. Similarly, the asset position of the households also has a positive relationship with income. It is interesting to note a positive relationship with non-food consumption expenditure. This indicates that as the income increases the consumption of non-food items also increases. Another aspect in the Table of correlation is that the area under rainfed conditions shows a negative relationship with the total income, thereby indicates that the farmers with larger area under dry lands do not have higher income. Surprisingly, size of landholding does not bear any significant relationship with any of the income concepts. The variables representing agricultural sector activities also have bearing on the effectiveness of the programme. Agricultural income shows a positive and high correlation with the total scheme assistance as well as with loans. A similar relationship is not seen with the other variables from the income group.

The variables relating to the scheme showed a positive relationship with assets, scheme income and scheme expenditure which was an expected result. Surprisingly, the landholdings showed a negative relationship with scheme expenditure. The consumption pattern has a definite positive relationship with asset holdings as well as land under irrigation. Though most of the correlations are not significant, they indicate a trend towards identification of the determinants of effectiveness.

In order to identify the major determinant of effectiveness of the programmes the study will consider selected variables and estimated the slope coefficient with the help of single variable simple additive model with the following specification:

$$Y = a + bX + u$$

Where,

Y = Effectiveness Index

X = Independent variable as indicated in Table

a = Regression constant (intercept)
b = Slope coefficient
u = Stochastic error term.

(*The analysis of the study is in progress*)

Conclusion

The study concludes that:

1. Most of the families particularly those families are unable to do labour activities faced the saviour problem of day-to-day consumption and majorities of families living and low level of living or in other words were below poverty line.
2. In the study area the sample households income generated activities are agricultural labour activities and labour activities involved uncertainties in availabilities of employment affects their family income and it reflects on standard of living.
3. The study observed that due to the non-availability of the micro-level data of the government, the implementing agency at the grassroot level finding major difficulties to achieve their objectives and targets and also the study notes that the development programmes are not effectively implemented.

The study suggests that:

1. There is an urgent need to collect micro-level data of socio-economic status, employment, assets, education, health, etc. to help to prepare micro-level planning, family-wise planning to help individual needs of family members of Scheduled Tribes for the effective implementation of socio-economic development programmes of Scheduled Tribes.
2. The programmes should provide employment at local level based on local needs. The skill training programmes should conduct and develop small scale entrepreneurship for the self-income generating activities in the village. Accordingly, the policies and programmes should be modified considering needs and requirements in the study area.
3. There is a need to identify areas and groups which continue

to suffer marked exclusion and neglect to enable a more focused implementation of positive discrimination policies. The study also emphasizes the need to invest greater financial and educational resources for their educational development.

Appendix 1: Definition of variables

Sl. No.	*Abrogation of Variables*	*Definition of Variables*
1.	m/pn	Male/PN
2.	f/pn	Female/PN
3.	m/f	Male/Female
4.	eh/pn	Education hostel beneficiary/PN
5.	19-a60/pn	Age 19 and above 60 Years/pn
6.	IAY/value	Indira Awas Yojana/Value Rs.
7.	self/value	IAY Self-Contribution/Value Rs.
8.	ainputc/ap	Agricultural input cost Rs./Agricultural Product Rs.
9.	apc/ap	Agricultural Product total cost Rs./Agricultural product Rs.
10.	lsv/lsi	Livestock value Rs./Livestock Income
11.	tfc/wlati	Total food consumption Rs./Wage, Livestock and agricultural total Income Rs.
12.	tnfc/wlati	Total non-food consumption Rs./Wage, Livestock and agricultural total Income Rs.
13.	tc/wlati	Total food consumption Rs./Wage, Livestock and agricultural total Income Rs.
14.	tmfw/wlati	Total Male-female wage income Rs./Wage, Livestock and agricultural total Income Rs.
15.	ntli/wlati	Net Livestock Income Rs./Wage, Livestock and agricultural total Income Rs.
16.	ntai/wlati	Net agricultural Income Rs./Wage, Livestock and agricultural total Income Rs.
17.	avim/avcm	Net Livestock Income Rs./Wage, Livestock and agricultural total Income Rs.
18.	rme/avinmo	Net agricultural Income Rs./Wage, Livestock and agricultural total Income Rs.
19.	avim/rme	Average Monthly Income Rs./Required Monthly Expenditure Rs.
20.	ratio wi/wlati	Ratio wage income/wage, Livestock and agricultural income
21.	tmfwi/iayv	Total Male-female wage income Rs./Indira AwasYojana Value
22.	nlin/iayv	Net Livestock income/Indira AwasYojana Value
23.	ntain/iayv	Net agricultural Income Rs./Indira AwasYojana Value
24.	wlain/iayv*100	Wage, Livestock and agricultural total Income Rs./Indira AwasYojana Value *100

Appendix 2: Correlation

Variables	m/pn	f/pn	m/f	eh/pn	19-a60/pn	IAY/value	self/value	ainputc/ap	apc/ap	lsv/lsi	tfc/wlati	tnfc/wlati	tc/wlati	tmfw/wlati	ntli/wlati	ntai/wlati	avim/avcm	rme/avinmo	avim/rme	ratio wi/wlati	tmfwi/iayv	nlin/iayv	ntain/iayv	wlain/iayv*100
	1	2	3	4	5	6	7	8	9	10	11	12	13	14	15	16	17	18	19	20	21	22	23	24
1.	1.00																							
2.	–0.95**	1.00																						
3.	0.82**	–0.81**	1.00																					
4.	–0.20	0.22**	–0.15**	1.00																				
5.	0.05	0.00	0.02	0.32**	1.00																			
6.	0.03	–0.02	0.00	–0.04	–0.01	1.00																		
7.	–0.01	0.03	–0.02	0.00	–0.01	–0.45**	1.00																	
8.	0.10	–0.10	0.15**	–0.02	–0.01	0.03	–0.01	1.00																
9.	0.09	–0.08	0.10	–0.10	0.00	0.05	–0.02	0.47**	1.00															
10.	0.06	–0.05	0.02	–0.09	0.02	0.06	–0.03	0.10	0.11	1.00														
11.	0.05	–0.04	0.14**	0.02	–0.02	0.01	–0.02	0.70**	0.14**	0.01	1.00													
12.	0.03	–0.02	0.12	–0.03	–0.03	–0.06	0.01	0.22**	0.02**	0.05	0.49**	1.00												
13.	0.05	–0.04	0.15**	0.01	–0.03	–0.01	–0.02	0.65**	0.13**	0.02	0.97**	0.69**	1.00											
14.	0.08	–0.07	0.14**	–0.05	0.02	0.04	–0.04	0.77**	0.15**	–0.02	0.90**	0.33**	0.84**	1.00										
15.	–0.13	0.13	–0.12**	0.10	0.06	–0.02	0.00	–0.01	–0.03	–0.02	0.01	0.08	0.03	–0.11*	1.00									
16.	–0.06	0.06	–0.12**	0.02	–0.02	–0.04	0.04	–0.77**	–0.15**	0.02	–0.90**	–0.34**	–0.85**	–0.99**	0.01	1.00								
17.	–0.05	0.05	–0.06	0.05	0.14**	0.09	–0.04	–0.02	0.04	–0.05	–0.06	–0.07	–0.07	–0.01	–0.01	0.02	1.00							
18.	–0.02	0.03	0.08	–0.09	–0.11**	0.00	–0.03	0.68**	0.15**	0.00	0.94**	0.49**	0.92**	0.89**	0.02	–0.89	–0.08	1.00						
19.	0.18**	–0.16**	0.05	0.14**	0.36	–0.03	0.06	–0.06	0.04	–0.05	–0.25**	–0.27**	–0.28**	–0.10	0.05	0.12	0.20	–0.34**	1.00					
20.	0.04	0.00	0.04	–0.16**	–0.03	0.00	–0.03	0.17**	–0.01	–0.01	0.27	0.20**	0.28**	0.43**	–0.29	–0.36	–0.02	0.37**	–0.10**	1.00				
21.	0.04	–0.04	–0.02	–0.11**	0.08	–0.13**	0.46**	–0.04	–0.06	–0.03	–0.12*	–0.13**	–0.14**	–0.01	–0.01	0.03	0.10	–0.11*	0.25**	0.03	1.00			
22.	0.05	–0.04	–0.09	0.04	0.07	–0.09	0.06	–0.01	–0.02	–0.02	–0.05	–0.05	–0.05	–0.05	0.44	0.01	0.01	–0.06	0.19**	–0.13**	0.32**	1.00		
23.	0.00	0.00	–0.03	–0.04	0.05	–0.08	0.30**	–0.05	0.11**	0.00	–0.09	–0.06	–0.09	–0.13**	–0.05	0.14	0.05	–0.10	0.15**	–0.25**	0.12**	0.01	1.00	
24.	0.05	–0.04	–0.05	–0.10	0.09	–0.15**	0.48**	–0.05	–0.03	–0.03	–0.14**	–0.14**	–0.16**	–0.05	0.07	0.06	0.10	–0.13**	0.29**	–0.06	0.95**	0.49**	0.37**	1.00

6

Impacting Development: Thought and Practice through Bhili Cultural Rejuvenation

Shankar Tadwal and *Rahul Banerjee*

Introductory Background

A fairly well established fact today is that the institutions set-up under the provisions of the Constitution of India for the protection of the *adivasis* have not functioned properly and the various laws and policies enacted from time-to-time for this purpose have not been implemented primarily due to the wrong development policies adopted by the state which have tended to strengthen rather than weaken the political and economic power of the non-*adivasis* *vis-à-vis* the *adivasis*. The state has also failed to provide good and adequate education services which has resulted in the *adivasis* remaining unequipped to negotiate the complexities of the modern centralised system of governance into which they have been forcefully integrated. The poverty induced by these wrong development policies has adversely affected the nutritional levels of the food intake of the *adivasis* and combined with the lack of good and cheap health services has led to a decline in their general health. Moreover, the even greater lack of both education and health services for the women has meant that they have not been able to smash age old patriarchal structures and their consequent lack of reproductive rights has led to a population explosion putting further pressure on already scarce resources. All these factors have combined to produce a scenario where in *adivasis* are being continually exploited by the improper functioning of the modern market system which has increasingly penetrated into their subsistence lifestyles and being forced to live on the edge. The condition of the Bhil *adivasis* of western Madhya Pradesh provides ample evidence of this decay.

The Bhils have not only lost their natural resource bases, but with the undermining of their subsistence agriculture-based lifestyle that this has led to, they have lost confidence in their own indigenous culture too. Poverty has led to community links breaking down and there has been a continuous downgrading of their culture by non-*adivasi* oppressors. Even their Gods are losing their shine as more and more Bhils have begun to worship Hindu or Christian Gods and Goddesses. The final blow has come in the form of dam building on the River Narmada and its tributaries which seeks to destroy completely not only the Bhils' habitat, but also, by displacing them into areas populated largely by non-*adivasis*, their unique culture.

The Bhil *adivasis* have a rich oral folklore. There is the creation myth centred on the River Narmada in some cases and in others on the Goddesses and Gods Velubai, Rani Kajal and Indiraja which is sung during the Diwasa festival allowing the Bhils to partake of the products of their lands during the *Kharif* season. Then there is the myth of the Goddess Kansari, who represents the staple cereal *sorghum*, which is sung at the time of the celebration of Indal which is a festival of thanks, giving to nature for having been bountiful with her harvests. Finally, there is the myth of Kalorano the God of Rain which is sung to appease him when the rains play truant during the monsoon season. Apart from these major myths there are a number of other stories. Their contents reflect the close empathic relations that the Bhils have traditionally had with their habitat given the fact that their very existence is directly dependent on the munificience of nature. This rich and valuable oral literary corpus has the potential for reviving not only the belief of the Bhils in themselves and thus motivating them to better participate as equal citizens in political and economic processes, but is also capable of providing theoretical and practical clues towards the formulation of a more sustainable agriculture-based developmental model than the one that is dominant today. However, this valuable heritage is in danger of being lost forever as the younger Bhils today have little regard for the traditional Bhil culture and its rich oral heritage given its inability at present to secure them a viable livelihood.

2. An Innovation that is Systems Changing

Historically, a major medium for the positing of a strong identity by any community has been its language. All literate cultures have thrived by developing a rich literature to strengthen their language. However, *adivasi* cultures being non-literate have not been able to do this and so have fallen behind and face extinction. Today, the lack of entertaining written literature in the Bhili language has resulted in most literate Bhils switching over to Hindi instead. So, transcribing the voluminous folklore of the Bhils and publishing it will provide the literate Bhils with enough reading materials of quality to entice them back to their mother tongue. New literature and the further development of the written Bhili language and a revival of their decaying culture will then follow as the night the day. The modern Indian languages have all developed in this way. Moreover, the experience of using the traditional myths and tunes in conveying modern developmental and cultural messages has shown that they are extremely effective for this purpose. This innovation is being done by various social and political developmental organisations in the western Madhya Pradesh region which are all affiliated to the federation *Adivasi* Ekta Parishad (AEP) which is active in the four contiguous states of Rajasthan, Madhya Pradesh, Gujarat and Maharashtra. Transcription of the whole of the folklore will also allow a systematic study of it and thus offer many more opportunities for innovation. The folklore is amenable to creative interpretation and copious material in support of the theory and practice of alternative, decentralised and sustainable development can be culled from it.

There is for example the creation myth sung in the villages near the Narmada which detail how God was suddenly beset with the idea to build the universe and he looked towards Relu Kabadi the woodsman to go into the jungle and fetch him wood. Thus, starts the whole story of how slowly all the animals and plants are created and finally the Rivers Narmada and Tapti. These rivers finally meet-up with the ocean Dudu Hamad in marriage and in the process of their journey all the various villages, hills and valleys are created. The whole song gives a sense of the vastness of nature and the strength of natural processes and inculcates a respect in the listener for these. This is in direct contrast to the hubris of modern man who has tried to subordinate nature to his own ends and given rise to the serious environmental problems that face him today. The *adivasis* have been sufferers of this process. Thus, by popularizing their creation myth and emphasising that their worldview is much more "rational" in the present context of serious ecological degradation will go a long way towards increasing their self-esteem.

Similarly, there is another story in one of the epic songs about a woman who has to answer for having questioned the authority of her husband. She is brought before the *panchayat* which is the traditional all male dispute resolution forum. There the *panchs* decree that she be punished for her disobedience and order that her tongue be cut off and given to the husband to swallow. The tongue then gets stuck in the throat of the husband where it has remained ever since. This story has been picked-up to depict the extent to which the Bhil society is patriarchally oppressive of women. At the same time the fact that the tongue has got stuck in the husband's throat offers the chance to the woman to recover it and so establish her right to speak out for her needs. This is the motif that has been used to organise the Bhil women to fight against diverse patriarchies inside the home and outside. Literature especially religious literature of an allegorical character has tremendous power to motivate people to act to change their socio-economic condition. Unfortunately, for *adivasis* in the Central Indian region in general and the Bhils in particular there has not been any significant effort till now to transcribe and use their rich oral literature.

Thus, what is being done here by the AEP and its affiliates is the systematic creation of a new written literature and performing arts of the Bhils not only for their value in themselves, but more for their utility as a crucial Developmental Tool through the transcription of their rich oral folklore by their own organic intellectuals who have risen from the process of the struggle to improve their socio-economic condition. While in the case of other modern Indian languages such forums sprang-up by themselves in the case of Bhili a special effort has to be made because it is not a written language and being the product of an indigenous culture which is under threat of extinction requires protective promotion.

The penetration of market oriented consumerist culture has led to the breaking down of traditional communitarian bonds not only in urban societies, but also in remote agrarian societies like those of the *adivasis*. Thus, the social system prevalent at present promotes cut throat competition among its members and hampers collective action. This in turn leads to violence and crime. This is extremely harmful for society as a whole. So, it is of utmost importance that *adivasi* societies which still retain communitarian social practices be encouraged to thrive and creatively build on these practices so that society as a whole can draw on this valuable resource to counter the threat of evolving into a consumerist mono-culture. For instance there is no sense of belonging in the cities these days leading to the problem of alienation. This is then sought to be corrected through identification with fundamentalist religious organizations which tend to divide society further into narrow communities. Thus, the present new intervention by conserving and positively developing one of the sources of rich communitarian culture, development and governance, that of the Bhils, will be a radically systems changing one in the long run.

The form of politics that has come to dominate the globe now is that of first past the post-competitive centralised electoral liberal democracy. In this system Central Governments of nation states tend to override the lower level governments. The local government institutions at the small town and village level suffer most as their needs and aspirations are sacrificed for the development of mega cities and industrial centres. The net result is that there is tremendous destruction of the environment and the livelihood opportunities of the urban and rural poor. This kind of political system is also extremely divisive socially as it tends to pit communities and groups against each other in the fight to gain control of state power which is crucial to secure a good livelihood. Thus, it is imperative that a more decentralised and localised form of democratic politics be promoted which works through consensus rather than by competition. The present intervention will provide an impetus for the revival of the traditional village council led management of affairs which is central to the lives of the Bhil *adivasis* and the eventual evolution of an alternative decentralised political system globally as an antidote to the ills of the present centralised one.

At the micro-level of western Madhya Pradesh this new intervention will over time contribute to the ongoing movement of the Bhils for attaining a strong self-identity based on a rich written literature that is capable of contending with the literature and culture of the non-*adivasis* and thus give them social equality with their oppressors. This will in turn help them to negotiate the modern political and economic systems on equal terms with the non-*adivasis* and thus gain a fair share of the developmental cake.

At the macro-level this new literature being the product of an agricultural society will first of all provide intellectual and cultural support for the ongoing national and worldwide efforts for the revival of agriculture which is in crisis all-over the world leading to serious problems of food and livelihood security. The modernisation of agriculture-based on artificial inputs has proved to be a failed enterprise and there is a growing trend towards the revival of sustainable organic agriculture. This is especially important for India which is primarily an agricultural country. The main agricultural areas in India have all come under the sway of modern agriculture and have lost the traditional seeds and processes and are suffering from severe erosion of soil quality and water sources.

The Bhils still retain traditional knowledge in this regard and a strengthening of their culture will lead to a strengthening of their agriculture too. At present the worldwide movement for sustainable agriculture lacks a mass base and a supporting culture which will help it to thrive. Sustainable ariculturists are perceived as quixotic deviants rather than as proponents of a serious alternative system. The AEP has actively promoted a sustainable agriculture-based socio-economic-political system as a comprehensive and viable alternative and the present intervention by strengthening its cultural dimensions will contribute positively to this movement. At a later point of time an alternative agriculture-based system of development that is less destructive of nature can develop from these preliminary efforts.

Finally, agricultural societies are all highly religious given their dependence on nature and the need to placate forces which are beyond their control. This is why despite the Nehruvian project of building a secular society and the specific injunction that the state will not function in support of any religion, in practice the majority of Indian society having rural agricultural roots has remained deeply religious and all the mainstream partics including the Communist Party of India in Bengal have to a greater or lesser extent promoted Hinduism. However, of late this has become overly problematical due to the aggressive fundamentalism of the Sangh Parivar. The Hindu fundamentalist organisations have embarked on a proselytisation campaign of the *adivasis* in violation of their fundamental right to follow freely their own religion as guaranteed under article 25 of the Constitution. The converted *adivasis* do not get an equal status with the high caste Hindus, but are inducted into Hindu society as menials who are even today treated as untouchables by the latter.

The reality of the power of religion in pre-modern agricultural societies has to be acknowledged and fundamentalism has to be countered through promotion of religious diversity. Religious diversity is as much a desired value as cultural diversity for the survival of the human race. The revival of their literature which is traditionally highly religious will automatically lead to a revival of the Bhili animist and nature friendly religion and provide them with an effective antidote to the proselytising thrust of the fundamentalist Hindu organisations.

3. A New Developmental Intervention

The two broad prevalent modes of developmental intervention for the improvement of the socio-economic condition of the *adivasis* in particular and the rural population in general among NGOs, social movements and the government are that of service delivery and political empowerment. The interventions in the cultural sphere mainly through the use of audio-visual media like street theatre for the purpose of information, education and communication (IEC) have not been independent developmental interventions, but have subserved the above mentioned two modes and the lack of a written literature of the *adivasis* has hampered these efforts. Thus, despite over two decades of developmental and empowerment interventions the impact in terms of creating a self-confident Bhil population capable of pinpointing and solving their problems independently has been less than desirable.

The intervention of the AEP makes a quantum jump both horizontally and vertically from the current practice. Horizontally, it makes the original assertion that the creation of a new living literature of the Bhils from their traditional folklore is itself a new and major developmental intervention that can parallel the prevailing two modes in the case of *adivasi* development because of their lack of a literate culture. Vertically, this intervention will result in considerably improving the content and style of the IEC campaigns which are a necessary part of the prevailing two modes of intervention. Moreover, the experience of service delivery and political mass organisation has shown that these processes rarely become self-supporting and have to be constantly reinforced with funding and professional assistance by outsiders. In this respect the creation of a literature has historically been a self-sustaining process once the initial critical mass of writers and readers has been established either through voluntary efforts or by some organised action.

This brings us to the existing interventions in the field of culture. Anthropologists Amita Baviskar and Engelbert Stiglmayer have studied some Bhili myths from an academic anthropological perspective so as to better understand the social dynamics of the Bhils. Jyotindra Jain has also studied some of these myths to assess their aesthetic qualities and to determine their relationship with the mainstream Hindu culture. Christian missionaries too have transcribed some of the myths, but not in any sustained manner and not with the objective of the creation of a new literature. Similarly, the Government departments of tribal development too have from time-to-time attempted to publish reading material in Bhili dialects, but these too have been haphazard and have necessarily lacked a mass character.

The decade of the nineteen nineties has seen yet another academic project launched by Ganesh Davy for the study of the languages of the *adivasis* of northern Maharashtra and Gujarat. In this externally funded venture a biannual journal is published by turns in four different Bhili dialects meaning that new written material is produced in a particular dialect only once in two years. Moreover, there is little attention being paid to the transcription of the folklore of the *adivasis*. Thus, this effort has spread itself thin by dealing with too many languages and so the output in terms of new literature in any of these is quite minimal and lacks the necessary critical mass of writers and readers to pose a strong challenge the hegemony of Marathi and Gujarati as the dominant languages.

The AEP effort, therefore, builds on all these previous interventions while giving them a new and purposeful thrust of reviving Bhili culture with the intention of positing it as a vehicle of sustainable development. The intervention thus seeks to protect and build on the fundamental right to culture of the Bhils guaranteed in article 29 of the Constitution of India. The Muslims and Sikhs have taken advantage of this provision, but there has been no such specific cultural rights intervention among *adivasis* in the central Indian region. Thus, what is being implemented by the AEP is a **best practice framework for *adivasi* cultural renewal** that can not only rejuvenate the living conditions of the Bhils, but can be gainfully replicated for the development of other *adivasi* cultures.

4. The Over-arching Social Problem being Addressed

This intervention addresses the serious problem that the culture of the Bhils is considered to be sub-human by the non-*adivasis* of the region and even the modern Indian state seeks to destroy the culture of the *adivasis* nationally by introducing a uniform modernising sweep through its developmental and educational policies. The problem assumes a vicious circle nature as the Bhils internalise this devaluation and tend to reject their culture. Given that most Bhils are not able to imbibe the modern non-*adivasi* culture in a successful manner this further reduces their ability to fight effectively in the competitive political and economic systems that prevail at present and leaves them even more disrespectful of their own culture.

The extent of this dehumanisation of the Bhils can be illustrated with an example. There was a great Bhil rebel named Tantia who fought the British and their subservient upper caste Hindu landlords valiantly in the latter half of the nineteenth century for over a decade and a half. He was a Robin Hood like character who used to distribute the loot from his raids on the British and the landlords among the poor Bhils. Thus, Bhil women used to consider him to be their brother and used to tell their children that Tantia Mama (maternal uncle) would bring gifts for them. He was finally apprehended by the British through treachery and hanged after a summary trial. Following the British the non-*adivasis* of the region regarded him not as a freedom fighter, but as a dacoit. Later the term *mama* too lost its value and degenerated into a pejorative name for the Bhils. The Bhils who have lost independent livelihood opportunities over the last century and a half are today forced to migrate to nearby cities and rich agricultural areas for employment. Thus, the Vadodara–Kota passenger which runs on the main Mumbai–Delhi trunk rail route is most of the time filled with Bhils going up and down from their homes to their places of work and back and has come to be called the "*mama gari*".

When the process of forming a forum for the revival of *adivasi* culture was begun, the major problem faced was the sense of shame that the educated *adivasis* felt about speaking and writing in Bhili in public places. A pamphlet in Bhili was published to popularise the whole idea. Even senior literate *adivasis* would go into peals of laughter on reading it. The process of reading the pamphlet itself proved to be labourious as there is no written literature in Bhili dialects. What more can be indicative of the extent of decay of a language than this reluctance of the literate Bhils to converse and write in it. Simultaneously, the illiterate Bhil masses are being wooed away by television and they do not spend as much time as they used to do to celebrate their own festivals. There is an increasing tendency to celebrate Hindu festivals such as *Ganesh Puja* and *Durga Navaratri* instead.

This lack of a positive self-image is a major obstacle in the search for a viable system of livelihood for the Bhils. Consequently, the core of the intervention draws from the glorious history of the European and modern Indian cultural renaissance movements and posits that the solution to this problem lies in the creation of a strong new literature using the rich classical resource of the Bhils' oral folklore as the cornerstone of the process of revival of a Bhili culture that can rival the dominant non-*adivasi* culture in all respects and so provide the Bhils with an equal cultural footing in their struggle for emancipation. At a higher level the successful implementation of this intervention will provide a replicable blueprint for the strengthening of non-literate *adivasi* cultures nationally and worldwide and so maintain cultural diversity. Indeed the whole point of the present intervention is to chart out a map for the revival and promotion of *adivasi* cultures in a sustainable way through mass participation.

As mentioned earlier the problem of the marginalisation of *adivasi* culture is closely linked to the proliferation of a consumerist monoculture worldwide which is proving to be dangerously harmful for future human development. Thus by seeking to strengthen *adivasi* cultures the present idea seeks to address this serious problem of loss of cultural diversity on a global scale as will be described in detail later.

5. The Main Systemic Problem being Addressed

The most serious systemic problem that the developmental initiatives in the western Madhya Pradesh region in particular and in *adivasi* areas in general have been unable to resolve is that they have not been able to inspire the *adivasis* to devise and then implement their own solutions to their problems of social, economic and cultural deprivation due to the culture of silence which stifles their articulation and innate genius giving rise to the problem of social devaluation described above. Invariably schemes and plans that have originated elsewhere have been dumped on the *adivasis* with the result that not only has any sustainable process of development not evolved, but that the *adivasis* have continued to remain mute recipients of the crumbs thrown to them. This has meant that the age-old exploitative structures have continued to hold sway. In many cases new developmental initiatives have been sabotaged by the non-*adivasis* who have been entrusted with their implementation.

For instance watershed development schemes have not addressed the basic lack of land resources with the *adivasis* in the region which has meant that even after successful completion of these schemes the *adivasis* have not been able to augment their incomes to higher levels sufficient for sustainable living from these small holdings because the enhanced production is not sufficient for the purpose. The response of the government has been the introduction of jersey cow based milk production and vermiculture. These, however, have failed because there is insufficient wasteland available for fodder development enough to make these latter schemes successful. The net result is that the *adivasis* who took government loans to start these projects are now in debt which they cannot possibly repay. This is in fact the situation with most subsidized poverty alleviation schemes of the government. The failure of the Integrated Rural Development Programme to bring about any widespread sustainable income generation due to this inability to take into account the views of the beneficiaries has been well documented.

Similarly, political empowerment interventions have addressed agenda close to the heart of the activists without paying attention to the actual demands of those who are being organised leading to the eventual dissipation of these movements. A very good example of this is the Narmada Bachao Andolan. The movement initially started by addressing the genuine fear voiced by the *adivasi* oustees of the Sardar Sarovar dam that they would be displaced from their lands without proper rehabilitation. Later, however, the movement was converted into a battle to stop the construction of the dam altogether mainly on the basis of the ideological predilections of the non-*adivasi* activists who led the movement. The pressure of the movement forced the government to better the rehabilitation package on offer and the *adivasis* plumped for this, but the activists went on fighting for the no-dam option with lesser and lesser people. This lack of articulation of the *adivasis* has meant that the two decades of work put in by various development and empowerment organisations has not been able to bring about self-sufficiency in the Bhils.

This lack of articulation can be seen also in the lack of effective implementation of two very important statutes. The fifth schedule of the Constitution of India provides for special governance of the notified scheduled *adivasi* areas in a state on the recommendations of the tribal advisory council comprised of *adivasi* legislators. Similarly, the Panchayati Raj Extension to Scheduled Areas Act (PESA) provides for the *adivasi gram sabhas* to be paramount in deciding on the use of the resources of the village and in resolving disputes. However, in reality these two powerful statutes are not being implemented in the way they should be because the *adivasis* and their elected representatives are not able to press for this in any articulate manner.

The urgent need therefore is that the *adivasis* be able to articulate their felt needs and act in an organised manner in accordance with their own genius, so that, they are fulfiled. The publication of literature in Bhili dialects addresses precisely this problem of lack of articulation among the Bhils. The Bhils are now writing about their problems and their culture and history in independent public fora that are funded by their own contributions and tremendous process of increasing articulation has been set into motion. The confidence created by this intervention among a new class of Bhili intellectuals has also lead them to write in other languages in the mainstream media.

The present intervention is thus an initial step in the direction of building-up the ability of effective articulation of Bhil *adivasis* as a prelude to breaking the deafening culture of silence that muzzles them. The vast Bhil masses remain unheard because what they say does not carry enough cultural clout to make any impact.

There are many NGOs and people's organisations in western Madhya Pradesh doing worthwhile work in the spheres of service delivery and political empowerment. There is a significant population associated with these organisations either directly as beneficiaries or participants or indirectly as well wishers and supporters. Workshops organised by these agencies and the AEP to critically analyse the results of the work done by them over the past decade and a half have clearly brought out the need for a concentrated intervention on the cultural front to give a wider base to their activities and also to counter the negative attitudes of the administration, the Hindu fundamentalist organisations and the non-*adivasi* development workers and social activists. This is the basis of the present intervention in this direction, the most important being the researching of the history of famous Bhil martyrs like Khajya Naik, Motia Bhil, Tantia Bhil, Chitu Kirar and others. Sustained lobbying and mass celebrations of the martyrdom of these heroes has resulted in their being acknowledged as freedom fighters of repute and the recognition that the Bhils had played a major resistive role against the British. Similarly, Bhili songs and stories and modern versions of these have been recorded and published.

6. Positive Local Impact of the Intervention

A narrative will bring out the way in which people's lives can change from a cultural initiative. The *adivasis* in Potla village in Dewas district were held in thrall by the only *sahukar* in the village who used to rule their lives in all respects. Some of them heard of the plans for holding the martyrdom celebrations of Tantia Bhil and came and told the rest of the villagers about it and distributed the pamphlets and booklets on Tantia's brave deeds to the educated *adivasi* youth. The result was that the villagers decided to participate in the *yatra* to Tantia's *Samadhi*. For this they needed to hire a truck to carry their possessions and they contacted their *sahukar* who initially agreed to give them his truck on hire. But on the day of their setting out the *sahukar* declined to give them the truck and also threatened not to give them any loans for the forthcoming cropping season.

This incensed the villagers so much that they decided to socially boycott the *sahukar* and his family and made alternative arrangements to participate in the *yatra*. There was no need for activists to go and organise the people as it just took a few pamphlets and a general milieu of cultural revival to bring about the end to generations of servitude. The emancipatory power of literature and its capability to bring about a positive change in the life of the oppressed has been established time and again throughout history and the French Revolution is the well-known example in this regard. The American freedom fighters were influenced by the writings of Thomas Paine to rebel against the British. The freedom fighters for India's Independence too were motivated by the publication of new and liberating literature. Indeed the *dalits* in this country have been far more enterprising in this regard as compared to the *adivasis* of the central and western Indian regions.

The important thing is that this new literature must be published as part of a general milieu of emancipatory socio-economic change. The work of the various civil society organisations of the Bhils over the past two decades in general and the activities of the AEP in particular have created such a milieu of change and it only needs a systematic and well articulated ideology for its further expansion which the present intervention intends to provide by encouraging the people to hark back to their rich oral folklore and their nature friendly animist beliefs and practices.

7. Potential for Wider Application

All-over the country and even worldwide *adivasi* cultures are on the verge of extinction. This has something to do with the decline of indigenous agriculture on which these cultures were based and with the homogenising culture of western consumerism which has been popularised through television soap operas, sports broadcasts and commercials. A global market is sought to be created for the products of the industrial west by washing away local cultural influences from the brains of people through this powerful cultural onslaught of western consumerism.

For instance the tremendous concentration of the audio-visual media on the Cricket World Cup in South Africa in 2003 seeped through to a remote *adivasi* village in the region where an old woman who did not know anything about cricket still lamented the fact that India had lost the final. The irony is that nationalism is being promoted through an unproductive symbol such as cricket when such poor people as this *adivasi* woman are on the edge of starvation because of a lack of viable livelihood opportunities just to sell various consumerist products of industry. A victory in the final would not in any way have improved the living conditions of poor people in this country, but a major improvement in their condition brought about by the adoption of more appropriate development policies would automatically ensure that we win more accolades in the international arena in sports which are played by more countries of the world than cricket.

This erosion of cultural diversity has come to be recognised as a serious impediment to the future of the human race. Thus, my innovation by stressing that the *adivasi* culture and the agricultural base from which it springs have the potential to offer an alternative to this destructive homogenisation of culture and livelihoods has vast areas of application not only in the preservation of *adivasi* cultures, but also that of the culture of more so called advanced societies. The AEP innovation provides a **best practice framework** for carrying out such a revival and preservation of cultural and livelihood diversity.

8. The Larger Impact of this Innovation

It is difficult to state exactly how many people have already benefited from the implementation of the innovation so far. The people who are consciously involved with the various organisations that are a part of this process number about one hundred thousand. However, many *adivasis* who may not be openly supportive of these efforts due to various reasons secretly go along with the process and try to move it forward in many ways. Thus, people even in remote areas have heard of the revival of the Tantia festival and have drawn heart from it without having participated in it. Many mainstream *adivasi* political figures from all parties have asserted in public fora that the revivalist movement of the Bhils is a positive development and some have even participated in the programmes of the AEP. The pressure created by the AEP so far has forced the government to take note of rising level of awareness of the *adivasis* and initiate beneficial development policies which have helped the whole of the *adivasi* population of the four States of Western India which is close to twelve million.

Today, we have a globalised world with far flung nations and communities tied together by trade in commodities and services, cross border manufacturing, financial transfers and also a massive communications industry. Thus, it is relatively easy for the more well endowed societies to press their social, economic and political thought on those who are not so advantaged. This process is happening at all levels from the village to the global. We have a situation in which cultural production is taking place in the affluent west and being broadcast for consumption by the world at large. The western cultural icons and agencies dominate the powerful medium of television, the newer and equally powerful medium of the internet as well as the various printed media.

This cultural domination favours the economic interests of the various corporate behemoths that control the world economy. It is in the interests of these corporations that the cultural tastes of the population of the whole world are homogenised. This has created a critical situation for human survival with the loss of diversity in the biological, economic and social spheres in addition to the cultural sphere. As mentioned earlier the only way in which this dangerous cultural homogenisation and erosion of diversity caused by thoughtless industrialism can be challenged is by rediscovering the virtues of traditional agriculture and the culture that it gave rise to. Today, it is the indigenous people worldwide who still retain the skills and knowledge of traditional agriculture and the accompanying culture. Thus, the work of the AEP by reviving and conserving the indigenous Bhil culture will challenge the dominant system of development and governance which is increasingly being adopted at all levels from the local to the global. Since, centralisation and homogenisation invariably necessitates violence which is so evident in various forms today the AEP's stress on decentralisation and difference presents a prospectus for peace and amity worldwide. This intervention, therefore, will impact development thought and practice and make it more amenable to the evolution of sustainable living and working patterns in the future at all levels from the local to the global.

7

Sustainable Agricultural Development and Poverty Reduction among the Tribal

A Case of Odisha

Ramya Ranjan Patel

Introduction

Environmental degradation is an inherent part of economic development. The precondition of present model of development and poverty reduction is to achieve high economic growth. On the other hand to achieve high economic growth, it is inevitable to destroy environment. Hence, comes the concept of sustainable development and became popular. World Commission on Environment and Development (1987) defines, Sustainable development as "a process of change in which the exploitation of resources, the direction of investments, the orientation of technological development, and institutional change are all in harmony and enhance both current and future potential to meet human needs and aspirations". But, no development activities could take place without the damage to the environment. The concept of sustainable development also has a component of damage to the environment, though it is minimum.

However, there is one such thing that has the potential of promoting development (and poverty reduction) with the true spirit of the idea of sustainability, without any damage to environment. That is tribal agricultural technology and practice. Tribal agriculture practice is mostly organic and sustainable in nature because of no use of chemical fertiliser and pesticides.

The tribal agricultural technology along with the proper marketing facilities of the tribal produce could remove poverty, food insecurity and overall development of the tribal, without any damage to environment. It is because nobody loves nature, the forests and the land more than the indigenous people. Their absolute dependence on nature for food supply and collection of it require no destruction or manipulation with natural resources.

On the other hand, the Government particularly in mineral resources states resorts to mining (based investment) as a panacea to improve the economic conditions of the tribal by causing large scale destruction to the environment and the Common Property Resources (CPRs), by destroying the forests, polluting the water sources, polluting the cultivable land and most importantly in many cases by displacing their tribal from their ancestral habitats. It is in this context the study seeks to answer the following objectives.

Objectives

1. To study the causes and extent of poverty and food insecurity among the tribal population with reference to Odisha.
2. To study the potential of their agricultural technology and practice in solving the problems of poverty through environment sustainability.

Data Sources and Methodology

The study will be based on both primary and secondary data. The secondary data sources mainly consists of the various rounds of consumer expenditure data of NSSO reports. The other sources of data are the Economic Survey of Odisha, Statistical Abstract of Odisha, District Statistical Handbook and others.

The study is a mixed one both quantitative and qualitative. The objectives are studied through evidences, observations and analysis of texts and literatures.

Poverty, Backwardness and Livelihood of Tribal in Odisha and India

Odisha is the poorest state in India (see Table 7.1) and it is even worse in terms of some of the African and Sub-Saharan Countries (see Table 7.2). The poverty and backwardness is not equally found in all the regions of the state; in some regions of the state the incidence of poverty is much higher in comparison to the other regions. For example poverty in the Southern region is as high as 87.05 per cent in comparison to 49.81 per cent in Northern and only 31.74 per cent in the Coastal region (Table 7.3). The same is the case for IMR, literacy rate and food insecurity for the region (Table 7.4). This is the region where, there is highest percentage of tribal living in the state. Among all the social groups the Scheduled Tribes (STs) are the poorest in the state. The Scheduled Tribes (STs) are poorest not only in the state, but also at the national level (Table 7.5) and all the states in India. The incidence of poverty among the tribal is even highest in the Southern region of the State of Odisha. The percentage of poor in this region is as high as 92.42, in comparison to 61.63 and 66.63 per cent in Northern and Coastal regions respectively (Table 7.3).

Question arises why such a huge percentage of people are poor and backward all-over India and Odisha in particular? It is obvious that they would not like to remain poor as they are. They are poor either because they are not able to adequately help themselves or not being helped by others (the Government or other agencies). Any society that lives well, earns well. Earnings on the other hand depend on the kind of livelihood and its paying capacity a society undertakes to meet its need. The income of any society engaged in production activities depends on the units of output it is producing and selling, and the price at which the commodities are sold or [Income (Y) = Units of Commodities (Q) * Prices (P)].

The tribal mostly depend on primary activities like agriculture and works either as cultivators, agricultural labourers or casual labourers and selling of NTFPs (Non-Timber Forests Products). The relationship between high percentage (77.75) of cultivators and agricultural labourers to total workers (Table 7.6), the percentage (43.20) of tribal population (Table 7.4) and the percentage (44.75) of forests cover (Table 7.7) in the southern region of the state confirm the above statement.

Table 7.1: Poverty, HDI and IMR in Indian States

States	*Poverty (Rural, 2004-05)*	*HDI Value (2011)*	*IMR (2000)*
Andhra Pradesh	10.5	0.485	65
Assam	22.1	0.474	75
Bihar	42.6	0.447	62
Chhattisgarh	40.8	0.449	
Gujarat	18.9	0.514	62
Haryana	13.3	0.545	67
Himachal Pradesh	10.5	0.558	
Jammu & Kashmir	4.3		
Jharkhand	46.2	0.464	
Karnataka	20.7	0.508	57
Kerala	13.2	0.625	14
Madhya Pradesh	36.8	0.454	87
Maharashtra	29.6	0.549	48
Odisha	**46.9**	**0.442**	**96**
Punjab	9	0.569	52
Rajasthan	18.3	0.468	79
Tamil Nadu	23	0.544	51
Uttarakhand	33.3	0.515	
Uttar Pradesh	40.7	0.468	83
West Bengal	28.4	0.509	51
India	**28.3**	**0.519**	**68**

Source: Col. 2. (NSSO 61st round), Col. 3, UNDP India 2011 (Inequality Adjusted Human Development Index for India's States), Col. 4, (Ministry of Health and Family Welfare, Government of India).

Table 7.2: HDI Value of Odisha and some African Countries

Countries	*HDI Value (2011)*
Eq. Guinea	0.538
Swaziland	0.498
Congo	0.489
Ghana	0.467
Cameroon	0.46
Odisha	0.442

Source: UNDP India 2011.

Table 7.3: Poverty (1999-2000) and IMR (1997-98) in Regions of Odisha by Social Groups

	ST	*SC*	*Other*	*All*	*IMR (1997-99)*
Coastal	66.63	42.18	24.32	31.74	92
Southern	92.42	88.9	77.65	87.05	125
Northern	61.69	57.22	34.67	49.81	93
Odisha	73.08	52.3	33.29	48.04	
Sub-Saharan Africa					108 (2002)

Source: Haan and Dubey, (EPW, May 28-June 4, 2005), Col. 6, (UNDP HDR, 2004 for Sub-Saharan Africa).

Table 7.4: Various Development Indicators in various regions of Odisha

Regions	*Literacy Rate (2001)*	*Male Literacy Rate*	*Female Literacy Rate*	*Literacy Rate of ST*	*Malnourished Children (grade 1-4) 2010*	*Food Security index, 2008*	*% of ST Population*
Coastal	69.73	81.56	59.16	39.90	45.93	0.50	10.21
Northern	62.96	75.07	48.30	48.11	55.37	0.41	31.45
Southern	41.84	56.34	27.54	29.50	58.76	0.34	43.20

Source: Census of India 2001, Department of Child and Women Development, Government of Odisha, *Food Security Atlas of Odisha*, 2008.

Table 7.5: Poverty Ratios by Social Groups, Odisha and India

	1983	*1987-88*	*1993-94*	*1999-2000*
Odisha				
ST	86.22	82.34	70.76	72.08
SC	75.38	65.35	49.39	55.08
Other	56.16	45.92	39.55	33.48
All	66.24	56.75	48.63	47.31
All India				
ST	63.27	55.93	46.29	43.67
SC	58.5	51.38	48.42	36.14
Other	40.66	34.48	30.46	21.04
All	45.57	39.31	35.95	25.87

Source: Hann and Dubey, *Economic and Political Weekly*, May 28-June 4, 2005.

Table 7.6: Percentage of Workers according to various Categories

Regions	*% of Total Workers*	*% of Cultivators to Workers*	*% of Agril. Labourers to Workers*	*% of Cultivators to Workers + % of Agril. Labourers to Workers*	*% of Workers in HHs Industry*
Coastal	35.38	29.05	30.67	59.72	4.09
Northern	41.01	30.23	35.28	65.51	6.73
Southern	47.56	35.66	42.09	77.75	3.54

Source: Census of India, 2001.

Table 7.7: Agricultural Statistics and Forests Coverage in various Regions of Odisha

Regions	*Net Sown Area to Total Cereal*	*Average Yield of Rice, 02-03*	*% Are of HYV seeds to NSA*	*Fertiliser Consumption in 2004-05 (kg/hect)*	*% of Govt. Forest (05-06)*	*% of NSA, 03-04 Irrigated*
Coastal	80.13	8.39	52.94	46.38	26.81	49.37692
Northern	81.58	7.2	70.32	45.33	32.43	29.58889
Southern	69.42	6.21	39.05	27.75	44.75	28.9425

Source: Directorate of Economics and Statistics, Government of Odisha, 2005.

There are certain prerequisite to enter the modern industrial sector or the service sector. There is requirement of good education, skills (or soft skills) or training to be productively engaged in those sectors. Sen (2002), suggests, "the ability of the poor to participate in the growth process depends on the presence of some enabling conditions like literacy, good health and information about the new opportunities," or popularly known as the 'capabilities' (alternative combinations of functioning from which a person can choose). However, Table 7.4 shows that, this region is grappled with low literacy rate (41.84%), lower rate of tribal literacy (29.5%), even lower rate of female literacy (27.54%) and quite high rate of food insecure people (reflected from 58.76% of child malnutrition). Questions arise, are the poor, uneducated, illiterate and unskilled rural tribal peasantry get any employment opportunities in the developed industrial sector? The scope is limited.

The low human capital formation scarcely give them any chance to enter into the modern industrial activity and are left only to work as casual labourer or agricultural labourer. But there is high percentage of poverty among the agricultural labourers because of low wage rates and unavailability of works. For example the average wage rate for field labourers in 2002-03 for the Southern region of the state is only Rs. 39.10, in comparison to a higher Rs. 47.13 for the coastal region (Table 7.8). The reasons for it are inadequate and ineffective public investment resulting into corruption and leakages. In tribal villages there is absence of class structure (Habib, 2006) or the absence of big farmers who use to give some employment to the labourers and lastly because of low productivity of the labourers. According to NSSO (Bhalla, 2006) per worker productivity in terms of rupee in Odisha (Rs. 6,856) is almost half and second lowest of India (Rs. 11,946).

Table 7.8: Average wage rate of Field Labourers in Regions of Odisha

Districts	*Average Wages of Field Labourers, Men (02-03)*	*Average Wages of Field Labourers, Women (02-03)*
Coastal	47.13	38.60
Northern	37.69	30.78
Southern	39.10	31.74
Odisha	42.16	34.42

Source: Statistical Abstracts of Odisha, 2005.

Similarly, there is need of capital (the past savings) to start a new economic activity. There is scarce possibility of generating saving, when more than 90 per cent of people living below poverty line, "since poor consumes more and saves less". Moreover, the concept of money is not very much penetrated into their life and they know little about the concept of saving (their life is more based on social relation and less on financial relation, unlike the modern industrial society). Let me share one of my experiences of field visit during Ph.D. to Boden Block of Nuapara, undivided Kalahandi. One of the NGOs promoting Self-Help Groups (SHGs) activities paid some money to a SHGs group run by a PTGs (Primitive Tribal Groups known as *Paharia*), a due which they are entitled to and asked them to count if the given amount is correct. None of the group members is willing to do that and looked at each others, out of a feeling of guilt that if they do count the money, the payer will think, they do not trust him. This is quite opposite to our society, where we do not trust even our family members in the matter of money, even if it is given by our parents.

Thus, they remain engaged in primary activities. However, these activities and particularly agriculture is least paying among any other activities in India. That is why many farmers do not wish to continue their profession and wants to come out of it. According to NSSO (59th round) as many as 40 per cent of the farmers want to leave their occupation, provided an alternative occupation. The situation is worst for the small and marginal farmers, who are in large numbers leaving agriculture. Despite being small farmers and despite the low paying capacity of their occupation, they love their occupation and willing to remain engaged in the activity of their own specialisation. My field visit to a backward tribal village also confirm the same experience, rather in the developed irrigated village the farmers are willing to leave their occupation. One of the reasons is the attachment to land for the tribal is much higher than the other social groups.

The tribal though majority of them are cultivators (44.7%) in India in comparison to 32.5 per cent for non-ST/SC (see Table 7.9) and despite owning highest area of land (Table 7.10) not only in India (0.8 hect.), but also in Odisha (0.6 hect.) and even in Southern part of Odisha (0.71 hect.) majority of them are poor. In India 34.85 per cent of the tribal population is poor in the land size groups of 4 hect. and above, in comparison to 17.26 for SC, 25.64 for OBC and 15.6

Table 7.9: Occupational Distribution of Social Groups (2001) in India

Type of Work	*ST*	*Other than ST/SC*
Cultivators	44.7	32.5
Agricultural Labourers	36.9	20.7
Household Industry	2.1	2.1
Other Work (Non-farm)	16.3	42.2

Source: Census 2001, Quoted from Planning Commission.

Table 7.10: Average Cultivable Landholding 1999-2000 (in hectares)

Social Groups	*India*	*Odisha*	*Coastal*	*Southern*	*Northern*
ST	0.8	0.6	0.52	0.71	0.55
SC	0.31	0.32	0.29	0.44	0.32
OBC	0.72	0.58	0.46	0.63	0.7
Other	0.98	0.55	0.51	0.54	0.71

Source: Haan and Dubey, 2005.

Table 7.11: Poverty in Different Land Size Groups in Rural Areas by Social Groups, 1999-2000

Land Size	*ST*	*SC*	*OBC*	*Others*	*Total*
Landless	40.39	36.14	27.36	17.23	28.62
0-0.4 hect.	48.85	37.28	30.7	21.85	31.44
0.4-1 hect.	47.78	34.18	24.82	15.13	26.42
1-2 hect.	38.84	31.25	21.68	12.52	22.16
2-4 hect.	39.62	25	16.28	7.8	16.95
4 and above	34.85	17.26	10.74	4.79	10.55
Total	**44.45**	**35.48**	**25.64**	**15.9**	**26.56**

Source: NSS 55th Round, quoted from IHD, 2006.

for Others (Table 7.11). A.K. Sen said poverty is because of two reasons the lack of assets or the lack of skills or education. The tribal despite owning asset (land), despite engaged in economic activities and despite working very hard (some say that they are poor because they do not work) they remain poor. It implies something wrong with their occupation or agricultural practice; either the level of output (productivity) is low or the price realised is low or both. In fact, the problems are both, it suffers from low productivity as well as low price that keeps their income low and makes them poor, vulnerable and food insecure.

Potential to Increase Productivity and Income through Sustainable Agriculture and Marketing Facilities

There is huge potential to improve both, the productivity or the price and overall their income, by providing them some facilities. Their productivity is low because of low use of chemical fertilisers, pesticides, HYVs seeds or use of machine or lack of irrigation facility (see Table 7.7). Though these agricultural inputs boost productivity, but is not sustainable in nature, since it pollutes water, pollutes soil, deplete water resources, and not good for human health. The disadvantage of tribal agriculture has huge potential to make it more advantageous for them, as they do not use these above inputs. The organic and sustainable in nature is the answer to their problem. Some of their own traditional variety of seeds are comparatively pest resistant and drought resistant and do not require pesticides and if at all, it could be controlled by promoting them to use organic pesticides. Similarly, the use of organic fertiliser or the compost fertiliser will go a long way in improving productivity. The compost could be made from the leaves of the forests and the wastage of their domesticated cattles that would be cost-effective for them. The use of organic fertiliser could also be promoted by supplying it from other areas and sold at reasonable prices. The Systemic Rice Intensification (SRI) method of cultivation would also be a good agricultural practice for them which is relatively labour intensive and the owner cultivators would not be hesitant to adopt this practice, since the tribal are mainly small farmers and the small farmers are mostly owner cultivators.

Because of the influence of commercial farming and to increase their productivity they are gradually adopting the modern agricultural practice and have started using the HYVs techniques. However, this trend has to be restricted to make it environment friendly. The above measures would not only increase productivity and income of the people, but also sustainable in nature.

Problems of Marketing and Reasons for Low Price

The tribal not only engaged in cereal production, but also substantially use their area to non-cereal crops (Table 7.7). The field survey of tribal village of Gajapati district of Odisha during M.Phil. in 2006 reflects that more than 94 per cent of the household in the surveyed villages of reported to have sold pineapple, 78 per cent cashew seeds, 56 per cent turmeric and 20 per cent lemon (Table 7.12). Similarly, the other tribal dominated district of Kandhamal is good in producing ginger and turmeric. The district of Nabarangpur produces good amount of corn. Despite producing substantial quantities of non-cereal output, which has relatively higher demand in comparison to cereal, they do not earn sufficient income because of low price of their product. The tribal in the Gajapati village lose a substantial amount of income in the marketing process. The price gap between villages and the district headquarter is almost double for pineapple (see Table 7.13). The marketing facilities and prices are comparatively well developed for foodgrains, particularly for rice and wheat, mainly because of strict implementation of MSPs, which is not well developed in case of other crops and particularly in the high land tribal regions.

Table 7.12: Percentage of Households Selling various Products

Name of Villages	*Pineapple*	*Cashew*	*Turmeric*	*Lime*
Dombarda	100	82.35	52.94	14.7
Jolanga	94.55	77.27	57.57	22.7
Total	94	78	56	20

Source: Field Survey.

Table 7.13: Quantity of Output Produced, Prices and their Values (Pineapple and Cashew)

Name of Village	*Pineapple*			*Cashew Seeds*		
	Output sold	*Price*	*Total value*	*Output sold*	*Price*	*Total value*
	(Quintal)	(Rs./kg)	(Rs.)	(Quintal)	(Rs./kg)	(Rs.)
Dombarda	147.4	5	73700	21.72	40	86900
Jolanga	231.75	4	92700	23.27	40	93100
Total	379.15	4.5	166400	44.99	40	180000
Parlakhemundi	379.15	10	379150	44.99	50	224950

Source: Field Survey.

Reasons for Low Prices

The reasons for income forgone due to low prices paid to the farmers can be explained mainly by two factors. The first one is due to the agency of buying in the villages being only traders who are mainly from big urban centres or are middlemen who sell ultimately to traders in those cities. There is no other alternative source of buying like the landlords, large farmers and village shopkeepers found in those regions.

Since, there are no alternative sources of buying, there is a complete buyer's monopoly or monopsony where the only sources of buying are the traders. In such a situation, it is the buyers who dictate the prices and other terms and conditions of buying. They dictate the prices in such a way for their gain at the cost of the income of the tribal households. The monopoly practice of the seller is even to the extent that they do not even weigh the product. The sellers had to sell their products at any cost, because they cannot postpone their sale. This is so because they have to meet their daily consumption needs. Another reason for them to not postpone their sale is that their items are perishable and by evening they have to reach their homes. This is how the marketing arrangement finally ends off in a distress sale by the sellers and is profitable for the buyers.

Secondly, there is no adequate connectivity to those villages and no road at all, not even the forest road or Gram Panchayat road, to carry their product to a market place or an urban centre which could have fetched them a decent price. Had this been realised, their income could have reached a significant level pushing them to meet their various demands, ofcourse including food.

Thirdly, there is lack of Government run marketing facilities or food processing centres in the regions. When there is absolute buyer's monopoly, where there is exploitation by the buyers of the sellers, there should be government intervention to correct the 'market failure' by providing various alternative sources of buying, but either that is non-existent or ineffective to solve the problem. That could be checked through providing proper marketing facilities and by establishing food processing centres that would ensure decent price to the poor tribal seller. The women should be given the responsibility to run those units.

Moreover, the organic nature of the tribal agricultural output has a huge potential to be sold at a much higher price. The organic products are sold almost at double the price of the common variety of the same product; be it at *FAB India*, be it at *Big Bazaar* or any other shop of a developed urban centre.

The problem of marketing does only lie in agricultural product, but also in the NTFPs, which is also a major source of income for the tribal. But they do not earn sufficient from its selling, again for the monopsony nature of the market. For example *Chiroungi* seeds, an edible forests product that the tribal sells at 5 to 12 rupees a kg, in the local market of Kalahandi district, is actually sold at 300 a kg (after processing) in the Raipur city of Chhattisgarh. In the tribal district of Gajapati, Rayagada and Koraput, though the declared price of tamarind by the Tribal Development Cooperative Corporation in the year 1998 was Rs. 4.50/kg, Tamarind has been actually sold at Rs. 1.25 per kg. Not only that they forgo a substantial amount of their income in selling the NTFPs again because of buyers monopoly.

There is only one way to make them come out of the poverty trap, by protecting their livelihood, sustaining their livelihood and making it profitable.

They cannot be transformed overnight as the Government contemplates. The Government thinks that if industries (mining-based heavy capital intensive industries) will be established in the tribal region, they will be transformed. But this policy will work negatively since, it would displace them from their original source of livelihood and being uneducated, unskilled and untrained, they do not find any employment in the modern sector. Rajendra Vadaka one of the tribal of the *Dongria Kond* tribe (a Primitive Tribal Group, that is fighting against the Vedanta Alumima group in Niyamgiri hills) said "we are tribal people, if we go outside we die". It will only destroy them further by polluting their land, polluting their rivers, destroying their livelihood and the forests. Rather helping them it will destroy them altogether. Social change is a slow gradual process. We have to empower them in their own field of livelihood, without imposing them anything alien to them. This will increase their income, help them to be educated and acquire human capital and enable them to join the modern sector.

Implications for Poverty, Food Security and Sustainability

The above measures of increasing agricultural productivity and marketing facilities will go a long way in solving the problems of poverty, food insecurity, gender inequality and promote sustainable agriculture in the following ways:

Poverty: The increase in productivity and marketing facilities will increase both number of quantity sold and fetch higher price for each unit. It increases income of the community and consumption expenditure of it. It will automatically reduce poverty.

Food Insecurity: The increase in output will help in both ways in meeting their needs of self-consumption and meeting other needs by selling a part of it in the market. It will also solve the problem of female food insecurity and anaemia, because the female members are worst sufferer of it, particularly in a poor family, who sacrifice most in terms of everything including food. Because of influence of modern agricultural practice they are gradually shifting from their traditional variety to only rice, and depend on market for the other products. But market is uncertain and unreliable which very often deprives them from the availability and accessibility of other items and causes food insecurity.

Gender Equality: The increase in income and particularly from the sale of NTFPs that are mainly collected and sold by the female member of the society will increase their income to a greater extent. The increase in income will increase their status in the society and in their family.

Sustainable Agriculture: The need of the hour is sustainability. Tribal agriculture practice is mostly organic and sustainable in nature because of low use of chemical fertiliser and pesticides. By promoting their agriculture it will be environment friendly and sustainable for long-time.

References

Bhalla, G.S. (2006), *Indian Agriculture Since Independence*, NBT 2006, p. 79.

Haan, A.D. and Dubey, A. (2005), Poverty, Disparities, or the Development of Underdevelopment in Orissa, *Economic and Political Weekly,* May 28-June 04, pp. 2321-2329.

Habib, I. (2006), *Economy (1858-1914), A People's History of India,* Tulika.

Orisaa Human Development Report, (2004), Planning and Coordination Department, Government of Orissa, Bhubaneswar, p. 39.

Patel, R.R. (2008) *Food Security among the Tribal Population of Orisha: A case study of Gajapati District* (Unpublished Dissertation) (New Delhi: Centre for the Study of Regional Development, Jawaharlal Nehru University).

Sen, A.K. (1996), *India, Economic Development and Social Opportunity*, New Delhi: Oxford University Press.

Sen, A.K. (2002), Globalisation, Inequality and Global Protest, *Development*, Vol. 45, No. 2, pp. 11-16.

8

Policy of Forest Development and Participation of Forest Dependent Tribal People

A Study in Andhra Pradesh

Satyam Sunkari

Introduction

Government of India has initiated Forest Development Agencies (FDA) in order to achieve more decentralized management of forest and forest development programmes. The Joint Forest Management Committees (JFMCs)/VSSs are central to the FDA. In this context, an attempt made to understand the forest policies and evolution of people oriented community forestry and its effectiveness with relation to ongoing programme.

In recent years, India has widely regarded forests are significant component for sustainable development and environmental conservation. Burgeoning populations of around 40 million are engaged in forest-based subsistence economy. It is a scenario which shows little sign of changing in the near future, and needs to be accommodated. Thus, role of forest dependent and dwelling communities sparked widespread concerns and initiated an intense drive to reforestation through the sustainable development approach. The historical and cultural significance of forest and forest resources to rural communities in India is an important article. It has been a long debate how forests provide a diverse range of critical resources, such as fuel wood, and fodder, materials for construction and agricultural implements, medicines, and how forests build-up sustainable environment because the forests are an integral part of the social fabric of tribals and sustainable development (http://www.ganesha.co.uk/JoPubWeb/Frontdiss.htm, access date 13/7/2011). Further, forests provide income-generating opportunities by producing materials such as bamboo, leaves, lac, honey, herbs and fruits. Under the Five Year Plans economy, the Government of India has given priority, as one of the thrust areas, to forestry. It is also noted that the First Five Year Plan was most concerned with food security while the Second and Third Five Year Plans reflected a drive towards industrialisation (Rawat, 1998) as a result forest was a casualty for focused industrialization and millions of hectares were leased out to industry with unsustainable silvicultural practices (Gadgil and Guha, 1992).

In this environment, the Second and Third Five Year Plans, along with food security and industrialization, the focus on the programmes concerning with the production of fast growing species, such as eucalyptus, and plantations were given, as a result, over 2.2 million hectares of plantations had been grown by 1980 (CSE, 1982). Plantations were also encouraged in a government-initiative to meet the rural need of biomass, which was becoming increasingly scarce. In the 1980's, under the augur of 'social forestry' 1.4 million hectares per year were planted with exotic species (Ravindranath and Hall, 1994). Although pragmatic in intent, social forestry is widely acknowledged as falling short of its remit on many counts, by environmentalists and foresters alike, from the suitability of the species, ecologically, and instrumentally (Shiva and Bandyopadhyay, 1983; Gadgil and Guha, 1995) to the issues of relieving the pressures on natural forests (Poffenberger and McGean, 1996), and providing for subsistence needs (Saxena, 1992), to the poor success rate, which was as low as 1 per cent in some areas (Pandey, 1998). For the responses of all such issues, the National Afforestation and Eco-Development Board (NAEB), set-up in August 1992, to promote afforestation, tree planting, ecological restoration and eco-development activities in the country, with special attention to the degraded forest areas and lands adjoining the forest areas, national parks, sanctuaries and other protected areas as well as the ecologically fragile areas like the Western Himalayas, Aravallis, Western Ghats, etc.

The detailed role and functions of the NAEB are "evolve mechanisms for ecological restoration of degraded forest areas and adjoining lands through systematic planning and implementation, in a cost-effective manner; restore through natural regeneration or appropriate intervention the forest cover in the country for ecological security and to meet the fuel wood, fodder and other needs of the rural communities; restore fuel wood, fodder, timber and other forest produce on the degraded forest and adjoining lands in order to meet the demands for these items; sponsor research and extension of research findings to disseminate new and proper technologies for the regeneration and development of degraded forest areas and adjoining lands; create general awareness and help foster people's movement for promoting afforestation and eco-development with the assistance of voluntary agencies, non-government organisations, Panchayati Raj institutions and others and promote participatory and sustainable management of degraded forest areas and adjoining lands; coordinate and monitor the Action Plans for afforestation, tree planting, ecological restoration and eco-development; and undertake all other measures necessary for promoting afforestation, tree planting, ecological restoration and eco-development activities in the country" (http://www.naeb.nic.in/, Access Date: 14/3/2011).

It continues to be the flagship scheme of NAEB, in so much as it provides support, both in physical and capacity-building terms, to the Forest Development Agencies (FDAs) which in turn are the main organs to move forward institutionalization of Joint Forest Management. The FDA has been conceived and established as a federation of Joint Forest Management Committees (JFMCs) at the Forest Division level to undertake holistic development in the forestry sector with people's participation. This is a paradigm shift from the earlier afforestation programmes wherein funds were routed through the State Governments. This decentralized two-tier institutional structure (FDA and JFMC) allows greater participation of the community, both in planning and implementation, to improve forests and livelihoods of the people living in and around forest areas. The village is reckoned as a unit of planning and implementation and all activities under the programme are conceptualized at the village level.

The two-tier approach, apart from building capacities at the grassroots level, significantly empowers the local people to participate in the decision-making process. Under Entry Point Activities, community assets are created with a 'care and share' concept.

1.1. Institutional Background

MoEF was operating four Centrally sponsored afforestation schemes during the Nineth Plan, i.e. Integrated Afforestation and Eco-development Project Scheme (IAEPS), Area Oriented Fuelwood and Fodder Project Scheme (AOFFPS), Conservation of Non-Timber Forest Produce including Medicinal Plants (NTFPS), and Association of ST and Rural Poor in Regeneration of Degraded Forests (ASTRPS). The Mid-Term Evaluation of the projects under these Schemes recommended a decentralised approach and speedy fund transfer mechanism. Taking cue from these recommendations, a Pilot Scheme, Samanvit Gram Vanikaran Samridhi Yojana (SGVSY) was launched in 2000-01 utilising the delivery mechanism of Forest Development Agency (FDA) and Joint Forest Management Committee (JFMC). As per Tenth Five Year Plan document of Planning Commission (the Forests and Environment Sector), the National Afforestation Programme (NAP) Scheme was initiated by scaling-up the SGVSY project experience and converging all afforestation schemes of the Nineth Five Year Plan period to avoid duplicity or redundancy, and at the same time keeping in focus the decentralization agenda of the government. NAP is being operated as a 100 per cent Central Sector Scheme".

The main objective of the NAP scheme is to develop the forest resources with people's participation, with focus on improvement in livelihoods of the forest-fringe communities, especially the poor. The scheme is targeted to support and accelerate the ongoing process of devolving forest protection, management and development functions to decentralized institutions of Joint Forest Management Committee (JFMC) at the village level, and Forest Development Agency (FDA) at the forest division level. The components under the scheme are Aided Natural Regeneration, Artificial Regeneration, Bamboo Plantation Cane Plantation, Mixed Plantation of trees having MFP and medicinal value, Regeneration of perennial herbs and shrubs of medicine value, Pasture Development/Silvipasture, Soil and

Moisture Conservation and Entry Point Activity for village development and it is estimated that average assistance would be Rs. 1.6 lakh per village; and Fencing, Monitoring and Evaluation, Training, Awareness raising in JFMC villages.

The NAP is being implemented through a two-tier structure of Forest Development Agency (FDA) at the Forest Division level and Joint Forest Management Committee (JFMC) at the village level. Thus, FDA is the confederation of JFMCs in that forest division. FDAs are registered under the Societies Registration Act. JFMCs are registered either with the Forest Department or under statutory provisions. The district-level officers of relevant line departments of the State Government and Panchayati Raj Institution are members of FDA.

According to official information of National Afforestation and Eco-Development Board, the recent experience with present institutional framework of FDA at the forest division level and JFMC at the village level is encouraging. All 28 States have adopted this institutional framework including in the Autonomous Hill Districts in Assam, Meghalaya and Mizoram (http://envfor.nic.in/naeb/sch/schnprg.html, access Date/23/3/2011). The report is also claimed that the institutions of FDAs and JFMCs are highly innovative resource transfer mechanisms whereby the Government of India channelises funds directly to the grassroot level implementing agency for the afforestation activities. It is noted in the documents of NAP guidelines, the focus was given to women, as gender concern, Scheduled Tribes and Scheduled Castes in the structure of FDAs and JFMCs. Moreover, women membership has been made mandatory in these bodies to the extent of 50 per cent.

According to the official website of NAEB (2009-10), there are 800 FDAs in operation of which 47 FDAs are in Andhra Pradesh, 32 in Chhattisgarh, 25 in Gujarat, 19 in Haryana, 30 in Himachal Pradesh, 31 in Jammu & Kashmir, 45 in Karnataka, 55 in Madhya Pradesh, 48 in Maharashtra, 46 in Odisha, 15 in Punjab, 33 in Rajasthan, 32 in Tamil Nadu, 69 in Uttar Pradesh, 38 in Uttarakhand, 3 in Goa, 34 in Jharkhand, 10 in Bihar, 27 in Kerala, 20 in West Bengal and remaining 141 FDAs are functioning in North-East states. It is obvious that the highest numbers of FDAs are functioning in the state of Uttar Pradesh with 14.54 per cent. As regards to JFMCs, 42535 are formed under the NAP from 2000-2001 to 2009-2010. Odisha has highest number of JFMCs (3547); followed by Madhya Pradesh (3270), Maharashtra (3092), Uttar Pradesh (2752), Chhattisgarh (2611), Andhra Pradesh (2555), Jharkhand (2495), Haryana (2265), Gujarat (2157) and remaining were distributed from other states of India including North-East states. The extent of coverage of area under the programme is 16.89 lakhs hectares.

Under the present programme, trainings were imparted to stakeholders and beneficiaries of FDA and JFMC by State Forest Departments, as well as by the Regional Centres of National Afforestation and Eco-development Board. There are 7 Regional Centres in the country. There is also a National-level Steering Committee of NAP and another at State-level called State-level Coordination committee chaired respectively by Secretary (Environment and Forests), Government of India, and Chief Secretary of the State Government to help and guide the FDAs and JFMCs. According to the Report of NAEB (2006), "Bamboo plantation, medicinal plants and Jatropha have been given adequate focus under NAP. State Governments have been advised to earmark 10 per cent of the project area under NAP, as per feasibility, for Jatropha plantation. Rehabilitation of shifting cultivation has been given specific focus under the programme, and so far 19 jhum projects have been sanctioned in NE States and in Odisha". According to the report of 2010, the NAP has covered, till March 2010, an area of 1547130 hectares of land under the FDA activities including private and forest lands and 10613.46 lakhs of seedlings have been planted in the same lands.

FDAs in Andhra Pradesh

Andhra Pradesh is the fifth largest state with an area of 2,75,045 sq. km. and accounting for 8.4 per cent of India's sovereign territory. It has a second longest coastline with 974 km. after the State of Gujarat. The forest area of the State is accounted about 22.58 per cent of the total geographic area. On par with an existing forest area, around half a million Scheduled Tribes (STs) are living in 5,936 villages in the nine ITDA areas of Andhra Pradesh. Moreover, the Scheduled Areas are inhabited by an estimated 2.8 million tribals who are entitled to the benefits of Tribal Sub-Plan projects and protective legislations (Gopinath Reddy, Anil Jumar, CESS Report). The tribal population in the State of Andhra Pradesh and in the country as a whole is the most deprived and vulnerable Community that faces severe economic exclusion. Although certain constitutional safeguards are provided, there has been no economic, social and political mobility across these communities. In the context of forest dependency of some tribal communities, the Government of Andhra Pradesh has taken-up seriously the "participatory aspect" for natural resource management since 1992. Prior to that, the Government of India (GoI) has given due importance to enabling community participation in Forest Protection and Management and issued a circular in 1990. Since then, there has been a major shift in management of forests. The local village communities that depend on the forests for meeting their needs were made partners in forest management through the concept of Joint Forest Management (JFM). Most important thing in this aspect is to increase the forest cover and there is a perceptible improvement in the forestry sector.

With the experience of JFM, in order to strengthen the institutionalized decentralization managerial responsibilities and to ensure steady flow of benefits to the communities, the Government of Andhra Pradesh launched Community Forest Management (CFM) in 2002. It is evident that Joint Forest Management and Community Forest Management primarily focus on treating forests as a common property resource and managing it for common use. Vana Samrakshana Samitis (VSSs) or Village Forest Protection Committees are formed in the forest-dependent villages under the CFM programme. Forests in the surrounding area of such villages are then allotted to these VSSs for protection and management. The VSSs are entitled for complete ownership of usufruct and are required to set apart 50 per cent of net proceeds from sale of timber and bamboos towards future forest management expenses.

The growth of formation of VSSs are very significant while 200 VSS in 1995, today there are as many as 6,726 VSS in the State managing 16.88 lakhs hectares of forest area. About 7.44 lakhs hectares of degraded forests have been treated through VSSs and around 13 lakh people, including 6 lakh women are actively participating in realizing the dream of bringing back greenery to the forests. SC/ST account for nearly 7 lakhs out of 13 lakhs beneficiaries. All the identified forest fringe villages have been covered under JFM stream (http://forest.ap.nic.in/about.htm, Workshop Proceedings 2002).

As it is detailed in previous pages that Government of India has formulated a scheme titled "National Afforestation Programme" by merging of Four IX Plans which are centrally sponsored afforestation schemes of the Ministry of Environment and Forests. According to the State of Forest Report 2009, so far, in Andhra Pradesh, 31 FDA projects have been initiated. Out of 31 projects, 13 projects were sanctioned during the year 2002-03, 10 projects during 2003-04 and 5 project during 2004-05 and 3 projects during 2005-06 (http://forest.ap.nic.in/about.htm, access date: 2/4/2011). The total of 1426 VSSs/EDCs are involved in implementing the project and an area of 14225 hectors are covered and thrust of the project is in the state is for raising plantations.

Purpose of the Study

In the context of NAP scheme, the study is intended to understand the people's participation, with focus on improvement in livelihoods of the forest-fringe communities, especially the poor. The scheme is targeted to support and accelerate the ongoing process of devolving forest protection, management and development functions to decentralized institutions of Joint Forest Management Committee (JFMC) or Vana Samrakshana Samitis (VSSs) at the village level, and Forest Development Agency (FDA) at the forest division level. As it is already explained, the components under the scheme are Aided Natural Regeneration, Artificial Regeneration, Bamboo Plantation Cane Plantation, Mixed Plantation of trees having MFP and medicinal value, Regeneration of perennial herbs and shrubs of medicine value, Pasture Development/Silvipasture, Soil and Moisture Conservation and Entry Point Activity for village development. So, the study focused in 100 VSSs as part of Centre for People's Forestry's commitment to understand the present scenario and people's perception with relation to institutional effectiveness of FDA to take-up further developmental activities in these areas of VSS.

Objectives of the Study

The main objective of the study is to Understanding the representation (in structure) and participation (in functioning) of people in FDA. The specific objectives are:

1. To analyze the structure and functioning of FDA (enabling/ disabling factors) in the guidelines and in practice.
2. To look in to the extent of people's participation in functioning of FDA.
3. To understand people's perceptions and aspirations with regard to better participation.
4. To understand perceptions of FD officials at different levels with regard to involvement of people.

Area of the Study

The study has been conducted in the 100 VSSs/EDCs of four forest divisions of Achamapet, Adilabad, Kurnool and Nellore of Andhra Pradesh. Detailed tables of selected VSSs are given in the table.

Research Methodology

The present study is based on empirical method involving comprehensive field study. A detailed schedule consisting of closed and open ended questions is prepared and group discussions held in all 100 selected VSS. Apart from the Group Discussions with community, formal discussions have been also held with the officials of Forest Department especially at the level of Divisional Forest Officers and Additional PCCF of FDA.

The field study has taken place during the month of January 2011 extensively in all the selected forest divisions with the help of four teams of field investigators. Initially, team of field investigators have built rapport with local communities and also took personnel views on the present functioning of FDAs activities from targeted people in some extent to understand virtual functioning and activities of the present programme. In addition to the collection of field data, substantiate literature with relation to forest policy in general and NAP (NAEB) in specific have been reviewed to understand the phenomenon.

Analysis on Participation of Forest Dependent Communities in Governance of Forest Development Agency

Forest Department in Andhra Pradesh is organized into territorial circles and divisions like circles, divisions, sections and beats in forest areas for effective and transparent governance. Forest Division of Achampet is part of Mahabubnagar District of Andhra Pradesh. The chapter structured into seven sections-based on the study questionnaire. The first section details, initially, physical structure and profile of selected VSSs/EDCs in terms of division, range, name of Grama Panchayat and name of specific VSS/EDC, formation year, compartment number and allotted forest area. Further, it examines the caste composition. It also presents status on forest types of VSSs/EDCs and activities of FDA taken-up such as Micro-planning, Entry point activity, SMC works, Afforestation, Natural regeneration, Artificial regeneration, Pasture/ Silvi development, Fencing and activities of Village Development.

Second section characterizes on peoples participation in FDA with detailed activities with relation to participation, especially, on involvement in preparation of plans, planning process and also gathered perceptions on "whether People's Opinions/Suggestions/ Local needs included in the plan" and on views of satisfaction with the works under the FDA. The section also presents constraints in the structure of FDA and other related issues.

Third section is broadly focused on capacity-building and income generation activities; fourth section is on monitoring and evaluation and fifth section details on awareness on the structure of the Forest Development Agency. Issues like people participation in FDA functioning, nomination process and memorandum of understanding is elaborated in sixth section; and gender related issues like representation, membership in committees of EC/GB, participation, training and role in decision-making process are analyzed in the last and seventh section-based on the responses of local community.

Peoples Participation in FDA Programme

In response to the question "Has your VSS/EDC prepared plans? Data presented in table 8.1. It shows that 50 per cent of VSSs/EDCs have agreed, 37 per cent have not accepted with a view to their VSSs/EDCs are prepared plans and 13 per cent of the total did not

Table 8.1: Preparation of Plans in VSSs/EDCs

Sl. No.	*Division-wise Responses of VSSs/EDCs*					
	Response	*Achampet*	*Adilabad*	*Kurnool*	*Nellore*	*Overall*
1.	Yes	8 (32%)	04 (16%)	17 (68%)	21 (84%)	50 (50%)
2.	No	12 (48%)	15 (60%)	06 (24%)	04 (16%)	37 (37%)
3.	No Response	5 (20%)	06 (24%)	02 (08%)	00 (00%)	13 (13%)
	Total	**25 (100%)**	**25 (100%)**	**25 (100%)**	**25 100%)**	**100 (100%)**

respond either way. It is obvious from the field data that half of the total members of VSSs are aware on the preparation of plans under FDAs. The division-wise break shows that significant per cent of VSSs/ EDCs have prepared plans in the division of Nellore, followed by Kurnool (68%), Achampet (32%) and Adilabad (16%) divisions.

Involvement of People in Planning Process

In order to know involvement of VSSs in planning process of FDA activities, this question was asked, "Have you involved in planning process of FDA activities at your VSS/EDC?" Information on this issue is gathered and presented in table 8.2. It shows that 46 per cent of VSSs/EDCs have accepted with a view to involvement in planning process under the activities of FDA. In their opinion, "we (members of VSSs/EDCs) have participated in the meetings, but could not involve in actual preparation of plans. Moreover, they (officials) did not take into account our views because we do not know how to do plans. So, the officials have initiated the preparation of plans and completed the task". 47 per cent have responded that they do not know about the planning in their VSSs/EDCs and remaining 7 per cent of members of VSSs/EDCs were not responded.

Table 8.2: Involvement in VSSs/EDCs

Sl. No.	*Division-wise Responses of VSSs/EDCs*					
	Response	*Achampet*	*Adilabad*	*Kurnool*	*Nellore*	*Overall*
1.	Yes	07 (28%)	04 (16%)	15 (60%)	20 (80%)	46 (46%)
2.	No	16 (64%)	16 (64%)	10 (40%)	05 (20%)	47 (47%)
3.	No Response	02 (08%)	05 (20%)	00 (00%)	00 (00%)	07 (07%)
	Total	**25 (100%)**	**25 (100%)**	**25 (100%)**	**25 (100%)**	**100 (100%)**

Table 8.3: Perceptions on "whether People's Opinions/Suggestions/Local needs included in the plan"

Sl. No.	*Division-wise Responses of VSSs/EDCs*					
	Response	*Achampet*	*Adilabad*	*Kurnool*	*Nellore*	*Overall*
1.	Yes	4 (16%)	05 (20%)	15 (60%)	18 (72%)	42 (42%)
2.	No	20 (80%)	20 (80%)	10 (40%)	05 (20%)	55 (55%)
3.	No Response	1 (4%)	00 (00%)	00 (00%)	02 (08%)	03 (03%)
	Total	**25 (100%)**	**25 (100%)**	**25 (100%)**	**25 (100%)**	**100 (100%)**

The study also tried to know people's perception on "whether opinion, suggestions and local needs of people included in the plan", responses presented in Table 8.2, shows that 42 per cent were said that their needs were given priority in the action plan in their respective habitations and 55 per cent have not accepted that priority is not given to their local needs and only 3 per cent VSSs/EDCs did not respond to this inquiry.

Table 8.4: Status on People's Satisfaction with the works under the FDA

Sl. No.	*Division-wise Responses of VSSs/EDCs*					
	Response	*Achampet*	*Adilabad*	*Kurnool*	*Nellore*	*Overall*
1.	Yes	02 (8%)	09 (36%)	08 (32%)	13 (52%)	32 (32%)
2.	No	20 (80%)	04 (16%)	10 (40%)	07 (28%)	41 (41%)
3.	No Response	03 (12%)	12 (48%)	07 (28%)	05 (20%)	27 (27%)
	Total	**25 (100%)**	**25 (100%)**	**25 (100%)**	**25 (100%)**	**100 (100%)**

In order to have general reflection on the implementation of FDA and whether the activities of FDA satisfied or dissatisfied, asked the following question to members of VSSs/EDCs; "Are you satisfied with the works of FDA?" The data presented in table 8.4. As regard to the people's satisfaction with the activities of FDA, 32 per cent have positively responded and 41 per cent negatively replied that they have not satisfied with the works of FDA and 27 per cent of local people are not responded with this question.

Constraints in the present structure of FDA are seen in almost all VSSs/EDCs because the outreach of the activities to the community under present initiation is not seen effectively. So, some constraints were emerged in the study such as lack of funds and cooperation;

Table 8.5: Constraints in the Present Structure of FDA

Sl. No.	*Division-wise Responses of VSSs/EDCs*					
	Response	*Achampet*	*Adilabad*	*Kurnool*	*Nellore*	*Overall*
1.	Lack of funds	08 (32%)	21 (84%)	19 (76%)	19 (76%)	67 (67%)
2.	Lack of cooperation	15 (60%)	02 (08%)	03 (12%)	03 (12%)	23 (23%)
3.	Political interference	0 (00%)	0 (00%)	01 (04%)	00 (00%)	01 (01%)
4.	Too many FD officials	02 (08%)	02 (08%)	02 (08%)	00 (00%)	06 (06%)
5.	Lack of people's interest	00 (00%)	00 (00%)	00 (00%)	03 (12%)	03 (03%)
	Total	**25 (100%)**	**25 (100%)**	**25 (100%)**	**25 (100%)**	**100 (100%)**

and to some extent involving forest officials in the functioning of FDA at grassroots. As it is shown in the above table 8.5, lack of funds is emerged as one of the main problems which account 67 per cent, while lack of cooperation is represented about 23 per cent, involvement of too many officials of Forest Department is evident in 06 per cent of VSSs/EDCs and 03 per cent responses are considered lack of people's interest as constraint and only one per cent opined that political interference is also problem in the proper functioning of FDA in VSSs/EDCs.

Additional Employment Opportunities under FDA

The study brought some information on whether additional employment or livelihoods have created under FDA, the details of perceptions of people have presented in Table 8.6. Of the total, 34 per cent of VSSs/EDCs have accepted with a view to creation of additional livelihoods and 55 per cent have not accepted with a view of creation of additional employment or livelihood sources and 11 per cent have not responded either way.

Table 8.6: Employment created under FDA

Sl. No.	*Division-wise Responses of VSSs/EDCs*					
	Response	*Achampet*	*Adilabad*	*Kurnool*	*Nellore*	*Overall*
1.	Yes	11 (44%)	14 (56%)	06 (24%)	03 (12%)	34 (34%)
2.	No	11 (44%)	06 (24%)	19 (76%)	19 (76%)	55 (55%)
3.	No Response	03 (12%)	05 (20%)	00 (00%)	03 (12%)	11 (11%)
	Total	**25 (100%)**	**25 (100%)**	**25 (100%)**	**25 (100%)**	**100 (100%)**

Table 8.7: Establishment of Village Development Fund (VDF)

Sl. No.	Response	Achampet	Adilabad	Kurnool	Nellore	Overall
1.	Yes	01 (04%)	03 (12%)	05 (20%)	01 (04%)	10 (10%)
2.	No	23 (92%)	22 (88%)	20 (80%)	24 (96%)	89 (55%)
3.	No Response	01 (04%)	00 (00%)	00 (00%)	00 (00%)	01 (01%)
	Total	**25 (100%)**	**25 (100%)**	**25 (100%)**	**25 (100%)**	**100 (100%)**

Division-wise Responses of VSSs/EDCs

The views on creation of village development fund are gathered and presented in table 8.7. The responses on these issues clearly shows that only 10 per cent of local people have accepted that the village development was created under the present structure of FDAs whereas 89 per cent of views have not accepted with a view that the village development fund was created and only one per cent of view was neither accepted not denied.

Capacity Building/Income Generation Activities

As part of trainings on capacity-building and income generation, the question was asked to the people that whether trainings are imparted under FDA or not? The details of perceptions of people have presented in Table 8.8. Of the total, 33 per cent of VSSs/EDCs have accepted with a view to trainings are given under FDA whereas 60 per cent of responses have expressed quite against that no trainings were imparted to the community; and 7 per cent have not given any response in the study. But, most of the general members of VSSs/EDCs have told that the trainings are never given on any specific point of view whether livelihoods, skills improvement or forest related as well. Nevertheless, some have expressed that the trainings were imparted on honey collection at Hyderabad, but changes in incomes have not seen.

Table 8.8: Training

Sl. No.	Response	Achampet	Adilabad	Kurnool	Nellore	Overall
1.	Yes	11 (44%)	01 (04%)	01 (04%)	20 (80%)	33 (33%)
2.	No	13 (52%)	23 (92%)	19 (76%)	05 (20%)	60 (60%)
3.	No Response	01 (04%)	01 (04%)	05 (20%)	00 (00%)	07 (07%)
	Total	**25 (100%)**	**25 (100%)**	**25 (100%)**	**25 (100%)**	**100 (100%)**

Division-wise Responses of VSSs/EDCs

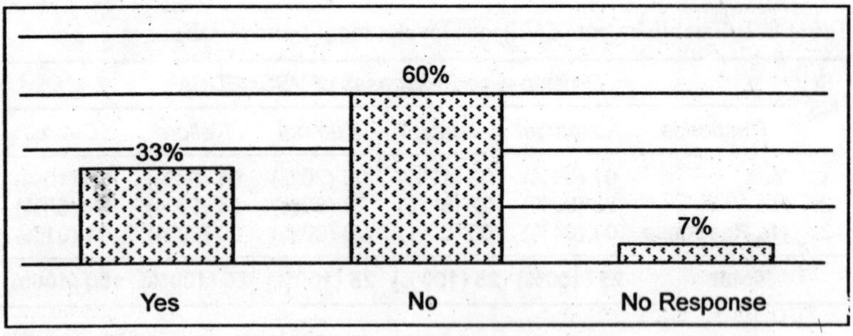

Graph 8.1: Status on Trainings Received by Community

Impact of Trainings on Livelihood or Capacity Building

The analysis is focused on with relation to views opined by local people on impact of trainings imparted to community (Table 8.9). Table 8.9 presents opinions on 'whether the trainings were changed community's incomes and strengthened community capacities, the data shows that only 12.12 per cent viewed that trainings were changed their incomes and remaining 87.87 per cent viewed that trainings are neither changed the incomes nor strengthened capacities of community.

Table 8.9: Impact of Training

Sl. No.	*Division-wise Responses of VSSs/EDCs*					
	Response	*Achampet*	*Adilabad*	*Kurnool*	*Nellore*	*Overall*
1.	Increased	00 (00%)	00 (00%)	00 (00%)	04 (10%)	04 (12.12%)
2.	No Change	11 (100%)	01 (100%)	01 (100%)	16 (45%)	29 (87.87%)
3.	Decreased	00 (00%)	00 (00%)	00 (00%)	00 (00%)	00 (00%)
4.	No Response	00 (00%)	00 (00%)	00 (00%)	00 (00%)	00 (00%)
	Total	**11 (100%)**	**01 (100%)**	**01 (100%)**	**20 (100%)**	**33 (100%)**

Officials of FD's Attendance for VSS/EDCs Meetings

As part of monitoring and evaluation of activities under FDA, the study is focused on whether officials of FD attending regularly meetings of VSS/EDCs, 25 per cent of members have said that officials are regularly attending the meetings, 40 per cent accepted with a view to need-based attendance, 15 per cent are agreed that the officials are visits and attend meetings sometimes only and around

Table 8.10: Monitoring and Evalution of Activities

Sl. No.	Response	Achampet	Adilabad	Kurnool	Nellore	Overall
		Division-wise Responses of VSSs/EDCs				
1.	Regular	06 (24%)	06 (24%)	02 (08%)	11 (44%)	25 (25%)
2.	Need Based	08 (32%)	08 (32%)	17 (68%)	07 (28%)	40 (40%)
3.	Sometimes only	04 (16%)	04 (16%)	02 (08%)	05 (20%)	15 (15%)
4.	Never attended	07 (28%)	07 (28%)	04 (16%)	02 (08%)	20 (20%)
	Total	**25 (100%)**	**25 (100%)**	**25 (100%)**	**25 (100%)**	**100 (100%)**

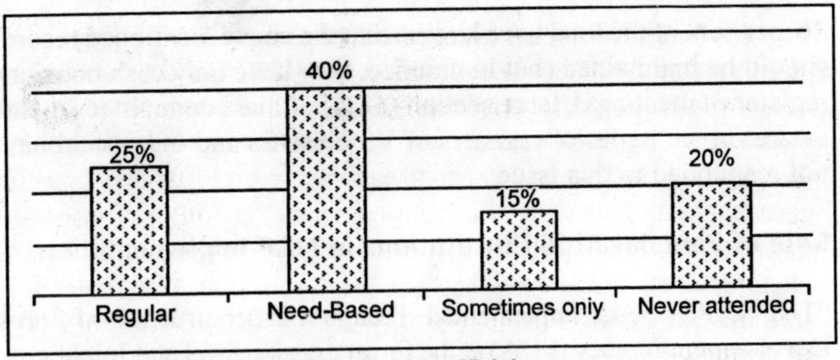

Graph 8.2: Pattern of Attandence of FD officials

20 per cent responded against to former responses that they never attended the meetings in respective areas of VSSs/EDCs. Similarly, with view to people's acceptance of officials attendance in meetings of General Body and Executive Committees, table 8.10 shows evidence on involvement of local community in planning process and community also replied that they could not involve in actual planning process, but preparation of plans virtually done by officials. This in turn, 55 per cent (including need based and sometimes attendance of officials visits) of responses further substantiate the officials inadequate response in FDAs activities.

Maintenance of Records by VSS Members

Virtually, all VSSs/EDCs have to maintain regularly Cash Book, Vouchers, Assets Register, Measurement Book, Register of Meetings, Resolutions and Minutes register (it gives brief note on conduct of General Body Meetings and subjects discussed and decisions/ resolutions passed). But, the study brought minimal responses on the maintenance of records in their respective areas of VSSs/EDCs. Only

Table 8.11: Maintenance of Records

Sl. No.	Division-wise Responses of VSSs/EDCs					
	Response	Achampet	Adilabad	Kurnool	Nellore	Overall
1.	Good	02 (08%)	04 (08%)	02 (08%)	18 (72%)	26 (26%)
2.	Average	21 (84%)	20 (80%)	23 (92%)	04 (16%)	68 (68%)
3.	Not Good	02 (08%)	01 (04%)	00 (00%)	03 (12%)	06 (06%)
	Total	**25 (100%)**	**25 (100%)**	**25 (100%)**	**25 (100%)**	**100 (100%)**

26 per cent of the total have known that the above mentioned records should be maintained (but in practice, they have only cash book and register of meetings), large section (68%) of these committees do not aware on the issues of registers of VSSs/EDCs and 6 per cent have not responded to this issue.

Role of Panchayati Raj Institutions in NAP Implementation

"The NAP is being implemented through a 2-tier structure of Forest Development Agency (FDA) at the forest division level and Joint Forest Management Committee (JFMC) at the village level. Thus, FDA is the confederation of JFMCs in that forest division. FDAs are registered under the Societies Registration Act. JFMCs are registered either with the Forest Department or under statutory provisions. The district-level officers of relevant line departments of the State Government and Panchayati Raj Institution are members of FDA" (Guidelines of National Afforestation Programme (NAP) Scheme, http://envfor.nic.in/naeb/). In this connection, the study also focused on institutional relation with Grama Panchayats and its involvement in regular activities of VSSs/EDCs. They revealed that only few (7%) of the total 100 VSSs/EDCs have accepted good

Table 8.12: Status of NAP Implementation through PRIs

Sl. No.	Division-wise Responses of VSSs/EDCs					
	Response	Achampet	Adilabad	Kurnool	Nellore	Overall
1.	Yes	02 (08%)	01 (04%)	01 (04%)	03 (12%)	07 (07%)
2.	No	02 (08%)	06 (24%)	06 (24%)	05 (20%)	19 (19%)
3.	No Response	14 (56%)	10 (40%)	18 (72%)	16 (64%)	58 (58%)
4.	Yes	07 (28%)	08 (32%)	00 (00%)	01 (04%)	16 (16%)
	Total	**25 (100%)**	**25 (100%)**	**25 (100%)**	**25 (100%)**	**100 (100%)**

relations with Grama Panchayats and many (58%) are not agreed with a view that there is a good relation with VSSs/EDCs as regard to activities of FDA. Moreover, 16 per cent are not even aware on the relation between the FDA activities in VSSs/EDCs and Grama Panchayats.

Section V: Awareness on the Structure of the Forest Development Agency

The study also sought to measure awareness about FDA in their respective areas. It had one important finding that only 21 per cent of the total respondents were aware about FDA as many as 75 per cent respondents unaware of what about they are supposed to know.

Table 8.13: Awareness on Forest Development Agency (FDA/NAP)

Sl. No.	*Response*	*Division-wise Responses of VSSs/EDCs*				
		Achampet	*Adilabad*	*Kurnool*	*Nellore*	*Overall*
1.	Yes	01 (04%)	00 (00%)	00 (00%)	20 (72%)	21 (21%)
2.	No	22 (88%)	24 (96%)	24 (96%)	05 (16%)	75 (75%)
3.	No Response	02 (08%)	01 (04%)	01 (04%)	00 (00%)	04 (04%)
	Total	**25 (100%)**	**25 (100%)**	**25 (100%)**	**25 (100%)**	**100 (100%)**

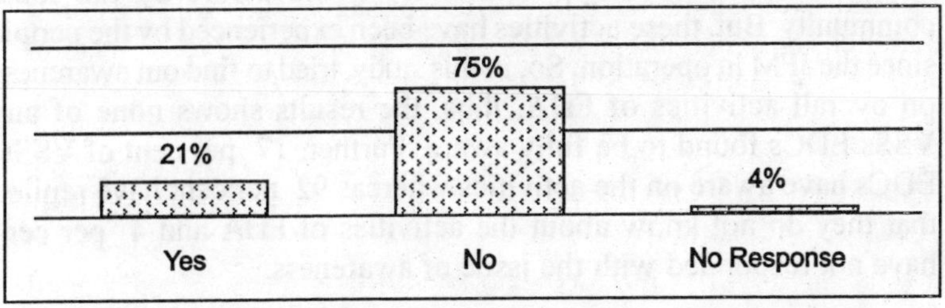

Graph 8.3: Awareness on FDA

Moreover, the study also found no responses on this specific issue which is being very important to overall success of the targeted objectives under the FDA. FDA, as an institution, has to reach to the grassroot whom it meant. But, the presented perceptions indicate the low level of awareness on the FDA among the targeted communities in 100 VSSs/EDCs.

Table 8.14: Awareness on activities of FDA in VSSs/EDCs

Sl. No.	Division-wise Responses of VSSs/EDCs					
	Response	Achampet	Adilabad	Kurnool	Nellore	Overall
1.	Yes	00 (00%)	00 (00%)	00 (00%)	17 (68%)	17 (17%)
2.	No	23 (92%)	24 (96%)	25 (100%)	07 (28%)	79 (79%)
3.	No Response	02 (08%)	01 (04%)	00 (00%)	01 (04%)	04 (04%)
	Total	**25 (100%)**	**25 (100%)**	**25 (100%)**	**25 (100%)**	**100 (100%)**

None of the total VSSs/EDCs had aware on activities of FDA. Here, some of grassroot issues need to be examined with regard to activities of FDA. Activities at VSSs/EDCs level are preparation of micro-planning in project villages and afforestation. Afforestation has different components like Aided Natural Regeneration, Artificial Regeneration, Bamboo Plantation, Cane Plantation, Mixed Plantation of trees having MFP and medicinal value, Regeneration of perennial herbs and shrubs of medicine value, Pasture Development/ Silvipasture, Soil and Moisture Conservation, Entry Point Activity (for village development; average assistance Rs. 1.6 lakh per village), Fencing, Training and Awareness raising. Of the total activities, only activities like preparation of micro-plans, Soil and Moisture Conservation and Entry Point Activity are aware by the local community. But, these activities have been experienced by the people since the JFM in operation. So, in this study, tried to find out awareness on overall activities of FDA, thus, the results shows none of any VSSs/EDCs found to be fully aware. Further, 17 per cent of VSSs/ EDCs have aware on the activities whereas 92 per cent have replied that they do not know about the activities of FDA and 4 per cent have not responded with the issue of awareness.

People Participation in FDA Functioning

VSS/EDCs Nomination for Membership in FDA

Further, the question was asked the members "Did your VSS/EDC get nominated to be a member of FDA"? The responses are presented briefly in Table 8.15. The data revealed very few (19%) of the members of VSSs/EDCs are familiar with the process of nomination and membership in FDA and similar proportions of VSSs/EDCs have replied that their *sanghas* have nominated for FDA membership; and

Table 8.15: Status of Membership Nomination

Sl. No.	Response	Achampet	Adilabad	Kurnool	Nellore	Overall
		Division-wise Responses of VSSs/EDCs				
1.	Yes	02 (08%)	00 (00%)	00 (00%)	17 (68%)	19 (19%)
2.	No	01 (04%)	20 (80%)	25 (100%)	05 (20%)	51 (51%)
3.	No Response	22 (88%)	05 (20%)	00 (00%)	03 (12%)	30 (30%)
	Total	**25 (100%)**	**25 (100%)**	**25 (100%)**	**25 (100%)**	**100 (100%)**

remaining 51 per cent have not nominated and 30 per cent of VSSs/EDCs have responded neither way.

Sharing of Information on Discussed Issues of GB/EC meetings of FDA

People's perception was gathered on whether the information regarding issues discussed in the meetings of FDA (General Body and Executive Body) are shared among the community members. The data shows that 15 per cent have accepted that information was shared among the members regarding issues discussed in EC/GB whereas 21 per cent have not agreed and 47 per cent of members of VSSs/EDCs have not given the response.

Table 8.16: Sharing of Information

Sl. No.	Response	Achampet	Adilabad	Kurnool	Nellore	Overall
		Division-wise Responses of VSSs/EDCs				
1.	Yes	09 (36%)	00 (00%)	00 (00%)	23 (68%)	32 (32%)
2.	No	09 (36%)	07 (28%)	03 (12%)	02 (20%)	21 (21%)
3.	Don't Know	07 (28%)	18 (72%)	22 (88%)	00 (00%)	47 (47%)
	Total	**25 (100%)**	**25 (100%)**	**25 (100%)**	**25 (100%)**	**100 (100%)**

Meetings by FDA: General Body

The responses on "whether General Body meetings are organised by FDA frequently" to understand effective and regular functioning of governance of VSSs/EDCs. The data shows that 27 per cent have agreed with a view to regular meetings of VSSs/EDCs and 16 per cent have not accepted and more than half of the total members have not

Table 8.17: Status of General Body Meetings

Sl. No.	*Response*	*Achampet*	*Adilabad*	*Kurnool*	*Nellore*	*Overall*
		Division-wise Responses of VSSs/EDCs				
1.	Yes	02 (08%)	03 (12%)	00 (00%)	22 (68%)	27 (27%)
2.	No	01 (04%)	14 (56%)	01 (04%)	00 (00%)	16 (16%)
3.	Don't Know	22 (88%)	08 (32%)	24 (96%)	03 (00%)	57 (57%)
	Total	**25 100%)**	**25 (100%)**	**25 (100%)**	**25 (100%)**	**100 (100%)**

said anything about these meetings. It may be understood that the local community is unaware about the meetings and its importance.

Participation of VSSs/EDCs in the Meetings of FDA (as a GB/EC member)

The other question put to the VSSs/EDCs was "Did your VSS/EDC participate in the meetings of FDA (as a GB/EC member)?" It is seen from Table 8.18 that about 20 per cent of the members of VSSs/EDCs felt that their organisations have participated, but, 72 per cent have not accepted with view to former responses and 24 per cent of the total have said that they do not know about all these things with relation to meetings and participation.

Table 8.18: Participation in Meetings

Sl. No.	*Response*	*Achampet*	*Adilabad*	*Kurnool*	*Nellore*	*Overall*
		Division-wise Responses of VSSs/EDCs				
1.	Yes	05 (20%)	01 (04%)	00 (00%)	21 (84%)	27 (27%)
2.	No	18 (72%)	23 (92%)	04 (16%)	04 (00%)	49 (49%)
3.	Don't Know	02 (08%)	01 (04%)	21 (84%)	00 (00%)	24 (24%)
	Total	**25 (100%)**	**25 (100%)**	**25 (100%)**	**25 (100%)**	**100 (100%)**

Perceptions on Satisfaction with the Present Structure of FDA

In order to find out the general perception of members of VSSs/EDCs on the structural–functional aspects, a specific question was asked like, "Are you satisfied with the existing structure of FDA?" According to Table 8.19, very limited and less responses emerged with a view to satisfaction that only 22 per cent have said that they

Table 8.19: Perception about the present structure

Sl. No.	*Response*	*Achampet*	*Adilabad*	*Kurnool*	*Nellore*	*Overall*
		Division-wise Responses of VSSs/EDCs				
1.	Yes	01 (04%)	01 (04%)	00 (00%)	20 (80%)	22 (22%)
2.	No	21 (84%)	18 (92%)	20 (8%)	05 (20%)	64 (64%)
3.	Don't Know	03 (12%)	06 (04%)	05 (20%)	00 (00%)	14 (14%)
	Total	**25 (100%)**	**25 (100%)**	**25 (100%)**	**25 (100%)**	**100 (100%)**

satisfied whereas 64 per cent of community members have not accepted with the view of satisfaction on the existing structure of FDA. And 12 per cent of local members have not given any response regarding above question.

Transparency and Accountability in Utilization of Fund

An attempt was made to know the opinion of members of VSSs/ EDCs on Transparency and Accountability in Utilization of Fund. In this regard, they were asked "Is fund utilization (income and expenditure) details are shared in GB/EC meetings?" The answers presented in Table 8.20, show that 25 per cent of the members felt that income and expenditure details of their VSSs/EDCs are shared in GB/EC meetings and contrarily, 45 per cent, a majority are replied that discussions regarding fund utilization are never held and 30 per cent said that they do not know about funds and fund utilization in their VSSs/EDCs.

Table 8.20: Transparency and Accountability of Funds

Sl. No.	*Response*	*Achampet*	*Adilabad*	*Kurnool*	*Nellore*	*Overall*
		Division-wise Responses of VSSs/EDCs				
1.	Yes	05 (20%)	02 (08%	00 (00%)	18 (72%)	25 (25%)
2.	No	15 (60%)	08 (32%)	16 (64%)	06 (24%)	45 (45%)
3.	Don't Know	05 (20%)	15 (60%)	09 (36%)	01 (04%)	30 (30%)
	Total	**25 (100%)**	**25 (100%)**	**25 (100%)**	**25 (100%)**	**100 (100%)**

Gender

Forest Development Authority is a district level organization developed under the guidelines of NAP, Government of India. It is the confederation of Joint Forest Management committees (VSSs/ EDCs) in a division. The main objective of FDA is to promote integrated ecosystem based management with people centred approach. The FDAs have given importance to the women in divisional level institutional set-up such as General Body and Executive Body with people's involvement especially members of VSSs/EDCs.

In this connection, the General Body, according to the Operational Guidelines (2004) of the National Afforestation Programme (NAP), constitutes with Chairperson-Conservator of Forests Members and Presidents of JFMC General Bodies, not more than 50 at any time, to be nominated by Chairperson on rotational basis for a period of one year, of which 20 would be women representatives and in Executive Body, fifteen nominees from the JFMCs of which minimum 7 would be women including Chairperson (Conservator of Forests), Member Secretary-*cum*-Chief Executive Officer (Divisional Forest Officer), Members from District Development Officer, District level Officers of Agriculture, Rural Development, Animal Husbandry, Soil Conservation, Tribal Welfare, Industries, Public Health and Engineering, Welfare, Horticulture, Minor Irrigation, Small Scale Industries/KVIC, Education Departments and the Lead Bank Officer ADM/AC to be nominated by DC/DM and others. In this background, the study also focused on women's representation, role and their voice in decision-making. In this section, women's views are only taken into account.

Representation of Women in FDA

The study also tried to find out the adequacy of representation of women in GB and ECs. For this purpose, the question was asked; "Is there women representation in FDA?" In their opinion, 24 per cent have accepted with a view of representation in FDA and 76 per cent of people said that there is no representation of women in GB/EC of FDAs. It is observed in the field that the names of women in the list of GB and ECs but women do not know that their names are in the list of respective committees. In connection with the above responses, further the question was asked, "If yes, whether membership in EC/ GB given to women?" the responses are presented table 8.21.

Table 8.21: Women's Reprentation in FDA

Sl. No.	Division-wise Responses of VSSs/EDCs					
	Response	*Achampet*	*Adilabad*	*Kurnool*	*Nellore*	*Overall*
1.	Yes	04 (16%)	00 (00%)	00 (00%)	20 (80%)	24 (24%)
2.	No	19 (76%)	22 (88%)	14 (56%)	04 (16%)	59 (59%)
3.	Don't Know	02 (08%)	03 (12%)	11 (44%)	01 (04%)	17 (17%)
	Total	**25 (100%)**	**25 (100%)**	**25 (100%)**	**25 (100%)**	**100 (100%)**

Women in Executive Committee or General Body (Whether)

Supplementary analysis is made based on the responses emerged from the table 8.22 with relation to women's membership in the executive Committee and General Body of FDAs structure. The responses evident that only 12 per cent of women are accepted with a view of membership given to women in ECs, 16 per cent of women have agreed that they were given membership in GBs and 72 per cent have not responded with this question.

Table 8.22: Women's Participation in Executive Committee

Sl. No.	Division-wise Responses of VSSs/EDCs					
	Response	*Achampet*	*Adilabad*	*Kurnool*	*Nellore*	*Overall*
1.	ECs	01 (04%)	00 (00%)	00 (00%)	11 (44%)	12 (12%)
2.	GBs	03 (12%)	01 (04%)	01 (04%)	11 (44%)	16 (16%)
3.	No Response	21 (84%)	24 (96%)	24 (96%)	03 (12%)	72 (72%)
	Total	**25 (100%)**	**25 (100%)**	**25 (100%)**	**25 (100%)**	**100 (100%)**

Women's Role in Decision-Making Process

In order to know women's role in decision-making process, this question was asked, "As a member in FDA, what is your role in decision-making process in GB/EC of FDA?" the data shows that only 16 per cent were responded with a view of women's role in decision-making and 53 per cent women have replied with an answer of 'no' very clearly. Remaining 31 per cent have not responded with this question. Thus, the women in FDA is not actively participated. There are different reasons such as lack of proper communication, negligence and women themselves were not ready at the time meetings due to heavy involvement in providing families essential services.

Table 8.23: Women's Role in Decision-Making Process

Sl. No.	Division-wise Responses of VSSs/EDCs					
	Response	*Achampet*	*Adilabad*	*Kurnool*	*Nellore*	*Overall*
1	Yes	00 (00%)	00 (00%)	00 (00%)	16 (64%)	16 (16%)
2	No	14 (56%)	13 (52%)	17 (68%)	09 (36%)	53 (53%)
3	Don't Know	11 (44%)	12 (48%)	08 (32%)	00 (00%)	31 (31%)
	Total	**25 (100%)**	**25 (100%)**	**25 (100%)**	**25 (100%)**	**100 (100%)**

Conclusion

As regard to the opinions on nomination of VSS/EDC's to be a member of FDA, data revealed that very few of the members are aware on the process of nomination and membership; and Memorandum of Understanding (MoU) in FDA. Sharing of information regarding issues discussed in the meetings of FDA between the chairpersons and general members; regular meetings (GB and EC) organised by FDA frequently is also not up to the satisfactory level. The reasonable participation of VSSs/EDCs in the meetings of FDA (as a GB/EC member) is not evident in the present study and only few of the total members expressed their satisfaction on the structural-functional aspects, especially the responses of the members of VSSs/EDCs on selection process of members of Executive Committee for Divisional level FDA. Majority of local people responded negatively on the meetings of VSS/EDC's General Body/Executive Committee because local level chairpersons have failed to inform about the meetings to all the members, but, it is obvious in the field, they inform only to those who are close to them and have connections regularly.

The few responses on selection process of members of Executive Committee for Divisional level FDA have satisfied and majority was differed. Importance to people's opinions/suggestions is modestly given, especially, at the time of meetings and preparation of micro-plan. One-fourth of the total members of VSSs/EDCs have accepted that transparency and accountability in utilization of fund (income and expenditure) are shared in GB/EC meetings and majority opinioned that such kind of sharing in the meetings is never seen.

The guidelines of NAP (FDAs), Government of India have given importance to the women in divisional level institutional set-up such as General Body and Executive Body with people's involvement especially members of VSSs/EDCs. It is clear from the study finding that there is inadequate representation of women in GB and ECs. Supplementary analysis of the study brought some important findings that women's membership in the executive Committee and General Body of FDA's structure is also not up to the mark as it in the NAP's guidelines. Information on meetings of FDA to women is also not appropriately passed and some of women members replied that they did not receive such kind of information.

Women's participation in trainings imparted by FDA is very low and role in decision-making process, based on the field level data, only very small per cent of women replied that they played key role and large number of women have not responded to this opinion. This study reflect there should be transparent and accountable mechanisms need to be evolved in general and taking the rate of women's voice in specific.

Important Findings in the Study

The following are the main issues found in the study:

- It is understood that there is low level of awareness on institutional issues like formation year, compartment number, allotted forest area and year of initiation of FDA in their respective VSSs/EDCs.
- There is the presence of all social groups (based on actual the presence of respective forest divisions), but participation is not as much as they present on the papers.
- A community perception on status of forest is not adequate and they expressed individually. People should be in a position to express commonly known fact about their forest.
- The awareness on activities under the FDA is not properly communicated. Consequently, people have missed the knowledge on different activities, especially afforestation, natural regeneration and artificial regeneration. These activities would have impacted on their respective forests positively.
- Some of the forest works were done with the help of motor vehicles, especially, the work of trench was taken up by JCP in Inole EDC.
- People's Participation in FDA Programme, especially in

preparation of micro-plans in VSSs/EDCs is not much progressive as a result diversified community views have been missing because community indigenous knowledge also helps in enhancing the overall natural resources including forests and also improve their regular incomes.

- Most of the VSSs/EDCs have not conducted meetings in regular intervals and no coordination found between members, chairpersons and forest officials.
- Lack of regular funds flow into VSSs/EDCs
- Most of the members of VSSs/EDCs have felt the constraints in the present structure of FDA are lack of funds, lack of people's interest, lack of cooperation and unstructured involvement of officials of Forest Department.
- There is no effective and efficient mechanism to include people's voice in micro-plans, no standard format is available.
- It is observed in the group discussions that transparency has become a much-debated issue among local people. Activities on additional employment or livelihoods, village development fund, trainings on capacity-building and income generation and skills improvement have not brought any changes in the lives of targeted community.
- Training activities and its objectives are not communicated to local people consequently trainings are in large extent not reached expected outcomes.
- The monitoring and evaluation (M&E) is not effective at the divisional as well as at grassroot level.
- Regular monitoring of forest officials is missing.
- The mixed perceptions of community expressed on the role of the officials of Forest Department in attending meetings of General Body and Executive Committee, in implementation and preparation of plans.
- Cash Book, Vouchers, Assets Register, Measurement Book, Register of Meetings, Resolutions and Minutes register of VSSs/EDCs have maintained, but there are only cash book and register of meetings and most of the members are not aware on the issues of maintenance of registers in their respective VSSs/EDCs.
- Most of the VSSs/EDCs' records are in the office of forest department, most of the cases in the present study, records are with the forest authority.

- Low level of awareness is observed on membership and most of the members are unaware about representation of chairperson in FDA.
- The relation between the FDA's and Grama Panchayats is not much better.
- Some of the members does not know about the institutional linkages between VSSs/EDECs and FDA which led to gap between the targets and outcomes of the FDA.
- Very few of the members are aware on the process of nomination and membership; and Memorandum of Understanding (MoU) in FDA.
- Sharing of information regarding issues discussed in the meetings of FDA between the chairpersons and general members; regular meetings (GB and EC) organised by FDA frequently is also not in satisfactory position.
- The participation of VSSs/EDCs in the meetings of FDA (as a GB/EC member) is not effective.
- Local people are not informed properly on selection process of members of Executive Committee for Divisional level FDA.
- Information on the meetings of VSS/EDC's General Body/ Executive Committee is sharing only too few of the total members.
- Selection process of members of Executive Committee for Divisional level FDA have not satisfied majority of the people.
- Discussion on transparency and accountability in utilization of fund (income and expenditure) is accounted very low with reference to community perception.
- Inadequate representation of women in GB and ECs, membership in the Executive Committee and General Body of FDA's, participation in trainings imparted by FDA and role in decision-making process is evidently very low.
- Dominance of traditional leadership is still predominantly influencing on people's minds because in VSSL. Bandla, field investigators requested the community members those who involved in group discussions for attendance signature, but they denied to put their signatures even the presence and attendance of respective VSSs' chairperson and vice-chairperson in the meeting and the field investigators

questioned 'why?', they replied that "we will sign after taking permission from our leader whose social background is Reddy. The social group of Reddy has traditional dominated character."

- Under the activities of village development and entry point, different types of activities are taken-up. The activities are varying from VSSs/EDCs to VSSs/EDCs. The activities includes supplying of Tent and allied goods, Sewing Machines to women, distribution of buffalos, goats, financial assistance as a loan for improving livelihoods, construction of bus stand, cattle troughs, water filters, solar power connections, chairs, water drums, borewells, distribution of submersible pump sets, hand pumps, cooking stoves (smokeless *Chulhas), Vermicompost, CC road (Pikklivanipalle, Kurnool division), community hall, pipelines for drinking water supply and distributed iron cooking stoves.*
- But, some of VSSs/EDCs experienced that the instruments like tent and allied goods are distributed to community and immediately took them back and kept in the guesthouse of forest office (Domalapenta EDCs, Achampet forest division).

Recommendations

The most efficient and effective long-term people's oriented policies have to consider for proper and expected results of the targeted goals in the present FDAs. The FDA with people's participation can make significant contributions toward meeting the goals of NAP if certain policy recommendations are effectively implemented. The following are the main recommendations:

- The need is to enhance awareness on institutional issues to all the members so as to improve people's participation in the present context of FDA which will help in future pro-people developmental programmes.
- There should be effective mechanisms to improve the participation of all social groups so that equitable social development possible.
- There should be proper communication channel to enhance awareness on activities under the FDA then people may be progressively involved to build local management capacity

consequently peoples participation in FDA, especially in preparation of micro-plans will be strengthened and it would be utilized diversified community's indigenous knowledge and also improve incomes of local community.

- There should be effective mechanism including both local people's representation and local forest officials to conduct meetings in regular intervals, to give priority to people's voice and to prepare micro-plans with people's participation; and this mechanism has to build coordination between members of VSSs/EDCs, its chairpersons and forest officials. This mechanism has to also work for transparent and accountable financial management at divisional as well as at grassroot.
- There should be planned and regular funds flow to VSSs/ EDCs through FDAs so that people may participate enthusiastically in these activities. Moreover, regular funds flow enhances the functional capacities of VSSs/EDCs and which leads effective natural resources management.
- There should be integrated effective mechanism to solve all the problems in VSSs/EDCs in the present structure of FDA in general and for efficient functioning of the JFMCs in specific. This mechanism has to act as monitoring and evaluation (M&E) effectively at the divisional as well as at grassroot level and also it has to look after the role of the officials of Forest Department in attending meetings regular intervals.
- Need-based training programmes with proper timelines has to be evolved so as to improve the utility of skills of trainings so as to improve the outcomes of targeted objectives of the FDA in general and to improve skills and income of people in specific.
- People should be trained thoroughly in maintenance of all records like Cash Book, Vouchers, Assets Register, Measurement Book, Register of Meetings, Resolutions, Minutes Register and Memorandum of Understanding (MoU) of VSSs/EDCs.
- Collaboration and networking with different departments like forest department, rural development department, Tribal Welfare department, Revenue Department and like has to be developed so as to improve the function of FDA especially at grassroots.

- Participation of people in meetings, sharing of information between the chairpersons and general members, information on selection process of members of GB/ECs have to be satisfactorily improved by conducting local level meetings regularly and mandatorily.
- Inadequate representation of women in GB and ECs, membership in the Executive Committee and General Body of FDA's, participation in trainings imparted by FDA and role in decision-making process is evidently very low.

Public policies should encourage sustainable development through people's participation and effective coordination, collaboration and networking with other appropriate departments to achieve overall objectives. The objectives of the NAP (FDAs) is to develop the forest resources with people's participation, with focus on improvement in livelihoods of the forest fringe communities, especially the poor and also it aimed to support and accelerate the ongoing process of devolving forest protection, management and development functions to decentralize institutions of Joint Forest Management Committees (JFMCs) at the village level, and Forest Development Agency (FDA) at the forest division level.

Note

1. This research was completed with the support of Centre for People's Forestry (CPF); Hyderabad based NGO where I worked as Programme Officer (Communication and Documentation and Analysis) during the period of 2010-2011. Later, this study further elaborated from Social Sciences Research approach. I have also taken inputs from Dr. D. Suryakumari, Director-CPF, and Jalaja, Daina Joseph, Nagaraj and K. Suresh were helped in preparing the questionnaire and orientation on questionnaire to the Field Level Investigators given by Dr. D. Suryakumari, K. Suresh, B. Jalaja, and D. Srinivasulu and Dr. Sunkari Satyam.

References

Agarwal, A. (1998): Myths about forest depletion; How India's rural poor are not denuding the country's forests. *Down to Earth*, Vol. 7, No. 1.

Agarwal, A., Chopra, R., Sharma, K. (1982): *State of India's Environment: The First Citizen's Report*. New Delhi: Centre for Science and Environment.

Agarwal, A., Narain, S. (1990): *Towards Green Villages: A Strategy for Environmentally Sound and Participatory Rural Development*. New Delhi: Centre for Science and Environment.

Andhra Pradesh Forest Department, Workshop Proceedings 2002, http://forest.ap.nic.in/about.htm, access date: 4/2/2001.

Bajaj, M. (1992): Natural Regeneration *vs.* Afforestation: An Examination of the Potential for Natural Regeneration with Community Participation. In: Agarwal, A. (Ed.) (1992): *The Price of Forests. Proceedings of a Seminar on the Economics of the Sustainable Use of Forest Resources*. New Delhi: Centre for Science and Environment (CSE).

Bryant, R.L., Bailey, S. (1997): *Third World Political Ecology*. London: Routledge.

Buchi, K.N. (1997): Shifting cultivation and its impact on forest ecosystem. In Mohapatra, P.M., Mohapatro, P.C. (eds.) (1997): *Forest Management in Tribal Areas: Forest Policy and Peoples' Participation*. New Delhi: Concept Publishing Company.

Chakrabarti, S.K., Gaharwar, K.S. (1998): A Study on Volume Estimation of Shorearobusta. *Indian Forester,* Vol. 124, No. 4.

Corbridge, S. (1986): *State, Tribe and Region: Policy and Politics in India's Jharkand, 1900-1980.* Unpublished Ph.D. dissertation, Department of Geography, Cambridge: University of Cambridge.

Corbridge, S., Jewitt, S. (1997): From forest struggles to forest citizens? Joint Forest Management in the unquiet woods of India's Jharkhand. *Environment and Planning A*. Vol. 29.

Fernandes, W. (Ed.) (1996): *Drafting a People's Forest Bill: The Forest Dweller-Social Activist Alternative*. New Delhi: Indian Social Institute.

Gadgil, M., Guha, R. (1992): *This Fissured Land: An Ecological History of India.* London: Oxford University Press.

Gadgil, M., Guha, R. (1995): *Ecology and Equity: The Use and Abuse of Nature in Contemporary India.* London: Routledge.

Guha, M. (1989): *The Unquiet Woods: Ecological Change and Peasant Resistance in the Himalaya.* New Delhi: Oxford University Press

Jain, A.K. (1998): Joint Forest Management in Cuddapah Forest Division: A Successful Example. *Indian Forester*, Vol. 124, No. 7.

Jewitt, S. (1995): Europe's 'Others'? Forestry policy and practices in colonial and postcolonial India. *Environment and Planning D: Society and Space*. Vol. 13.

Jewitt, S. (1995): Voluntary and 'official' forest protection committees in Bihar: solutions to India's deforestation? *Journal of Biogeography,* Vol. 22.

Jo Lawbuary, (1999): Reclaiming the Forests?, People's Participation in Forest Management, East India, http://www.ganesha.co.uk/JoPubWeb/Frontdiss.htm, access date 13/6/2011.

Khan, I. (1998): Protection Woes. *Down to Earth/Centre for Science and Environment Campaigns Supplement.* January 15.

Kulkarni, S. (1983): The forest policy and forest bill: A critique and suggestion for change. In: W Fernandes, S. Kulkarni (eds.) (1983). *Towards a New Forest Policy: Peoples' Rights and Environmental Needs.* New Delhi: Indian Social Institute, pp. 84-102.

Malhotra, K.C., Deb, D. (1998): History of Deforestation and Regeneration/ Plantation in Midnapore District of West Bengal, India. In: Roy, S.B., Chatterjee, M., Yadav, G., Mukherjee, R., (Eds.) (1998): *Policy to Practice of Joint Forest Management.* New Delhi: Indian Institute of Bio-Social Research and Development (IBRAD). pp. 279-300.

Malhotra, K.C., Deb, D., Dutta, M., Vasulu, T.S., Yadav, G., Adhikari, M. (1998): Role of Non-Timber Forest Product (NTFP) in Village Economy. In: Roy, S.B., Chatterjee, M., Yadav, G., Mukherjee, R., (Eds.) (1998): *Policy to Practice of Joint Forest Management.* New Delhi: Indian Institute of Bio-Social Research and Development (IBRAD). pp. 160-207.

Maslekar, A.R., (1977): *Forester's Companion.* Dehra Dun: Surya International Publications.

Ministry of Environment and Forests (1998): *State of the Forest Report, 1997.* http://envfor.nic.in/naeb/sch/schnprg.html, access Date/23/3/2011

Ministry of Environment and Forests (1999): *Annual Report 1997-98.* http:// envfor.nic.in/naeb/sch/schnprg.html, access Date/23/3/2011.

National Afforestation and Eco-development Board, http://www.naeb.nic.in/, Access Date: 07/2/2011

Palit, S. (1998): Indian Forest Departments in Transition. In: Poffenberger, M., McGean, B. (1998): *Village Voices, Forest Choices. Joint Forest Management in India.* New Delhi: Oxford University Press.

Poffenberger, M. (1995): The resurgence of community forest management in the jungle mahals of West Bengal. In Arnold, D., Guha, R. (1995): *Nature, Culture and Imperialism: Essays on the Environmental History of South Asia.* New Delhi: Oxford University Press.

Poffenberger, M. (Ed.) (1996): *Communities and Forest Management: IUCN Working Group on Community Involvement in Forest Management.* IUCN.

Poffenberger, M., McGean, B. (1998): *Village Voices, Forest Choices. Joint Forest Management in India.* New Delhi: Oxford University Press.

Ravindranath, N.H., Gadgil, M., Campbell, J. (1998): Ecological Stabilization and Community Needs: Managing India's Forest by Objective. In Poffenberger, M., McGean, B. (1998): *Village Voices, Forest Choices. Joint Forest Management in India.* New Delhi: Oxford University Press.

Reddy, Gopinath, Anil Kumar (2010): Political Economy of Tribal Development: A Case Study of Andhra Pradesh, Working Paper No. 85, CESS Report, Hyderabad. http://www.cess.ac.in/cesshome/wp/WP_85.pdf, access Date: 4/3/2011.

Roy, S.B., Mahapatra, T., Giri, D., Mukhopadhyay, D., Chowdhury, S. (1998):

Vegetation Monitoring by the People. In: Roy, S.B., Chatterjee, M., Yadav, G., Mukherjee, R. (Eds.) (1998): *Policy to Practice of Joint Forest Management*. New Delhi: Indian Institute of Bio-Social Research and Development (IBRAD).

Samal, J. (1997): Role of forest in a poor resource base tribal economy: A micro-analysis. In Mohapatra, P.M., Mohapatro, P.C. (eds.) (1997): *Forest Management in Tribal Areas: Forest Policy and Peoples' Participation*. New Delhi: Concept Publishing Co.

Saxena, N.C. (1992): Adoption of a long-gestation crop—eucalyptus growers in north-west India. *Journal of Agricultural Economics*. Vol. 43, No. 2, pp. 257-267.

Shiva, V., Bandyopadhyay, J. (1983): Eucalyptus: A disastrous tree for India. *The Ecologist*. Vol. 13, No. 5, pp. 184-187.

Thakur, B.N. (1997): Impact of shifting cultivation on forest ecosystem. In Mohapatra, P.M., Mohapatro, P.C. (eds.) (1997): *Forest Management in Tribal Areas: Forest Policy and Peoples' Participation*. New Delhi: Concept Publishing Co.

Vardhan, R., Kurian, M. (Eds.) (1996): *The JFM Experience: Proceedings of the National Workshop in Process Documentation*. New Delhi: TERI (Tata Energy Research Institute) and Haryana Forest Department, pp. 32-34.

9

Tribals and Protected Areas

Protest Dynamics in a Conservation Project in Odisha

Sthitapragyan Ray

Introduction

The establishment of protected areas (PAs), has been the principal conservation strategy in most parts of the world, including India (Adams, 2004; Neumann, 2002). In India, the dominance of the "forests" over the "sustainable use" model of conservation, has led to the creation of centralised state-administered wildlife reserves.[1] The spatial strategy of separating people from nature for conservation through creation of PAs, reflects the manner in which modern state seeks to manipulate and control nature by applying scientific knowledge (see Scott, 1998). This exclusionary conservation paradigm has had significant implications both for wildlife and forest-dependent population (Kothari *et al.*, 1996; Rangarajan and Shahabuddin, 2006; Kabra, 2009) living in India's five per cent geographic space and 668 PAs (Government of India, 2012).[2] In Odisha, the PAs comprising two national parks and 18 sanctuaries, constitute 4.25 per cent of total area of the state (Government of Odisha, 2012). According to a World Bank supported study (Kumar *et al.*, 2006), a total of 8,11,155 hectares of area and 771 villages have been affected by the creation of sanctuaries and national parks in the state. Most of the existing and proposed PAs in the state are situated in tribal-dominated areas, with the later forming 44 per cent of Odisha's geographic and almost 70 per cent of its forest area.[3]

The growing recognition of economic and socio-cultural costs of PAs for local communities particularly tribals since the 1980s (IUCN, 1980; World Bank, 1984; WPC, 2003; CBD, 2004), has led to putting a premium on inclusion and sustainability rather than on exclusion and damage limitation in the creation of PAs. Consequently, major policy changes have taken place (World Bank, 2001; AfDB, 2003; ADB, 2003), which seek to recognise "restricted access" as a form of involuntary displacement even when people are not physically removed from forests declared as PAs, as restriction of access inevitably causes impoverishment as long as alternative income generating options are not provided (Cernia & Schmidt-soltau, 2006). But the paradigm shift in global approach towards conservation-induced displacement, is not reflected in Odisha Government's Resettlement and Rehabilitation Policy, 2006, projected as one of the most progressive policies of this genre in India. Precisely because of the official non-recognition of "restricted access" as a form of displacement even when people are not physically removed from PAs, that only one out of the fourteen wildlife wardens covered in our study, reported any displacement of population in their sanctuaries. Displacement was officially recognized only in the Chandaka-Dampara sanctuary of the state, where there was actual physical displacement and relocation of 1322 persons, all of whom were tribals (GoO, 2012).

The Present Study

It is in this context that the present study of the protest movement of tribals and other forest dwellers affected by the proclamation of Kuldiha Wildlife Sanctuary, covering an area of 272.75 square kilometers in Kuldiha and Debgiri reserve forests under the scheduled Nilgiri sub-division in the south-western part of Balasore district in Odisha, assumes significance. Compared to studies on protest movements against defence, dam, mining, industrial and other commercial projects including shrimp farming in Odisha (Patel, 2001; Das & Das, 2006; Padel & Das, 2010; Padhi & Panigrahi, 2011; Nayak & Berkes, 2011), those on PAs remain relatively sporadic (Sarangai, 1999; Vasundhara, 2007). The current work, carried out during 2010-12, seeks to bridge this gap.

The information used in the study has been collected through various means and from various sources. The absence of relevant information and the reluctance of authorities to part with available information which was considered to be "sensitive", led to filing of several Right to Information (RTI) applications with the Departments of Forest, Revenue, Panchayati Raj and Tribal Development to put together a clear picture of the problem. Several tranches of field trips were made to Kuildiha to grasp the ground realities.[4] Semi-structured interviews were conducted with government officials at state and district-levels including the Principal and Special Secretaries, Department of Forest and Environment; Chief Conservator of Forests (Wildlife); 14 Wildlife Divisional Forest Officers (WDFOs) including Balasore WDFO; Collector, Balasore; Principal Secretary and Director, Department of Panchayati Raj; Revenue Divisional Commissioner (RDC), Central Division (CD); Director, Tribal Development; Director, Tribal Research Institute; office bearers of political parties; movement leaders; Sarpanches and ward members of affected Panchayats; lawyers advocating the case and affected people. Content analysis of relevant acts, rules, policies, government notifications, affidavits and counter affidavits filed in the High Court, Supreme Court order and related documents was done. Village-level population and amenities data were collected from the Census Directorate to cross-check the veracity of affected population figures provided by the Forest and Revenue departments.

Contextualising the Issues

Kuldiha, located at the trijunction of Balasore, Mayurbhanj and Keonjhar districts and part of a mega-habitat belonging to Mahanadian bio-geographical region (a transition zone between the Eastern Ghats and North-East India bio-geographical zone), was declared a sanctuary by the Department of Forest, Government of Odisha, on 4.1.1984 under Section 18 of the Wildlife Protection Act (WPA), 1972 (*vide* Notification No. 243-FF&AH) for protecting, propagating and developing wildlife over an area of 272.75 sq.km.[5] The settlement of claims and rights as laid down in the WPA, 1972 (Sections 19-25) had not taken place in Kuldiha. As per Section 21 of the WPA, 1972, the Collector shall issue proclamation within a period of sixty days from the date of issue of notification under Section 18 to enquire and determine the rights of any person in or over the land within the limit of the sanctuary. Accordingly, the Collector, Balasore had issued proclamation on 30.4.1984 and had informed the Principal Secretary to Government of Odisha, Forest and Environment Department on 27.6.1998 (*vide* Letter No. 922/LR) that as no claim or right in prescribed manner (Form No. 8) had been received from any person, the proceeding had thus been concluded. But recognizing that there were human habitations within the sanctuary, the report of the Collector was not accepted by the State Government. The Collector, Balasore was again asked by State Government during 2004 and 2006, through the offices of Chief Wildlife Warden and the RDC (CD) (*vide* their Letter No. 379, No. 3660 and No. XLII-12/04-310/Gen.) to complete the proceedings under Sections 19-25 of the WPA, for final notification of the sanctuary under Section 26 (A), in order to implement the directions of the Supreme Court of India [Writ Petition (Civil) No. 337 of 1995 in the case of Centre for Environmental Law-WWF(I) *vs*. Union of India and others]. Accordingly, the survey and demarcation of sanctuary boundary had been executed by the Forest and Revenue department during 2009-2010 as per boundary description in the gazette notification (*vide* No. 5, dt. 3.2.1984).

Following this and twenty-seven years after the Section 18 notification and first proclamation of 1984, another proclamation [*vide* No. 7 1(16)] was issued by the Collector, Balasore on 16.6.2011 under Section 21 of the WPA, wherein persons in possession of any right over land within the boundaries of the Kuldiha Sanctuary were invited to submit their written claims to the Collector on or before 17.8.2011.

But a major bone of contention arises here. Section 21 of the WPA specifies that after issuance of a notification under Section 18, the Collector is bound to issue a proclamation specifying the situation and inviting written claims under Section 19 of the WPA within two months (60 days) from the date of issuance of such proclamation. But here the Collector had issued the second proclamation after 27 years from the issuance of Section 18 notification and first proclamation during 1984. Notwithstanding the claim of the Forest department that 569 individual claims had been recognized in Kuldiha, the second proclamation was challenged in the Odisha High Court for being illegal, arbitrary and contrary to provisions of the WPA. The district administration had sought to defend the action by terming it as an opportunity given to the affected community living within the sanctuary to put forth their claims for proper enquiry and settlement of genuine rights in accordance with the spirit of the WPA and direction of the Supreme Court (Writ Civil Petition No. 337 of 1995).

But on the ground, the district wildlife administration, taking the plea of the provision on declaration of sanctuary leading to suspension of rights even in case of non-completion of proceedings of determination and acquisition of rights [Section 25A of WPA (Amendment) Act, 2002], had tried to impose restrictions on people living inside the boundaries of Kuldiha Sanctuary. These restrictions had inevitable socio-economic costs (Chatty & Colchester, 2002; Rangarajan & Shahabuddin, 2006; Agrawal & Redford, 2007) for the 8767 tribals and forest-dwellers living in 12 revenue villages of the eight affected Gram Panchayats (GPs) in Kuldiha sanctuary area (GoO, 2012; GoI, 2001). Scheduled Tribes belonging to Santhal, Bhumij, Bathudi, Kolho constitute the vast majority of population (93.6%) in the sanctuary-affected villages with some exclusive tribal villages like Ambajhar with a population size of 208 people, Bishnupur with a population size of 99, Hatikholia with 1389 people, Ranipokhari with 291 people and Pindabasa with 172 people. Tribals constitute little less than 60 per cent of Nilgiri population and their concentration in a compact area has led to designating Nilgiri as a scheduled area with an Integrated Tribal Development Agency (ITDA), which covers all the sanctuary-affected villages in Kuldiha (GoO, 2009). Considering the relative backwardness of Nilgiri region, the perceptive Collector of Balasore referred to these areas as the KBK region of the district. It may be mentioned here that the KBK refers to the undivided tribal-dominated Kalahandi, Bolangir and Koraput districts of south-western Odisha, infamous for their structural poverty, starvation deaths and chronic underdevelopment.

First, these measures went against the customary *nistar* rights and privileges granted by the Durbar Administration of erstwhile Nilgiri Princely State to its tenants (both tribal and non-tribal) after the famous Prajamandal agitation during 1938 to use the forest including access to forests for fodder (including grazing of cattle), fuel (firewood collection) and timber for household purposes for which the people still pay a special forest cess to the government (see Nanda, 1998; Rath, 2005). This move also violated provisions of the Administration of Orissa States Order, 1948; Section 5 of the Merged States (Laws) Act, 1949 and Article 372 of the Constitution of India.[6] The sanctuary proclamation move negated the assurances made by the then Deputy Prime Minister of India Sardar Vallabhbhai Patel on 15.12.1947 that the Union and State Governments would take adequate measures for the rapid progress of the former princely states in general and Nilgiri in particular as it had the distinction of being the first Garjat State to merge with the Indian Union. On the contrary, sanctuary proclamation had considerable negative development implications for forest-dependent population in Kuldiha as a 2000 Supreme Court order and consequent amendment to the WPA in 2002 (Section, 29) restricted non-timber forest produce collection in PAs. It may be mentioned here that Kuldiha tribals had a composite yet precarious livelihood structure in which they used to supplement their uncertain incomes from dry-land agriculture and wage labour through work on stone quarries, minor forest produce (MFP) collection and fishing in the Risia reservoir on the mouth of the Tangnariver. The complete and abrupt ban on quarrying, MFP collection and fishing, which used to supplement their irregular incomes, had hit them hard. For instance, the cultivation of paddy (*aasudhana*), corn and vegetable (brinjal) by the tribals on forest land had been completely stopped. While irrigation through the Mukhachaturi Nalah had come to an end, water had not been released from the Risia dam, thereby putting cultivation of *kharif* crops at risk. Also the plucking and collection of leaves particularly sal leaves had been completely banned. Apart from this, the notified sanctuary area would engulf at least one third of Nilgiri Notified Council area including the royal palace, Jagannath temple and many government establishments. Hence, there was a popular demand to confine the sanctuary limits to a realistic area of 57 sq. km, which was earmarked as core area.

Second, with the 2002 amendment to the WPA (Section 27), restrictions on entry into and mobility within Kuldiha sanctuary had come into effect with the declaration of intention to create a PA. This had also put a brake on implementation of development programmes particularly rural road and electrification schemes like the Pradhan Mantri Gram Sadak Yojana and Rajiv Gandhi Grameen Vidyutikaran Yojana in the 12 affected revenue villages affecting the well-being of about 9000 people. Other development activities like the construction of community centres by the ITDA in the affected K.C. Pur GP and

Sarva Shiksha Abhiyan primary schools in Telipal GP had been put on hold.

Third, these developments also brought into sharp focus the implementation of protective measures for tribals living in scheduled areas. The affected people of the 12 revenue villages in Kuldiha had never been consulted before the issuance of sanctuary proclamation notwithstanding the operation of Panchayats Extension to the Scheduled Areas Act (PESA), 1996 (Section 4) and the Scheduled Tribes and Other Traditional Forest Dwellers (Recognition of Forest Rights) Act (FRA), 2006 [Sections 5 and 2(a)] which vest the forest dwellers and their *Gram Sabha*s and Panchayats with extensive statutory rights for protection and management of their habitats and cultural and natural heritage even in sanctuaries and national parks.[7] Notwithstanding the assertion by the Balasore WDFO that 569 individual claims had been recognized within the sanctuary, not a single title certificate for either community or individual claims had been distributed under the FRA in the affected villages.

Fourth, the enabling provisions in the WPA (Amendment), 2002, for Constitution of sanctuary advisory committees with representation from Panchayats, seeking to ensure participatory and sustainable conservation, had never been implemented in Kuldiha. The FRA also recognized displacement, as more than the loss of tribal homestead land and as loss of access to and control over their forests, pastures etc. Considering the adverse development implications of Kuldiha sanctuary for its tribal inhabitants in terms of their loss of access to forests, rivers and basic services, it could be argued that it had effectively led to displacement in the livelihood if not in the physical sense of the term (World Bank, 2001; ADB, 2003), but which was not recognized as such by the State Government.

Finally, a proposal for constitution of critical wildlife habitat (CWH) in Kuldiha had been submitted by the WDFO, Balasore on 7.2.2008 (*vide* Memo No. 737) to the State Government. As per the FRA, 2006 and the WPA (Amendment), 2006, CWHs are envisaged as inviolate areas for sustenance of viable populations of tiger and other wildlife umbrella species in PAs and identified corridors to conserve entire bio-diversity of the area. Kuldiha is part of a vital wildlife corridor linking Hadagarh Sanctuary to Simlipal Tiger Reserve, which is the traditional migratory route of elephants. Due to its ecological importance (it being the largest catchment feeding the major rivers of Balasore district and having the rare distinction of a high forest eco-system near the coast), Kuldiha is already included in the Mayurbhanj elephant reserve spread over 7043.74 sq.km. area (*vide* notification no. 8F(W)42/2001-15806/F&E, dt. 29.9.2001 and corrigendum no. 8F(W)42/2001-18639/F&E, dt. 28.11.2001). Detailed provisions have been provided for declaration of CWHs by the Union Ministry of Environment and Forest, based on the recommendations of State Governments. Two expert committees, one at the State and the other at the Central level have been constituted to consider proposals on case by case basis, with a significant role given to *Gram Sabha*s of affected areas. But in a clear violation of the provisions for declaration of CWH, the Balasore WDFO had neither consulted nor obtained resolutions of the eight affected *Gram Sabhas*/ Panchayats certifying that in areas included within the proposed Kuldiha CWH, the process of recognition and vesting of rights had been completed. As the wildlife administration had not completed the process of recognition and vesting of rights over land in Kuldiha for the last 27 years (under Sections 19-25 of WPA) and had not bothered to inform the affected people of the eight Panchayats of its plan to include their habitations in the proposed CWH, logically, it had failed to procure resolutions of the eight affected *Gram Sabha*s certifying that they had been informed in writing and had been provided with a copy of the complete proposal by the government. This was not only a major contravention of the mandatory requirements for declaration of Kuldiha as a CWH, but is also a denial of the legal and democratic rights of the affected tribals and other forest dwellers of the area.

Unravelling the Nilgiri Dynamics

To fight for their rights, the affected population of the area consisting primarily, but not exclusively of tribals had come together under the banner of the *Bhita-mati Jivan Jivika Surkhya Manch* (BJSM) (Homestead, Life and Livelihood Protection Front). The battle was being fought on two related yet different fronts i.e., legal and political. On the legal side, the filing of a Public Interest Litigation (PIL) by the BJSM (Raghunath Singh and others *versus* State of Odisha and others in Writ Petition (Civil) No. 22/40 of 2011) had led the Odisha High

Court to putting a stay on the sanctuary proclamation order of the government. More important was the political struggle of BJSM and the ideology which animated its protest. The movement by the encysted tribes of Nilgiri was a protest against the disparities of development (Roy, Burman, 1979, Singh, 1966, Desai, 1977, cf. Oommen, 1990: 74-81). It sought to challenge the simultaneous yet contradictory attempts at expansion of state power and de-politicisation of development (Ferguson, 1994). In a sense the BJSM-led protest questioned received notions of "the powerless" project-affected tribal (Beazley, 2009), who failed to counteract top-down and unilateral state conservation interventions and succumb to impoverishment risks (Brockington, 2004; Rangarajan and Shahabuddin, 2006; Kabra, 2009). The history, geography and socio-political dynamics of Nilgiri ensured adequate politicization of the issues, thereby contributing to considerable flow of information, effective organization of oppositional movement and finally, enhancing the socio-political clout of the affected. The grassroots political mobilization of the project-affected tribals, though might be viewed as an instance of top-down elite activism, lends support to the thesis (Kohli, 1987; Das, 2000) that the active presence of a pro-poor communist party i.e., the Communist Party of India (Marxist) [CPI(M)] in Nilgiri, was indeed a key factor in subjecting state action to organised struggle of the tribal poor and thereby influencing the balance of power between the state actors and the project-affected on the ground. Also the presence of a pro-tribal district collector or "a reformist" (Evans, 1997) for a short period during 2011-12 provided some sort of a favourable "climate of opinion" for the demands of the movement.

The movement was rooted in the historical context of Nilgiri, which was the first Princely Garjat State to be integrated into the Union of India after Independence. The BJSM was banking on the tradition of left-led popular mobilization, particularly among the tribals in the area, as the peoples' movement was instrumental in forcing the Nilgiri State to sign the Instrument of Accession with the Indian Union on November 14, 1947. Right from the beginning of the popular democratic Prajamandal movement of the 1930s against the predatory and exploitative Garjat ruler of Nilgiri, communist leaders of the area like Banamali Das did a lot in politically mobilizing local tribals through the *ashrams* (political recruiting and training centres) and raising issues pertaining to tribals like reduction of disproportionately high rent charged from them compared to fellow non-tribal tenants, abolition of license fees on *handia* (rice liquor) and *puchwai* (unprocessed liquor) (see Nanda, 1998). Though the Nilgiri assembly constituency is currently represented by the Bharatiya Janata Party (BJP), it has traditionally been a Communist Party of India's (Marxist) [CPI(M)] strong-hold. The party had retained the seat during 1967, 1971, 1974 and 2000 assembly elections.[8] The party still enjoys considerable grassroots presence in the tribal tracts of the area. In the 2012 Panchayat elections, the CPI(M)-backed candidates won in six panchayats like Telipal, Kesipur, Kandagardi, Chatrapur etc. which had become the nerve centres of the movement. It may be mentioned here that GP elections in Odisha are fought, on paper at least, along non-party lines, though political parties remain *de facto* players in the game. The physical and cultural location of the Nilgiri tribals amidst the coastal Hindus, made certain upto a point, the prevalence of comparable patterns of materialistic orientations and political articulations among the tribals as among the surrounding non-tribal communities.

Approaching the Tribal Protest

The three popular approaches (Corbridge, 1988) are found inadequate in dealing with the BJSM-led movement.[9] The Sons of the Soil model (Jha, 1968; Weiner, 1978), seeks to interpret tribal movements as a manifestation of some kind of ethno-territorial aspirations to restore their economic, political and cultural hegemony over an area where they were the original inhabitants and have progressively been displaced by non-tribal outsiders, the hated "*dikus*". Thus, the notions of ethnic and physical space are used to interpret tribal revolts as nothing more than a demonstration of primordial ethnic antagonism against the *diku* (i.e., outsider). The tribals of inland Odisha, notably the Kondhs, Gonds and Bhuiyans had led bloody rebellions during nineteenth century to protest against the denial of their rights over land and resources and their subjugation to non-tribals (Bailey, 1963; Pathy, 1987; Pati, 1997; Padel, 1995). A strong belief in "restoration" of the original tribal rule, which underpins these revolts, continues to inform the outlook of contemporary movements. During the 1980s, the Jharkhand Mukti Morcha led an agitation of local tribals in the steel city of Rourkela against the domination by non-tribal outsiders including caste Hindus of coastal Odisha and those from outside the State, demanding exclusive employment of tribals in the up-coming projects in Sundergarh district (Meher, 1998). The on-going movement by the pro-Maoist *Chasi Mulia Adivasi Sangha* in southern Odisha, demanding the restoration of land and by extension of "lost" power and status to tribals, is another instance of it. Forcible occupations of non-tribal land by tribals on the pretext that the latter were the original owners of the land, have been reported from interior areas of southern districts like Gajapati.[10] But this approach fails to see through the current movement as the tribal protest consciousness here was made-up not only of mutually consistent elements and tendencies, but also those which apparently clash and conflict with one another. The tribal consciousness in Nilgiri has often transcended the limits of ethnic ties as defined within the confines of a shared habitat (see for instance Guha, 1983). Nilgiri does not belong to the tribal hinterland of the State, but is a part of coastal Odisha. Nilgiri has a tradition of class rather than ethnicity-based mobilization at least since colonial times when the peoples' movement supported by both non-tribals and tribals, against Garjat rulers was led by both Congress and communists. But this is also a fact that the Garjat rulers had unsuccessfully tried to divide the movement by playing the tribal card and inciting tribals against non-tribals of the area. The current movement was also being nurtured by the CPI(M). The tribals of Nilgiri, particularly the major ones like the Bathudis and the Bhumij have been considerably Hinduised.[11] The movement from the beginning, by virtue of its very ecological and cultural location, was primarily, but not exclusively based on tribal identity. Given the location of the tribals *vis-à-vis* the core peasant matrix of Nilgiri (Sinha, 1972; *cf.* Oommen 1990), the movement represented the interests of a number of disparate non-tribal groups and communities of the area as well. The inner dynamic of the movement reflected a fortuitous synthesis of two apparently antithetical interests i.e., the profit motive of the quarry and transport owners, who were mostly upper caste Hindus from outside Kuldiha, with the survival interest of the quarry and transport sub-contractors and workers, majority of whom were Kuldiha tribals. Though formally exhibiting an exclusive tribal identity, the BJSM movement served, explicitly or implicitly, the interests of both tribals and caste Hindus as that of workers and petty bourgeoisie. It was also interesting to note that the BJSM had no formal association with the *Adivasi* Mahasabha, the tribal wing of the CPI(M), though many of the leading tribal figures of the movement like Raghu Singh, Ratha Singh, Ramchandra Murmu and Sasmita Singh were active CPI(M) and Mahasabha members. Though rooted in "ethnic" tribal identities, at a broader level, the movement assumes a "regional" dimension (Singh, 1977; *cf.* Oommen, 1990) by seeking to project the economic interests of both the tribals and non-tribals of the area. The *real politik* of the movement challenges the representation of tribals as an internally undifferentiated yet externally distinctive mass, variously exploited by the non-tribals (Weiner, 1978; Jones, 1978; Mandelbaum, 1970). It brings out the 'duplex' character of the movement, wherein ethnicity and class got intertwined.

The perversity model (Rungta, 1978, *cf.* Corbridge, 1988), with roots in conventional colonial discourse, is prone to treating tribal protest as 'pre-political' phenomenon, as a mere 'law and order' problem. This perspective mostly held in some bureaucratic and police circles, sees tribal assertions as a "perverse and irrational" response to the State policies in post-independent India, which are progressive when compared with the retrograde isolationist policies of the colonial rule. Tribal issues are treated pre-eminently as matters of administrative concern, necessitating 'counter-insurgency' measures to prevent their occurrence in future (*see* Guha, 1983; Government of India, 2010).[12] The Odisha forest bureaucracy both at the local and state-levels including the views of DFO (Wildlife), Balasore, Chief Conservator of Forests (Wildlife) appeared to subscribe to this view. These officers also remained blissfully ignorant of the special Constitutional rights of Kuldiha tribals residing in a scheduled area. But more interesting was the considered opinion of the Director, Tribal Welfare in the Government of Odisha, who happened to be an Indian Forest Service officer. Notwithstanding, his official position, he most explicitly and aggressively seemed to promote wildlife interests at the cost of Kuldiha tribals. Despite these official attempts, the movement far from being a "perverse and irrational" reaction, was an eminently rational response to undemocratic and extra-legal state action. And as already pointed out, this movement, though articulated through the political use of the "tribal" identity, also represents the needs and aspirations of the affected non-tribal population of the area. Non-tribals like the former CPI(M) MLA of Nilgiri Pradipta Panda, CPI(M) State Secretary Santosh Das and State and local-level leaders of other parties including the ruling BJD like Upendra Das, Gangadhar

Mishra, Gati Krushna Nanda etc. were also associated with the movement. To that extent, the Nilgiri movement has succeeded in rising above its local and ethnic roots and in maintaining its apparently non-party political character. The maturity and sophistication of the movement was exemplified by the fact that it had sought to pursue its demands within the Constitutional framework by using the liberal democratic means of protest including the employment of legal strategy. Thus, it successfully managed in securing a stay from the Odisha High Court on sanctuary proclamation order of the State Government. The leaders of the movement were quite clear in maintaining a studious and publicly proclaimed distance from Naxal ideology and strategy, notwithstanding the proximity of the area to the Maoist-affected Mayurbhanj district.

Finally, some versions of Marxist and neo-Marxist approaches including the internal colonialism thesis (Wallerstein, 1979; Jones, 1978) used considerably in the context of Odisha tribes (Mohanty 1990; Das & Das, 2006; Das, 2007; Padhi & Panigrahi, 2011), could not fully address the issues involved. Combined with the classical natural resource-curse hypothesis (Sachs and Warner, 1995), this approach reasons that (Das, 2007; Padel & Das, 2010) the paradox of tribal poverty and natural resource abundance is maintained and perpetuated by not attacking the power of the upper caste and class non-tribal oligarchy and by treating the tribal areas as an internal colony for extraction of resources, which greatly outweighs the funds allocated by the state for tribal development. It argues that tribal protest movements like the one led by the Dongria Kondh tribals of the Niyamgiri Hills during the first decade of 2000 in the scheduled Lanjigarh block of Kalahandi district against bauxite mining by the multi-national company Vedanta Alumina or the protest by the Kalinga Nagar tribals in Jajpur district against land acquisition for the Tata Steel plant and their subsequent killing in police firing during 2006, however, well-organised, have to contend with the interests of powerful non-tribal economic elite and industrial capital—both domestic and foreign (Padhi & Panigrahi, 2011) who, with the active connivance of a subservient state, have facilitated resource transfers from tribal periphery to developed non-tribal centres located in coastal Odisha and other national and global capitalist metropolis (Mohanty, 1990; Das & Das, 2006; Padel & Das, 2010).[13]

But Kuldiha is located in coastal Odisha and is not a part of the mineral rich in-land tribal belt of the State, which has been historically exploited through resource extraction. And in the instant case at least, the State instead of promoting commercial exploitation of forests, had taken steps for their protection from quarrying activities. While it would be naive to pretend that all tribals gained as much from the quarrying activities, yet the internal colonialism thesis that the working class of tribal quarry workers had been systematically and collectively exploited by a class of external non-tribal capitalists, is betrayed by evidence. On the contrary, the movement succeeded in establishing cross-cutting alliance with outside non-tribal quarry and transport owners and they were found actively supporting the movement as their material interests were affected by the proclamation of expanded sanctuary boundaries leading to closure of stone quarries. Also, local tribals themselves were found to have quarry ownership and transport business, either working independently or as sub-contractors for outside non-tribal owners. For example, Ratha Singh, a Bhumij tribal and convener of the BJSM, was himself a quarry-owner and employed a number of tribal wage labourers. In the absence of sustainable livelihood sources, there was evidence that many tribals gained remunerative employment in the stone quarries and ancillary transport activities, earning on an average Rs. 5000 to Rs. 6000 per month. The quarrying activities were also in consonance with the traditional skills and preference of some tribals like the Kolhos, who traditionally specialized in stone-cutting activities and despised earth work provided to them under the NREGS.

The Movement and its Rationale

As a red-green movement (Martinez-Alier, 2002; Forsyth, 2007), BJSM was trying to balance wildlife conservation and development in the context of Kuldiha sanctuary by recognizing their dialectical complementarity. The political ecology approach (Forsyth, 2005) combined with the perspectives of populism (Laclau, 1977; Canovan, 1981) seems to provide a more nuanced interpretation of the kind of localized environmental politics represented by the BJSM. In trying to understand the role of the state as the central agent in the direction, legitimisation and exercise of power and control in the name of conservation (Neumann, 1998), the socio-economic implications of conservation through establishment of PAs and the politics of environmental action in Kuldiha as rooted in its geography, sociology and environmental history, the political-ecology perspective highlights the inextricable links between the social and the natural and how ideas about nature are formed, shaped and applied in ways that are inherently political. It questions the way the modern state classifies, organises and simplifies complexity by demarcating separate spaces for wildlife and human settlement (*see* Scott, 1998).

The differing perceptions of and demands over the forest resources in Kuldiha reflect an environmental conflict between the local tribals and the forest department over the establishment and expansion of sanctuary boundaries (*see* Bryant and Bailey, 1997). While the Kuldiha forests were seen only in terms of their capacity for wildlife conservation by the forest department, the tribals had sought to identify a plurality of ecological functions for the forest including its livelihood functions, which appears to be counter to the conservation logic of the State. The utilization of land as sanctuary led to the exclusion of groups living inside the designated space from accessing the forest for purposes other than protecting the wilderness. The political-ecology approach thus questions "scientific forest management" and its predefined interpretation of eco-system functions as these have been shaped by the political influences of a few "powerful" stakeholders with the exclusion of others. It draws attention to the fact that forest policies rarely develop in a vacuum and Forest departments are rarely independent bodies, with their actions having seen or unseen relationships with a variety of political objectives.[14]

The Movement Entrepreneurs and the Little Men

Unlike some interpretations of tribal movements as being spontaneous and autonomous (Guha, 1982; Hardiman, 1987), this movement was nurtured and guided by a political party i.e., the CPI(M). From a resource mobilization perspective (Tilly, 1986; McCarthy & Zald, 1977; McAdam *et al.,* 1996), it could be argued that the party acted as a movement "entrepreneur" by mobilizing resources—material, human, cognitive, technical and channelizing the popular discontent into organized forms. Thus, while looking at the movement basically as interest group politics played out by socially connected groups of tribals and non-tribals, the structural bases of the conflict had not been lost sight of. The party remained committed to popular mobilization on the basis of a subtle anti-status quoist ideology, which stops short of radical change.[15] And this blend of change and stability orientations, pursued simultaneously in the movement, was reflected in its pragmatic and flexible approach to the problem. While the establishment of the sanctuary and wildlife conservation was not questioned, what was demanded were the delimitation of its boundaries and protection of land and livelihood of the forest-dependent population. Except for some sporadic show of solidarity by the other major parties like the Congress, BJD and BJP, there was no serious attempt by them to support this movement. These parties were initially on the defensive on the issue, but made a *volte face* after sensing the popular mood. In fact, in a meeting of the movement leaders with the State Forest Minister, the sitting Nilgiri MLA from the BJP took a stand favouring the Kuldiha elephants over the tribals. The Congress was in a sticky wicket as it was during its rule in 1984 that the sanctuary was established. The local wing of the ruling BJD led by a former MLA of the area made some belated and confusing attempts like forming a regressive and feudal association called the Garjat Praja Samiti to mobilize the people. But it was the CPI(M)-backed BJSM and its PIL in the Odisha High Court leading to a stay on the sanctuary proclamation that had caught the popular imagination. Also the CPI(M) vernacular mouthpiece *Samyabadee* had been effectively used to regularly report on the movement. Its electoral implications were evident from the 2012 panchayat election results where the CPI(M)-backed candidates were able to control six of the affected GPs.

In a sense, the movement as a collective mode of adaptation reflects the dialectic tension between popular needs and aspirations of the Kuldiha tribals and inadequate systemic means to meet them. And this asynchronism has been used as a mobilizing ideology by the movement leaders. The Nilgiri tribals historical association with and exposure to the surrounding Hindu communities' political articulations, particularly their political socialization in terms of the communist strand of the Prajamandal movement of 1930s, had come in handy for the left-led popular mobilization in the area.

Given the context, the CPI(M) had tried to rely on some variant of democratic populism (*see* DiTella, 1965) i.e., a "populism of the little man" (Canovan, 1981) as contrasted with the authoritarian populism of right-wing elements like the BJP which had liberally employed monetary and communal incentives like *sadhus* in their election campaigns in Nilgiri or the revolutionary populism of the Maoists, lurking in the neighbouring Simlipal forests of the adjacent Mayurbhanj district. Following DiTella (1965) populism could be construed here as "a political movement which enjoys the support of the mass of the working class and/or the peasantry, but which does not result from the autonomous organizational power of either of these two sectors. It is also supported by non-working class sectors upholding an anti-status quo ideology." The CPI(M) had sought to mobilize both the landless tribal and non-tribal wage workers and small proprietors of Kuldiha including the tribal and non-tribal peasants, quarry owners, transporters, shop-keepers and other petty businessmen etc., who were distrustful of government, dominant political parties and politicians because of their stand on the issue. True to a populist mobilization strategy, the CPI(M) had sought to project an 'above politics' mobilization (Brass, 1997) on the basis of a tribal myth by trying to limit if not eliminate the mediating role of political parties and establishing direct relationship between the affected people of Kuldiha and the Government. The BJSM, the front leading the movement, was promoted by the CPI(M) and many of the front's leading tribal leaders belonged to the *Adivasi* Mahasabha, the tribal arm of the CPI(M). Thus, Raghu Singh, a Bhumij tribal and one of the most articulate members of the BJSM, contested the 2012 Zilla Parishad elections with active support from the CPI(M). Yet, theoretically the BJSM functioned on non-party lines with its membership open to all the affected persons of Kuldiha irrespective of their party affiliations and ethnic identity. Also the class identity of the quarry workers and subsistence peasants who participated in the movement, were expressed mostly in non-class ethnic terms, i.e., as tribals. This brings out how issues of "indigenousness" and identity provided a more immediate political context and also added complexity to the dialectical relationship between people and protected areas. Thus contrary to some arguments (Brass, 1997), this brand of populism is associated with the political left rather than with the political right.[16] Notwithstanding, the constraints and in true Marxist tradition (*see* McLellan, 1977;

Thompson, 1986), the BJSM had focused not on the tribals' weaknesses and powerlessness, but on their perspectives and agency to gain access to forests by linking them to the enabling properties of state structure and by strategically using the resources at their disposition to unfold idiosyncratic outcomes (Giddens, 1984).

Conclusion

The rationale of the BJSM movement was based on what is called "rightful resistance" (O'Brien and Lianjiang 2006) reflecting an attempt by the tribals to defend the rights already granted by the Constitution, yet often denied by the local state. These were the rights Kuldiha tribals believed could be derived from the legitimating ideology of the Indian Union. Thus, the tribal protest discourse here represents the deployment of an acceptable "grammar" embedded within the system to voice doubts about the system itself (*see* Shue, 2004). That is, it constitutes a discourse that is critical of state power and policies, albeit in a necessarily coded form, one that is permitted within the current climate of opinion.[17] But the movement also derived its sustenance from a more important source by linking the "dense cluster of claims and usages" of the Kuldiha tribals to a particular ideology i.e., a form of radical moral economy (*see* Thompson, 1986, 1990), which sought to legitimize the rights and claims of tribals and forest dwellers by opposing the elite ideology of exclusionary conservation. As has been rightly observed (*see* Thompson, 1990), conflict over forest resources and claim and counter-claim by the poor on one hand and the state and the elite on the other, had been "the condition of forest life for centuries" and the Nilgiri forests and its tribals were no exception to it.

Notes

1. The Wildlife (Protection) Act, 1972, a Central act, deals with the creation and management of PAs such as national parks and sanctuaries. The strong regulatory focus of the Act restricts almost all human activities inside PAs including restrictions on entry (Section 27), NTFP collection (except for bona-fide self-consumption), grazing or movement of livestock etc. Enforcement of WPA is complemented by other Acts *viz.*, Forest

(Conservation) Act, 1980, Environment (Protection) Act, 1986, Biological Diversity Act, 2002 and the Scheduled Tribes and Other Traditional Forest Dwellers (Recognition of Forest Rights) Act, 2006.

2. India has 102 national parks, 515 wildlife sanctuaries, 47 conservation and four community reserves.
3. Odisha, home to 11 per cent of the national tribal population, accommodates 62 tribal communities. The scheduled areas cover 13 districts (six wholly and seven partially), 120 blocks and 1941 *Gram Panchayats* of the State.
4. Interestingly the request for permission to conduct field work in Kuldiha was rejected by the Chief Wildlife Warden, Odisha *vide* their letter no. 5431/1WL-E-196/10, dtd. 31st July, 2010 on the ground that this was not allowed under the Wildlife Protection Act, which was a contradiction of Section 28 (C) of the Act itself i.e., grant of permission for scientific research in a sanctuary.
5. Under the WPA, Sections 18-26A deal with the creation of wildlife sanctuaries including the declaration of intention by the Government to create a sanctuary (Section 18), determination of land rights within sanctuary limits by the Collector (Section 19), issuance of proclamation by Collector (Section 21), commencement of enquiry by Collector in the claims preferred by admitting or rejecting such claims (Sections 22, 24.1 and 24.2), initiation of acquisition proceedings for land which are to be included in the sanctuary under the Land Acquisition Act, 1894 and for which claims have been admitted (Section 25) and issuance of final notification declaring area as sanctuary (Section 26A). A process of time-bound serving of notice, submission of claim by affected persons, inquiry into the submissions and acquisition of rights have been provided for in the Act.
6. While Article 372 deals with the continuance and adaptation of laws which were in force immediately before the commencement of the Constitution, until their alteration, repeal or amendment by a competent Legislature or other competent authority, Section 5 of the Merged States (Laws) Act, 1949 stipulates the provisions for the repeal of laws in merged States like Nilgiri. Though not given any revenue/management rights over forests, the Panchayats under the Nilgiri State Panchayat Act of 1946, had the power to regulate the plantation and preservation of trees, forests and grazing grounds.
7. The 12 revenue villages of Rissia, Betakata, Dwarikasuni, Ambajhar, Bisnupur, Hatikholia, Siadimal, Tenda, Nizgarh, Ranipokhari, Betei and Pindabasa belong to eight Panchayats i.e., K.C. Pur, Garadihi, Kandagaradi, Shyamsundarpur, Sajanagarh, Siadimal, Chatrapur, Telipal including a part of the Nilgiri NAC.
8. CPI(M)'s defeat and BJP's victory in 2004 and 2009 assembly elections could be attributed to a fortuitous combination of factors including, but not limited to the use of moneypower, communal card, delimitation of constituencies, unpredictable and unprincipled political permutations and combinations at the micro and macro-levels, etc.

9. Notwithstanding the prominence of the "identity" dimension, the movement was not viewed from the New Social Movement (NSM) perspective. The focus of contention here was not so much with conserving what Touraine calls a "way of life" of tribals with their culture, mores, forms of knowledge etc. as with protecting their land and livelihood interests. The movement was directed at the state and as such scholars like Touraine would like to exclude it from the NSM category. Unlike what Melucci, Touraine and others would argue, BJSM had very specific instrumental objectives and participation in the movement was never a goal in itself for its tribal and non-tribal supporters.
10. A large-scale attempt at tribal occupation of land originally allotted to the Tibetan refugees by the Government in the Chandragiri area of Mohana block in Gajapati district has lately been reported. Similar individual cases of unauthorized occupation of non-tribal land by the tribals, leading to law and order problems, have been reported from interior areas of the district. Here, the Sauras are a dominant tribe, followed by the Kondhs. The area has a history of violent conflict between tribals and non-tribals, particularly the scheduled caste Pano community over land and identity issues like language, SC, ST status etc.
11. During the first-half of the nineteenth century, the Bhumij in the neighbouring south-west Bengal had led one of the notable tribal rebellions in Indian history. The revolt of the Bhumij grew out of the ill-judged disruption of local institutions by the British resulting in accelerated Hinduization of tribals, expropriation of their land, depredations of money-lenders, increasing penetration of market etc. After the revolt of 1832-33, the British restored, so far as they could, the traditional structures to buy peace in the area.
12. There is a long tradition in colonial historiography of treating tribal movements like the Bhumij uprising, the Kol insurrection and the Santal revolt during the nineteenth century, against the *sarkari*, *sahukari*, and *zamindari* oppression, as merely 'law and order' problems, which need to be dealt with by 'counter-insurgency' measures to prevent their recurrence. This also forms a vital strand of the current strategy of the government in Independent India to deal with the Naxal problem, primarily located in the scheduled areas of Central Indian tribal belt including Odisha.
13. Interestingly, there seems to be an official recognition of the existence of a tribal periphery as public policies, court judgements like the Odisha R&R Policy, 2006, Supreme Court ruling on the Vedanta and the State Government's ORISED Act seek to develop these areas through the Constitution of Periphery Development Funds to be financed from a marginal share of the huge profits made by mining and industrial companies operating in tribal belts.
14. Among many cases, the one involving bauxite mining activities of the multi-national company Vedanta Alumina in the eco-sensitive Niyamgiri hills in

the scheduled Lanjigarh block of Kalahandi district, puts the issue in proper perspective. As per a 2010 expert group report of the Union Ministry of Environment and Forest, the Odisha Government in its eagerness to facilitate mining, completely disregarded concerns for tribal, environmental and wildlife protection and violated key provisions of Forest Conservation Act, Odisha Forest Act, Environmental Protection Act, Forest Rights Act and the Panchayats (Extension to the Scheduled Areas) Act. Notwithstanding the official recognition of high wildlife value of the area, the proposed Niyamgiri Wildlife Sanctuary and the South Odisha Elephant Reserve passing through this zone, never materialized thanks to the Vedanta proposal for mining in the Niyamgiri hills.

15. In a situation of inequality and political vacuum, the protest by the resource-poor tribals of Kuldiha, could have ended-up either in a radical Maoist mobilization, capitalizing on simmering tribal discontent or, to use the words of Melucci and Scott, in some kind of "submerged" or "hidden" forms of resistance, but for the CPI(M) involvement. The party's support to the movement, which might have been prompted by the need to recover lost ground in the area, led to limiting movement objectives to material rather than to broad cultural elements and in generating apparent tensions between the identity and economic aspects of the movement.
16. The CPI(M) policy document on the issue seeks to look at the tribals as an important part of Indian proletariat and the tribal question as a class question. Notwithstanding this claim, the movement has ended up putting a premium on the ethnic rather than on the class identity of the tribals.It thus represents an ethnic route to class mobilization as the CPI(M) State Secretary was hard-pressed to explain in which the material rather than the cultural interests of the affected tribals mattered the most.
17. Notwithstanding the existence of a number of protective measures to safeguard forests and tribals, the overall thrust of Odisha Government as reflected in its Industrial Policies of 2001 and 2007, is in the direction of industrialization and commercial exploitation of the state's natural resources at the cost of its people. The State policies and actions aim at making Odisha an "investor friendly" destination by providing various concessions and State support for industrialists: for instance, by acquiring land including tribal and forest land in scheduled areas for private industries and mines.

References

Adams, W.M. (2004). *Against Extinction: The Story of Conservation*. London: Earthscan.

African Development Bank (2003). Involuntary Resettlement Policy. Available on http://www.afdb.org/psdu/involuntary_resettlement.

Asian Development Bank (2003). Involuntary Resettlement Policy. Manila: ADB.

Beazley, K. (2009). "Interrogating Notions of the Powerless Oustee", *Development and Change*, 40(2): 219-248.

Brass, T. (1997). "The Agrarian Myth, the 'New' Populism and the 'New' Right", *Economic and Political Weekly*, 32(4): PE27-PE42.

Brockington, D. (2004). "Community Conservation, Inequality and Injustice: Myths of Power in Protected Area Management", *Conservation and Society*, 2(2):411-32.

Bryant, R. and S. Bailey (1997). *Third-World Political Ecology*, London: Routledge.

Canovan, Margaret. (1981). *Populism*. New York: Harcourt Brace Jovanovich.

Cernea, M.M. and K. Schmidt-Soltau. (2006). "Poverty Risks and National Parks: Policy Issues in Conservation and Resettlement", *World Development*, 34(10): 1808-30.

Convention on Biological Diversity. 2004. Governance, Participation, Equity and Benefit-sharing. Available on http://www.biodiv.org/doc/meetings/cop/cop-07/official/cop-07-l-32-en.doc.

Corbridge, S. (1988). "The Ideology of Tribal Economy and Society: Politics in the Jharkhand, 1950-1980", *Modern Asian Studies*, 22(1): 1-42.

Das, A. and V. Das, (2006). *Chronicle of a Struggle and Other Writings*. Kashipur: Agragamee Publications.

Das, M. (2007). *Draft Concept Note on Odisha: Addressing Social Inclusion in the Context of Growth*. World Bank.

Das, R.J. (2000). "The State-Society Relation: The Case of an Anti-poverty Policy", *Environment and Planning C: Government and Policy*, 18(6): 631-650.

DiTella, T.S. (1965). "Populism and Reform in Latin America," in Claudio Veliz (ed.) *Obstacles to Change in Latin America*. London: Oxford University Press: 47.

Ferguson, J. (1990). *The Anti-Politics Machine: Development, Depoliticization and Bureaucratic Power in Lesotho*. St. Paul: University of Minnesota Press.

Forsyth, T. (2005). "The Political Ecology of the Ecosystem Approach for Forests", in J. Sayer and S. Maginnis (eds.). *Forests in Landscapes: Ecosystem Approaches to Sustainability*. London: Earthscan: 165-176.

Forsyth, T. (2007). Are Environmental Social Movements Socially Exclusive? An Historical Study from Thailand, *World Development*, 35(12): 2110–2130.

Giddens, A. (1984). *The Constitution of Society*, Berkeley: University of California Press.

Government of India, (1972). Wildlife Protection Act, 1972, New Delhi: Ministry of Law and Justice.

Government of India, (1996). The Provisions of the Panchayats (Extension to the Scheduled Areas) Act, 1996. New Delhi: Ministry of Law and Justice.

Government of India, (2001). Balasore District Village Amenities Survey, Bhubaneswar: Directorate of Census Operations, Odisha.

Government of India, (2007). The Scheduled Tribes and Other Traditional Forest Dwellers (Recognition of Forest Rights) Act, 2006. New Delhi: Ministry of Law and Justice.

Government of India, (2010). Annual Report 2009-10, New Delhi: Ministry of Home Affairs.

Government of India, (2011). Annual Report 2010-11, New Delhi: Ministry of Environment & Forest.

Government of Odisha, (2006). Odisha Resettlement and Rehabilitation Policy, 2006, Bhubaneswar: Department of Revenue.

Government of Odisha, (2011). Annual Report 2010-11, Bhubaneswar: Department of Forest and Environment.

Government of Odisha (1984). *Odisha Gazette Notification on Kuldiha Wildlife Sanctuary*, Bhubaneswar: Department of Forest, Fisheries & Animal Husbandry.

Government of Odisha, (2012). Reports Submitted under Right to Information Act, 2005 by the Offices of Fourteen Divisional Forest Officers-*cum*-Wildlife Wardens, Department of Forest and Environment.

Government of Odisha, (2012). Reports Submitted under Right to Information Act, 2005 by the Offices of Block Development Officers, Oupada and Nilgiri Blocks, Department of Panchayati Raj.

Government of Odisha, (2011). Reports Submitted under Right to Information Act, 2005 by the Office of Tehsildar, Nilgiri, Departmemt of Revenue.

Government of Odisha, (20110. Notification for Declaration of Kuldiha Wildlife Sanctuary, dated 16.6.2011, Balasore: Office of Collector.

Guha, Ranajit (ed.). (1982). *Subaltern Studies-Writings on South Asian History and Society*, Vol. I, New Delhi: Oxford University Press: 2-3.

Hardiman, D. (1987). *The Coming of the Devi: Adivasi Assertion in Western India*, New Delhi: Oxford University Press.

Jha, S. (1968). "Tribal Leadership in Bihar", *Economic and Political Weekly*, 3(5): 603-8.

Jones, S. (1978). "Tribal Underdevelopment in India", *Development and Change*, 9: 41-70.

Kabra, A. (2009). "Conservation-induced Displacement: A comparative study of two Indian protected areas", *Conservation & Society*. 7(4): 249-267.

Kohli, A. (1987). *The State and Poverty in India: The Political Economy of Reform*, Cambridge: Cambridge University Press.

Kothari, A., P. Pande *et al.* (1989). *Management of National Parks and Sanctuaries in India—A Status Report*, New Delhi: Indian Institute of Public Administration.

Kumar, K., P.R. Choudhary, *et al.* (2006). "A Socio-Economic and Legal Study of Scheduled Tribes" *Land in Odisha*. World Bank.

Laclau, E. (1977). *Politics and Ideology in Marxist Theory: Capitalism, Fascism, Populism*. London: New Left Books.

Mandelbaum, D. (1970). *Society in India*: 2 Vols., Berkeley: University of California Press.

Martinez-Alier, J. (2002). *The Environmentalism of the Poor: A Study of Ecological Conflicts and Valuation*. London: Elgar.

McAdam, D., J.D. McCarthy, *et al.* (1996). 'Introduction', *Comparative Perspectives on Social Movements: Politicai Opportunities, Mobilizing*

Structures and Cultural Framings. Cambridge: Cambridge University Press: 1-20.

McLellan, D. (1977). *Karl Marx: Selected Writings*. Oxford: Oxford University Press.

Mohanty, M. (1990). "Class, Caste and Dominance in a Backward State: Orissa", in F. Frankel and M.S.A. Rao (eds.). *Dominance and State Power in Modern India: Decline of a Social Order*, Vol. 2. New Delhi: Oxford University Press, 321-366.

Nanda, C.P. (1998). "National Politics and Popular Struggles in the Princely States: Rethinking Nilgiri State (1937-39)", in *Odisha State Archives—Towards Merger*: 84-119.

Neumann, R.P. (1998). *Imposing Wilderness: Struggles over Livelihood and Nature*.

Neumann, R.P. (2002). The Post-war Conservation Boom in British Colonial Africa. *Environmental History*, 7: 22-47.

Preservation in Africa, Los Angeles and Berkeley: University of California Press.

O'Brien, K.J. and L. Li. (2006). *Rightful Resistance in Rural China*. New York and Cambridge: Cambridge University Press.

Oommen, T.K. (1990). *Protest and Change: Studies in Social Movements*. New Delhi: Sage Publications, 74-81.

Padel, F. and S. Das. (2010). *Out of this Earth: East India Adivasis and the Aluminium Cartel*.

Padhi, S. and N. Panigrahi. (2011). *Tribal Movements and Livelihoods: Recent Developments in Orissa*. New Delhi: Chronic Poverty Research Centre, IIPA.

Patel, S. 2001. "Community, Identity and Politics: The Baliapal Movement", in S.S. Jodhka (ed.). *Community and Identities: Contemporary Discourses on Culture and Politics in India*. New Delhi: Sage Publications, 140-159.

Rangarajan, M. and G. Shahabuddin. (2006). "Displacement and Relocation from Protected Areas: Towards a Biological and Historical Synthesis", *Conservation and Society*, 4(3): 359-78.

Rath, B. (2005). *Aspects of Garjat Forestry*, Vasundhara.

Sachs, J.D. and A.M. Warner, (1995). *Natural Resource Abundance and Economic Growth*. NBER Working Paper No. 5398.

Sarangai, D. (1999). "Orissa: Struggles against Sanctuaries', *Economic and Political Weekly*, 34(12).

Scott, J. (1998). *Seeing like a State: How Certain Schemes to Improve the Human Condition Have Failed*, New Haven: Yale University Press.

Shue, V. (2004). "Legitimacy Crisis in China?" in P.H. Gries and S. Rosen (eds.). *State and Society in Twenty-First Century China: Crisis, Contention, and Legitimation*, New York: Routledge, 24-49.

Thompson, E.P. (1986). *The Making of the English Working Class*. Harmondsworth: Penguin.

Tilly, C. (1986). *The Contentious French*, Cambridge, MA: Harvard University Press.

Vasundhara (2007). *Draft Report on Eviction from Sunabeda Sanctuary.* Bhubaneswar: Odisha Protected Area Netrwork.

Wallerstein, I. (1979). *The Capitalist World-Economy*. Paris: Cambridge University Press.

Weiner, Myron. (1978). *Sons of the Soil*, Princeton: Princeton University Press.

World Bank. (2001). *Operational Policy 4.12: Involuntary Resettlement.* Washington, DC, USA: World Bank.

World Park Congress. (2003). Recommendations available on http://www.iucn.org/themes/wcpa/wpc2003/english/outputs/recommendations.

10

Infrastructure Development and Population Growth in Tribal Belt

Gujarat Experience

Prabha Shastri Ranade

Introduction

"Scheduled Tribes" constitute 14.8 per cent of the population of Gujarat, which is much higher than the national average of 8.2 per cent. Gujarat stands eleventh among the Indian States in terms of proportion of Scheduled tribe's population to total population. The 7 North-eastern states occupy the first 7 ranks. Though Gujarat's population constitutes 4.98 per cent of India's total population, its tribal population constitutes 8.87 per cent of India's tribal population. Over 89 lakh tribal inhabitants belonging to 29 notified Scheduled Tribes (as per 2011 Census) are concentrated in 12 districts located in the eastern and southern parts of Gujarat bordering Rajasthan, Madhya Pradesh and Maharashtra. These districts constituting the tribal belt of Gujarat are the focus of this study.

Gujarat is one of the developed States in the country, known for its high rate of economic development especially during the last decade. ASSOCHAM study of 2013 reveals that out of the 20 emerging industrial States in India, Gujarat tops in terms of investments. Over the period the entire Gujarat State including its tribal belt has witnessed rapid economic and infrastructure development and urbanization. The tribal population of Gujarat was so far known for its seasonal outward migration. With the degradation of forests in the recent past, the livelihood of the tribal population was badly affected which compelled them to move out of the area in search of livelihood from other ways and means. The recent 2011 Census has noted appreciable increase in the population of the tribal belt. It has recorded population growth higher than the State and National average. Gujarat appears to be the fastest growing urbanising State of India. This chapter discusses the population growth in the tribal belt of Gujarat, its infrastructure development and urbanization. The process of urbanization in the tribal belt is studied in details as it is associated with infrastructure development. Among the various types of infrastructure, the present research takes into consideration public health infrastructure, facilities of drinking water and development of roads in tribal areas. Several economists have pointed out that the development in Gujarat is largely roads, electricity and water. The chapter considers diversion of forest land for infrastructure development.

Gujarat Infrastructure

Good infrastructure is the key to ensuring development. The Government of Gujarat launched a number of schemes to improve infrastructure in the State. Gujarat was the first State in the country to enact the Gujarat Infrastructure Development Act. This was done to boost investments in infrastructural projects. The Gujarat Infrastructure Development Board was set-up in 1995 under this Act. It facilitates the flow of funds from private sector into the infrastructure sector and ensures coordination among various agencies.

Urbanization in Tribal Belt of Gujarat

According to Census of India's 2011 figures, 31.16 per cent of India's population (i.e. 377 million people out of 1.21 billion people live in urban areas, whereas in Gujarat 42.58 per cent of the population, i.e. 2.57 crores out of 6.03 crores live in urban areas. Gujarat's high-speed urbanization (35.83% urban population in the last one decade), is the highest in the country. Gujarat's total population constitutes 4.98 per cent of India's population, whereas Gujarat's urban population constitutes 6.82 per cent of India's urban population.

Tribal areas are characterized by low level of urbanization. Seven districts of the tribal belt represent extremely low level of urbanization where urban population constitutes 9 to 15 per cent of district's population. Surat and Vadodara districts, each having 3 to 4 talukas with sizeable tribal population have a high level of urbanization (urban population over 45%). In 2001, 37.36 per cent of Gujarat's population was residing in urban areas, while in tribal districts, this proportion was 33.51 per cent, which increased to 37 per cent in 2011. Urban population in tribal districts constitutes 38.66 per cent of Gujarat's urban population. Number of towns in tribal districts increased from 85 in 2001 to 163 in 2011.

Table shows district-wise statistics of urbanisation in tribal districts of Gujarat as per 2011 Census.

District	No. of Towns, (2001)	No. of Towns (2011)	Percentage of urban population. (2001)	Percentage of urban population. (2011)	Percentage decadal growth Total population	Percentage. decadal growth Urban population
Banaskantha	6	12	11.00	13.27	24.43	50.05
Sabarkantha	8	15	10.81	14.96	16.56	50.05
Panchmahals	6	9	12.51	14.00	17.92	32.00
Dohad	4	6	9.55	8.99	29.95	22.24
Vadodara	16	25	45.20	49.54	14.16	25.12
Narmada	3	5	10.13	10.44	14.77	18.25
Bharuch	8	21	25.72	34.07	13.14	49.88
The Dangs	0	3	nil	10.89	21.44	Na
Navsari	9	13	27.36	30.74	8.24	21.63
Valsad	17	28	27.02	37.23	20.74	66.35
Surat	18	22	68.44	79.68	42.19	65.52
Tapi	—	4	9.66	9.79	12.07	13.61
Gujarat	**242**	**348**	**37.36**	**42.58**	**19.17**	**35.83**

In Gujarat the decadal growth rate of urban population is impressive as compared to States like Tamil Nadu (27.16%), Chandigarh (26.86%), NCT of Delhi (26.56%), Punjab (25.72%) and Maharashtra (23.67%). Urban population has increased at a higher rate than total population in all tribal districts except Dohad. Five districts in the tribal belt have recorded higher rate of urbanization than the national average of 35.83 per cent. A phenomenal increase in urban population has been registered in the tribal districts of Valsad, (66.35%) followed by Surat (65.52%). Surat City has recorded the highest decadal growth of 66.4 per cent against the decadal growth rate of all municipal corporations of Gujarat (46.51%). Sabarkantha

Banaskantha and Bharuch are the other districts, which recorded around 50 per cent increase in urban population as the number of towns in each district has almost doubled. The Dangs district was entirely rural without any Census town in 2001, where 3 new towns have been recognized in this district. Surat's population growth is attributed to urbanization and immigration from other parts of Gujarat as well as other States of India. In Dohad district though the number of towns has increased from 4 to 6, the proportion of urban to total population has marginally declined due to slower urban growth compared to total population growth. In spite of its small urban base, Dohad has witnessed accelerated population growth.

Urbanisation at Taluka Level

In Gujarat, 43 talukas of the 12 tribal districts where the scheduled tribes population constitute over 50 per cent of total population are selected under Integrated Tribal Development Programme (ITDP) for special assistance and upliftment of tribal population. These are the most backward areas of the tribal belt with extremely low level of economic development. No census or statutory town was recorded in 26 out of these talukas in 2001. In 2011 census this number has come down to 14. In 13 talukas new towns are recorded for the first time in 2011 census. 14 talukas of 8 districts still remain entirely rural throughout the period. They include 3 talukas each of Dohad and Tapi districts. In order to study the process of urbanization, the percentage of urban to total population in 2001 is compared with the percentage in 2011. It is observed that in 5 talukas the percentage of urban to total population has remained the same, reduced in 6 talukas and significantly increased in 5 talukas. Most notable rapid increase is found in Pardi and Umbargaon talukas in Valsad district and Mangrol and Bardoli talukas of Surat district. This is a pointer to the fact that urbanization in Gujarat is unevenly spread out in tribal talukas. This also indicates that the momentum of urban growth in Gujarat is fuelled by medium sized towns as is evident by the impressive figures registered in the tribal talukas.

Forest Cover in Tribal Belt

Forests play a very significant role in tribal economy and in maintaining ecological balance. Tribal areas are comparatively rich in forest cover and forest resources. All the socio-cultural practices of tribal are woven around forests. Therefore, it is very important to monitor and analyze the forest cover situation in the tribal areas. It is an inevitable truth that the poorest people of India live in the richest forests. From the policy and planning point of view, it is necessary to know the extent and quality of forest cover within recorded forest area and outside it. In tribal districts 37.25 per cent of geographical area is covered by forest against the national average of 21.05 per cent under forest cover. The recorded forest area in Gujarat is 18,927 sq. km, which works out to 9.66 per cent of the geographical area. (As per Bureau of Economics and Statistics, Government of Gujarat, 2010) Reserved, Protected and Un-classed forests constitute 74.61 per cent, 2.53 per cent and 22.86 per cent of this total forest area. As per the State of Forest Report 2011, the forest cover in Gujarat state is 14,619 sq. kms. This works out to 7.46 per cent of State's geographical area, much below the national average.

Tribal areas being hilly and forested face major environmental challenges. The challenges identified are decline in forest cover, (deforestation) conversion of dense forest into open forest, as revealed by satellite data, diversion of forest land for infrastructure and other projects and forest fires. Gujarat reported a declining trend in area under forest in tribal districts during the decade. Area under forest in tribal districts together has declined from 9514 km to 8716 km during the decade. There has been a significant decline in area under dense forest in all tribal districts. Dense forests constituted 63.9 per cent of total forests in tribal districts in 2001. Their share have come down to 46.5 per cent in 2011, which is highly deplorable.

Decrease in forest area in 10 districts is mainly attributed to divergence of forest land for development projects, illicit felling of trees, encroachments, submergence of forest areas in the catchments of dams. Increase in forest area in two districts is attributed to success of afforestation projects such as Social Forestry and Wasteland Development. Enhanced plantation activity is noted outside forest area. Local needs also exert pressure on forests. Road widening has claimed the largest forest land (651 ha.) in Surat district, approach road 74 ha in Sabarkantha. Forest land was diverted for mining (171 ha.) and gas pipeline (37 ha.) in Banaskantha. For

Optical Fibre Cables 17 ha. of forest land was acquired in Surat district, for Industry 9.46 ha. and for cargo port 38 ha. in Bharuch district. Other causes of diversion were irrigation drainage pipeline, sewer line and for education trust. Forest land diversion had been the lowest in Dangs and Narmada districts. They remain backward and least urbanized tracts of Gujarat.

The dwindling forest cover in tribal areas needs to be protected from environmental challenges and diversion for various activities. Enriching biodiversity of the forest through afforestation activities with the aim of providing firewood, fodder, timber and food security would improve the quality of life of the tribal population. Plantation and nursery development have the potential to generate maximum wage employment. More investment is needed in tribal areas in forest related activities for rapid economic development of tribal communities.

Public Healthcare Infrastructure in Tribal Belt

It has been observed that public health facilities in reaching out to the tribal population are extremely limited in our country. The infrastructure developed in public health sector in Gujarat's tribal areas during the last decade and various schemes implemented by Gujarat Government in health sector for tribal population are taken into consideration for this study. The availability of Primary Health Centres and sub-centres along with other medical facilities in all tribal districts is examined. Gujarat has scored well in the healthcare sector as its Health Index has always remained higher than the all India average. Gujarat's focus on health began in 2007. The Health Department of Gujarat Government has created infrastructure for provision of health care services.

Anaemia and malnutrition are high among tribal regions mainly due to lack of food security and water scarcity. Diseases of poverty continue to afflict a section of the tribal population. Sickle Cell Anaemia is one of the most common hereditary disease and traditional illnesses which affects tribal communities of Gujarat. In the year 2012-13 there were 446 centres in 12 tribal districts involved in comprehensive care of Sickle Cell Anaemia patients. Special human resource has been created to carry forward the comprehensive health care programme in all tribal districts. Tribal people get regular free medicines at their doorstep. Sickle cell anemia control programme run by Gujarat Government has been awarded with "Prime Minister's award for Excellence in Public Administration" for the activities carried out in tribal districts.

The state currently has 13 medical colleges, 1,072 Primary Health Centres (PHC), 7,274 Sub-Centres, 273 Community Health Centres (CHC) and 85 mobile health care units. The PHCs and CHCs in tribal districts constitute 51.4 and 42.6 per cent of Gujarat's total number. Chiranjeevi Scheme has been introduced by the Government in the wake of reducing the rate of maternal and infant mortality. As per the scheme, the Government and private sector specialists are collaborating and jointly work towards providing safe child delivery services. The scheme has been especially implemented for socially economic weaker sections.

There is a shortfall of PHC, CHC and sub-centres throughout the State and there is a shortfall of medical specialists and personnel as well. In terms of average number of villages served by PHC and CHC, Gujarat's position is better that the Indian average. In the area of health care delivery services, public private partnerships are taking place a number of super speciality hospitals have been established in tribal belt since the year 2000 on Public Private Partnership (PPP) and operated by Trusts. Through them super-speciality services are made available to the poorest of the poor through use of modern day technology. They provide medical services free of cost or at nominal rates to the inhabitants of the areas. They work in partnership with various NGOs and Government units like Primary Health Centres, Aanganwadis, etc. to reach out to more underprivileged patients in need of treatment. They are full service Hospitals and serve the Tribal population with complete health services. These include Shamlaji Hospital located in Sabarkantha district, which is a CHC running on PPP basis. They have appointed visiting specialists of different specialty. All services are provided free of charge. Some of the prominent Trust Hospitals include Heart Institute and Drishti Netralaya at Dohad, Pramukh Swami General Hospital, Dabhoi, situated near tribal area of Vadodara district. Shrimad Rajchandra Hospital (SRH), a charitable, multi-speciality hospital in Dharampur town of Valsad district, a world-class Oral Rehabilitation Centre in the Dang district. Health services are also provided by major industrial and corporate houses to their surrounding rural and tribal areas **under Corporate Social Responsibility obligation.** Medical camps are organized by all sites benefiting patients from nearby villages and tribal areas. National Rural Health Mission (NRHM) is helping to reach the vulnerable and marginalized tribal groups through expanding outreach and linking with gram and Block level panchayats. An NGO has opened 10 centres in the five predominantly tribal areas that are connected through telemedicine to the super speciality hospitals at Ahmedabad and other places with an objective to promote better healthcare. Emergency Medical Research Institute (EMRI) with the Gujarat Government takes care of road and fire accident victims on a 24-hour basis through the year by just dialling 108. The objective is provision of emergency medical services for road and fire accidents through a centralized ambulance system. Budgetary allocations are made for 50 primary health centres, 10 community health centres, and to start 400 sub-centres that would increase the healthcare reach to tribal areas. Lots of changes have taken place in the tribal way of life. Schemes to improve the health of tribal population have benefited tribal women from BPL families.

Infrastructure for Drinking Water in Tribal Belt

Most of the tribal areas are hilly and rocky with undulating terrain and covered with forests. Supplying drinking water to them poses challenges. Deforestation and degradation of environmental resources in tribal belt has led to serious shortage of water after monsoon. Tribal women are worst affected by water scarcity. In order to provide drinking water to tribal households, various projects and schemes are implemented by Government agencies and NGOs. Water delivery at household level in villages is ensuring water security at village level.

The topography and scattered nature of habitations in tribal villages make conventional water supply schemes ineffective and call for innovative measures. A variety of technologies are adopted to provide safe water in rural areas. UNICEF has provided technical assistance. The focus of new water supply projects in tribal areas is on creation of alternative source for increasing quantity and improved quality of water both seasonally and perennially. Gujarat constituted Water and Sanitation Management Organization (WASMO) in 2002, ensuring participation of communities and women in water supply management. WASMO has done commendable work in providing drinking water, particularly in tribal areas. WASMO aims to make Gujarat a "water-secure state, from a water scarce state". WASMO works in partnership with 75 non-governmental organizations and other civil society groups. Private sector business houses are also collaborating with WASMO to supply drinking water in areas adjacent to their factories. Free of charge electricity supply is available for drinking water supply throughout the state through a dedicated feeder 24 x 7 around the year. In 2009 WASMO won the prestigious UN Public Service Award for "fostering participation in policy-making decisions through innovative mechanisms." During 2010-11, 554 village water supply schemes were completed by WASMO in tribal areas. As hand pump technology is relatively more feasible in tribal areas, this is the most important source of water at several places, In tribal areas of Gujarat one hand pump is provided for an average of 50 persons. NGOs have also come forward in installation of hand pumps in tribal areas. For proper storage of rainwater, rooftop rainwater harvesting scheme is introduced in tribal villages. Individual rainwater harvesting storage tanks are built at household level. Government bears 80 per cent cost of work and remaining 20 per cent is contributed by beneficiaries. 7819 rooftop rainwater storage tanks with 1000 litre capacity have been provided to tribal families. Solar pumps are running successfully to meet drinking water requirements of tribals. In order to serve small tribal pockets mini pipeline scheme was introduced. This scheme involve less financial burden and ensures access to adequate and safe water throughout the year to tribal population spread in dispersed hamlets. During 2010-11, 1562 mini pipe water supply schemes were completed in tribal areas. Water quality monitoring and surveillance is carried out with active involvement of ASHA workers and medical officer-in-charge of Primary Health Centre, Every ASHA is trained for testing water quality and is provided the Field Test Kit. Families getting water at household level in rural areas has increased from 48,698 (3.9%) in 2001 to 8,59,676 (43.25%) in 2011. As safe drinking water has reached the tribal households in rural areas through taps, it has resulted in tremendous improvement in quality of life of tribals. Improvement in quality of life has reduced malnutrition among women and children. Access to adequate water has facilitated the tribals to practice safe sanitation practices, which has improved the health of people.

Transport Infrastructure (Roads) in Tribal Belt

The road network in Gujarat has always been good. A pioneer in innovation, Gujarat Government launched number of schemes to improve infrastructure in the State highways. It placed **great emphasis on highways in its development journey.** The road network has been improved over the last ten years. Gujarat has an extensive road network of 74,038 km. which includes the National Highways (2,848 km.), State Highways (18,409 km.) and Expressways (93 km.), District Roads (30,270) and Village Approach Roads (19,656) and the target of Gujarat is to increase the network and take it to 1,14,866 km. 38.2 per cent of total expressways and National Highways in the state are multi-lane; 87.9 per cent of total roads are asphalt-surfaced. Travellers shower all kinds of praises on the Highways in Gujarat. Over 90 per cent of rural connectivity in Gujarat is through its weather roads, which is believed to be the highest in India. The railway network is also quite vast and is around 5,309 km. Road length in 12 tribal districts is 17,918 km. which constitutes 24.2 per cent of the state's road network. Average road length per 100 sq.km. of area in tribal districts is 55.1 and per one lakh of population is 309.

The goal of the Pragatipath Yojana, launched in 2005, was to "connect tribal belts, coastal, industrial and rural areas with mainstream areas and the extremities of the state." The Pragatipath Yojana entailed widening and Strengthening of 9 High Speed Corridors connecting ends of the state. Total length of the project was 3710 km. at a total cost of 2488 crores. Under **Kisan Path Yojana** 7830 km. of roads have been taken-up for improvement and 3364 villages have benefited. The state has total 18066 villages, out of these villages, 17856 villages are connected with "*pucca*" roads. Hence, 98.84 per cent villages are connected by "*pucca*" roads. Out of these 17856 villages, 17478 villages are connected with asphalt surfaced roads where as 378 villages are connected with WBM surface road.

Gujarat is the first State in India to have a law governing Built Own and Transfer (BOT) transaction along with private participation in infrastructure projects. A Planning Commission study, supported by World Bank, has said that "Gujarat offers an example of international best practice in roads management. Reforms in Gujarat in the roads sector come closer to international standards for other states and developing countries to follow." In 2010, the Gujarat State Rural Road Development Authority initiated a project to use Global Positioning System (GPS) for preparing a Geographic Information System (GIS) database to implement the PMGSY in all the districts of Gujarat. **The GPS mapping and creation of a GIS database has been completed in 20 districts.** A GIS based database for building the country's rural road network is a significant achievement.

11

Translating Communitization in Health

A Case of Village Health and Sanitation Committees (VHSCs) within National Rural Health Mission (NRHM) in Jharkhand

Minashree Horo

Introduction

The Primary Health Care Approach is for addressing the health problems of the developing countries like India where the health status of its people is very poor. This approach has concern for the poor people who do not have the accessibility and affordability to the health care services. The major contributing factors to this that have been identified were the inequity that is existed within the society such as within the community, among the people and the geography. The rural areas and its people are seen as more disadvantaged group in terms of having good health care services as it hardly or improperly reached out to them. The main factors that are taking the rural areas and the poor people away from the better health care was because of the model that is techno-centric, expensive and mostly the urban based health care system. So, the approach came into existence for ensuring universal accessibility of the better health care to every individual and the community through making it more responsive by practical, scientifically sound and socially acceptable methods and technology. Thus, the approach has basic thrust upon the full community participation and the reasonable cost that community can afford and for ensuring this the approach emphasizes on giving people the responsibility of their health in their hands with the spirit of self-reliance and self-determination.

The moment health responsibility came into the hands of the people the components such as community participation becomes pivotal. And in ensuring this the governance system was approached by devolving them the powers to get the full involvement of the local people in the managements starting from the planning to its implementation. The local governance system creates a space for addressing the local health issues by involving and ensuring every individuals and the families concerns and needs. This ultimately enhances their participation and results in the fulfilment of people's health needs by the people themselves. The whole idea was conceptualized as the new approach known to be the "Communitization approach" in which government trust the community and allow them to participate in their health developments. They believe that people value health more and the returns are immediate and the sufferings are intense, so, they will be keen to participate in the process of improving the quality of services and accountability through the political control such as with the local governance. In the Communitization process, community is seen as partners with the government where they handle the management parts of the health institutions and resources set-up for their use and the government looks after the skill development part for enhancing their knowledge and confidence in taking care of these institutions.

This concept was not new in our country. Since, the Bhore Committee's recommendation of 1946, it has been suggested to involve communities in the healthcare services. Many initiatives such as Community Health Worker (CHW), Village Health Worker (VHW) schemes has been introduced in 1970s and, 1980s, but seen to be the major failure and being vulnerable because they do not seem to be firmly embedded in the communities themselves due to the lack of ownership and not driven by the community. So, the greater urge for ensuring the community participation risen and it was integrated in the health care delivery system by institutionalizing and mainstreaming it for the management and community financing to sustain the local resources as a necessity for the country where the people are poor and the environment is not so conducive for the easy accessibility of the health care services. This ultimately pointed towards the need of the political leadership, substantial and consistent financial, technical and material support.

The NRHM came into existence with the same line of thoughts and adopted the same approach for ensuring the primary healthcare for all the citizens of the country. The mission adopted the Communitization approach as per the demand of the situation by advocating the institutionalization of local health committees by giving them resources and powers for its management and utilization. VHSCs is seen as an important tool for the Communitization process under NRHM. It has the potential to ensure the community participation in the health planning and could increase the health demands from the community itself. Though there are many other components under NRHM that have been used for the communitization process such as Accredited Social Health Assistant (ASHA), Rogi Kalyan Samiti (RKS), but the VHSCs are seen to be the most important component in terms of ensuring participation straight from the grassroots level. It is capable of achieving the health goals through the collective efforts that underlying with the social capital and bonding within it, with the involvement and by representation from all the sections of the community. There is no apprehension that the collective efforts can help in making the development journey much smoother by ensuring and providing platform for the communities to address their issues and grievances related to health and other health related activities and enhance the accountability and control for better quality of health services. By undertaking this architectural correction in the health system the mission intends to ensure the better delivery of healthcare services through increased community ownership, decentralization of the programmes to the local level, inter-sectoral convergence and improved primary health care. It can be possible only if they are given much space for decision-making that increases ownerships for the resources leading to the full participation, and enhancement of their skills through capacity-building on a regular basis. After reviewing the related literatures concord with the idea that the VHSCs an important model for the communitization to enhance people's participation and accountability at the grassroots level healthcare services.

The present study is focused on the model of communitized institutions so adopted at the primary/village level, i.e. Village Health and Sanitation Committees (VHSCs). It has explored the communitization process through the VHSCs in Jharkhand a newly formed state (that) comes under the Fifth Schedule Areas with around twenty eight per cent of the tribal population (according to census 2001) along with the mandate of Indian Parliament legislation of Panchayat (Extension to Scheduled Areas) Act, 1996 (PESA). This was introduced to devolve certain political, administrative and fiscal powers to local government elected by the tribal communities in their jurisdiction allowing tribal communities with the 'radical powers' to preserve their traditions and confining them with the authority to manage their community resources (Kurup, 2008). After the separation of state from Bihar the implementation of programmes has improved, but still the state faces significant challenges in overcoming the growing weaknesses of the implementation capacity. The weak institutional performances, the newly formed local government/Panchayati Raj Institutions, inequalities in health status that exists across districts, between ethnic and social groups, and the poor and non-poor, inadequate rural primary health care services all translates into the poor service delivery including the healthcare.

So, the study is keen to look upon the communitization process through the VHSCs in the newly formed state of Jharkhand with adverse initial conditions with low average income, high incidence of poverty and little social development. At the situation where the state is at its primordial stage of development initiatives, already with the existence of the local governance system recently replaced by the Panchayati Raj Institutions (PRIs) as a forum to discuss the developmental issues that subsist, the study will try to look upon how VHSCs will help in revamping the value of the health system in the Jharkhand.

1. Methodology

1.1 Selection of the Study Area

The core objective of the study was to explore the process of communitization within the VHSCs under the NRHM through analysis of its conceptualization, implementation and community involvement. Through critically examined the designs of communitization model—Village Health and Sanitation Committee

(VHSCs) and by contrasting the outcomes of communitization in the intervention and non-intervention areas of two districts of Jharkhand. For the purpose of understanding the implementation of the VHSCs at the village level and explore its functioning, coordination with the stakeholders such as ANM, AWW and Animators and the outcomes of their functions.

The field study was carried out in the State of Jharkhand due to its newly formed status and the Economic Empowered Groups (EEG) state where the developmental initiatives are in its primordial stage. Fieldwork was conducted in the two districts of the state based on the intervention where the NGO is intervening and the non-intervention area where there is only the government's interposition.

The Gumla District was selected purposively as the non-intervention area where there is no other developmental agency apart from the government present those working for the development of the VHSCs. This was one of the oldest districts of the state which was established in 1984 (Singh, 2006: 334) and already having an established health delivery health services system. This was also purposively selected because of the researcher's convenience of familiarity with the local dialects and the availability of transportation and accommodation facility which helps in carrying out the research in good manner.

The Khunti District was selected as the Intervention area for the study because of the NGO implementations. Though the NGO was intervening in both the Khunti and the Gumla district, but the district was chosen purposively by the researcher according to her convenience with respect to the transportation and accommodation facility and also because of the familiarity with the local dialects. The district is a newly formed district in the year 2007 after the formation of the state. The district was on its primeval stage establishing its health institutions and systems. So, the researcher also chose it for having a clear understanding the effects of the NGO intervention in the newly formed district without government prior inputs for the VHSCs developments.

The Ghaghra Block of the Gumla district and the Khunti Block of the Khunti district was selected purposively by the researcher as per the convenience of the transportation and accommodation facility and the familiarity of the dialect.

The four villages of the Ghaghra block of the Gumla District (non-intervention area) were selected on the basis of the distance from the Block PHC/CHC. The four villages namely Salgi village of Adar Panchayat within the distance of 18 km, Sirkoat village of Puto Panchayat within 8 km, Sarango village of Sarango Panchayat within 12 km and the Ranhe village of Kugaon Panchayat within the distance of 3 km belongs were selected by the researcher.

Another four villages of the Khunti block of the Khunti District (Intervention area) were selected on the basis of the NGO intervention villages. The villages namely Fudi village of Fudi Panchayat, Kalamati village of Kalamati Panchayat, Manhu village of Siladone Panchayat and Chikor village of Hesahatu Panchayat were selected.

1.2 Data Sources

The researcher collected both secondary and primary data for the study.

1.2.1 *Secondary data*: The secondary data was collected from reports available with State VHSC-Sahiyya Resource Centre VSRC, evaluation reports of VHSC, Common review missions of NRHM and other articles, books and journals related to VHSC. And also at the field level documentations such as VHSC Registers, Log Books, SOE copy of the VHSC.

1.2.2 *Primary data*: The primary data was collected through semi-structured interview schedule and observation. The interviews were conducted of the respondents and the key respondents that have been selected purposively by the researcher.

(a) *Respondents:* The stakeholders in the study are village level Health functionaries such as ASHAs, AWWs and ANMs, VHSC president, VHC members, PRI members, SHGs members, Technical supporters like Sahiyya sathi (ASHA facilitator), Block Training Team, Animators, NGOs (CINI) representatives and Block & District-level officials.

(b) *Number of Respondents:* The total numbers of the respondent interviewed are 74. The Key Informants interviews were conducted with the 8 VHSC presidents, and the In-depth Interviews were conducted with the 12 ANM, 8 AWW, 15 Sahiyya (ASHA), 12 SHG Members, 8 PRI Member, 2 BTT,

2 Sahiyya Sathi (Sahiyya Supervisor), 2 NGO Animators. Using the Semi-structured interview schedule the Key Informant Interviews was conducted with 2 District Programme Coordinator (DPC), 2 Block Programme Manager (BPM) each from both the blocks, and 1 NGO Nodal Officer at state-level.

1.3 Data Collection Process

The different techniques used were in-depth interviews, key Informant Interviews, questionnaires, semi-structured schedules and observations.

1.3.1 *Interviews*: The Key Informant interviews were conducted with the VHSC President and government and development agencies' nodal officers. They were interviewed in detail. The VHSC presidents were interviewed in their respective village. And the officials were interviewed in their offices. The VHSCs other members were such as Sahiyya, PRI members and other health functionaries of the village were interviewed in their villages, at their home and also at the AWC of their village using as the centre meeting place by the villagers. An interview guide meant for interviewing them was designed for pre-test. The broad questions to meet the objectives of the study were asked. In Early December 2011, the interview guide was tested with the few VHSC and required changes in the tool were made. Certain questions were replaced with somewhat more relevant questions that emerged up during the pre-test. Also, the pre-test helped in clustering a few related questions under a broad theme. Also, pre-test helped in identifying certain broader themes, which could be explored in-depth among various respondents.

Interviews were not recorded during the pre-test, and short notes were made while conversing with the respondents and later incorporated with necessary details. The process of researcher often posed interruption on part of the respondent's in terms of enquiry about the details being noted down which often disturb the free flow of information. As later the whole interview were recorded as due to the researcher's may face problem in recording the interviews that were taking place in the local dialects. But later it is being run smoothly without any interruptions as the whole interviews were recorded and later transcribed.

The interviews were recorded by taking notes with the official respondents and also some of them agreed to record the interviews.

1.3.2 *In-Depth Interviews:* The interviews conducted during this were recorded. Before recordings, the consent of the respondent was taken and the purpose was distinctly clarified. In case of refusal, the interviews were sought to note down the necessary details. None objected on recordings the necessary details. At times memory based additions were made.

1.3.3 *Conducting the Interviews:* The respondents chosen for the study were the members of the VHSCs of the respective villages and the blocks and intervention area. The time taken by the respondents to complete one interview would vary from 40-45 minutes to 100 minutes. Since, the respondent has a busy schedule, meetings were fixed as an appointment, so that, they can give interview when they have with ample time. At the village level it was difficult for them to convince them for a long interviews session. Moreover, ethically it is unfair so the interviews were re-scheduled for the next day to continue with the other phase of the interviews with the same respondent.

1.3.4 *Other key-informants Interviews:* Apart from the interviews conducted with the VHSCs members at the village level, frequently the health officials were also interviewed in order to understand the Village health institutions and the linkages of the members with the governments and the officials. At the same time interaction with the officials responsible for the block health activities, the villagers, the headman of the village and with the PRI members were done often; give an insight of the life in the village and the institutions dynamics. Field notes about the experiences of researcher in the village were also made.

1.3.5 *Observations:* Observations were an inherent part of the study often yielded valuable information on areas where sufficient data could not be collected through interviews. For instance, the meeting regularities, the discussions on the health issues, record keeping and the sustainability of the activities that were conducted, and the power relationships and bonding between the committee members, the conflict between the members were all observed by the researcher. Apart from that the condition of the village, its people, their clothing, concern for hygiene, eating habits, social relations, beliefs etc. were also observed.

1.4 Methods used in Processing and Analyzing Data

The recorded interviews were transcribed and translated. The qualitative data was analyzed separately for each category of respondents and then re-arranged to assess similarities and differences. The domains identified after reviewing the literatures and data were collected on the basis of domains such as on community participation, decentralization, social mobilization and the communitization processes. Under these broad domain the sub-domain were identified and those are formation process, composition, roles and responsibilities under community participation, powers such as political powers, administrative powers and fiscal powers and the power structure under the decentralization, the capacity-building supports systems from the state, its structure, facilitation by the NGOs, trainings under social mobilization, and accessibility, plan, implementation, monitoring, cooperation, collaboration, knowledge and awareness in VHSC and its output under the communitization. During this the new themes were allowed to emerge through the constant connections of the sub-domains. The various qualitative data were cross studied in order to understand the inter-relation of the categories with each other. The best suited narratives were added at the times to bring the true picture that existed.

1.5 Problems Encountered during the Study

The problem of the fixed timing and appointments sometimes had hindered the interviews because the interviewees are eager to switch into the other activities that were appointed to them. The researcher took care of that the respondent does not get affected in their routine work. The distraction would often drag the respondent away from the researcher. The researcher had to try at times to bring back the respondents to the area being already discussed.

1.6 Limitations of the Study

The purposive sampling selection of the study area due to reasons of ease of the communication and familiarity with the socio-cultural set-up upto some extent has already been mentioned. Also, the study areas are having low accessibility as most of them do not have the good facility of the conveyance system. The most of the study area were got affected by the extremist (Naxal affected area) due to which researcher has to take precaution in terms of early completion of the interviews as to get her place back before late evening. Due to this many a times she has to leave the interview and postpone for the next day. Also the study deals with the VHSC of the Jharkhand with respect to various socio-economic and political factors prevalent in the area, the findings of the study cannot be generalized.

1.7 Ethical Consideration

The researcher took permission and introduced herself before conducting interviews to the respondent at the field. The informed consent was taken from the respondent before recording the data both in writings and recording with the help of voice recorder. At the village level the respondent allow researcher to use the recording device for recording the data. After the permission only she used the recording device so that he/she may not get offended.

2. Major Findings and Discussion

The whole VHSC visualized as a simple and effective management structure at the lowest level, comprising representatives from the village to initiate the community-led action.

The key function of the VHSC is to prepare the Village Health Plan (VHP), implement it and manage the fund which ventured as per the need of the community. The committee is the facilitating body for the village development programme relating to health and sanitation, and reflects the aspiration of the local community.

2.1 Community Participation

2.1.1 Formation Process

In contrast to the guideline the formation process was not followed by the proposed steps and mode of dissemination and orientation. It has been done without any concept seeding around the ideas, purposes and the role assignments to the VHSC members, village community and office bearers. The male members were discouraged to participate being an office bearers which ideally, needs to be the involvement of both the genders to ensure the better participation of the community. The whole formation and selection process of the VHSC was compromised by some dominant sections and interest groups of the community which already had a say in all the village affairs. This leaving behind the core idea of equal representation and accessibility led towards the community participation with the facilitation and acknowledgement of the perspective, view points, consents, inputs and knowledge awareness of all the major sections such as all men, women hailing from rest of the village hamlets, differing clans and pre-existing committees of a village at the entire village level. An influence exertions and pressurization from the health functionaries at block level and the PHCs such as ANMs in the selection of the Sahiyyas and VHSC President of the village and it was apparent that they were somehow already chosen prior to the village meeting. Thus, the agencies that were expected to act as facilitators assumed the role of pressure groups and reinforced their choice in the process of selection coupled with the dominance of certain sections.

2.1.2 Lack of Self-Motivated Office Bearers

In practice, taking of the responsibilities by the person for being the part of the VHSCs becomes the central issues as one cannot compel eligible persons without their interest. The criteria followed for the selection process were based on nomination by someone, status of the person, proven participation in village affairs in the past, vocal behaviour to represent villagers, articulation abilities and basic literacy to handle bank accounts and registers, sometimes leads towards the scarcity of the kind of eligible persons. Then community usually does not have any choice. And if the chosen one are not self-motivated and enthusiastic enough to take-up responsibility in serious manner then it affects in their ownership level and thus negating the core idea of communitization that "empower the motivated one instead of wasting time and money on unmotivated empowered one" this ultimately led towards the lackadaisical of the ownership an important step to achieve the participation.

2.1.3 Gender Specific Construction of the Health Schemes and Programmes

Male counterparts in the village got an impression of often disqualify or unsuitable for taking part in the activities basically for the females. Such as distributing Iron folic tablets, RCH programmes and immunization related activities.

2.1.4 Stake of the VHSC President and the Other Committee Members

President was subjected to very insignificant roles and had limited opportunities to exercise power and struggling for marinating their stake in the committees. Other committee members lack interest due to their role obscurity and involvement in the committees functions.

As a result VHSCs were not taken as serious committee lacking representation of most of the worthy and active people of the villages contributing themselves to the other committees.

2.1.5 Facilitator NGOs Performance

Facilitator NGO (CINI) completed their work in the target oriented manner just to complete the numbers that they were asked to achieve bond with MoUs.

2.1A. Composition

2.1A.1 Vivid Dichotomy between the Guidelines in Principle and Practice

Other vital aspects were compromised at the first place in order to fulfil the said criteria as per the guidelines regarding the committee's composition such as women reservation and ensuring the ST category representative in the village. In many ways these criteria proved constrains in realizing the complete participation from every sections and residents of the village resulting in exclusion of males and other social categories. The facilitators have an easy access to the local elites, dominant clans of the village, petty local contractors and mostly literate (neo-literate) avoiding residents of other hamlets difficult to access due to tough tiresome terrains with low connectivity and illiteracy of the marginal clans residing in those so-called unimportant hamlets.

The guideline generalizes ST and SC categories within which

even many marginal clans and primitive/endangered population exists in these villages were bypassed who in reality often contests with the dominant tribal population for their say and schemes that come to the village. Guideline unable to take much care of the inclusion and say of the women by focusing on the fact that women participating hails from marginal or dominant groups and due to the prior information of the major criteria few of them who resides in the same hamlet lack interest in participating as they felt already excluded with the programme. The other excluding factors were that the members are supposed to be a women and to ensure this only committee were approached was SHG of the hamlets/village by ignoring the other important committees of the village, giving an impression of VHSC as a women groups headed by the Sahiyya. It appears as if the same guidelines were misused by the facilitators to avoid taking pain and smoothen their way for getting done their work in their hand faster. The homogenizing nature of the said guidelines was realized as constrains in ensuring communitization in true spirit wherein these marginal groups within the stratified village should give proper representation by design.

2.1. A.2 Focus of State Health Policy in Strengthening Process

The State Health Policy basically focuses on the Sahiyyas for ensuring the better healthcare delivery system at the local level and undervaluing the strength of the VHSCs. It seems as patronizing Sahiyyas by making them sole player in the committee, overshadowing the roles, responsibilities and power of decision-making of the president and the other VHSC members.

2.1. A.3 Wide Information and Knowledge Gap

The Sahiyyas more powerfulness in terms of decision-making and through direct linkages and contacts with the Government officials at the block level or PHC level, and by regular knowledge upgradation through meetings and trainings widen the gap between her and the other committee members. So, the president and the other members lack the interest and ownership for the committee in them. This develops an impression that the VHSC is all got to do with the Sahiyya and she is the sole player giving a back-up and proof to emerged nomenclature of VHSC untied fund as a 'Sahiyya Fund' from the community itself. It seems supporting the people's perception and gives a glimpse of centralization of the power and resources against the decentralization a basic approach of communitization at the institutional level.

2.1. A.4 VHSCs and the Sahiyyas Role into it are seen as a Separate Entity

The other health extension workers of the village such as Auxiliary Nurse Midwifery (ANM) and Anganwadi Worker (AWW) shows least interest in taking responsibility pertaining to the VHSCs because they are already founded overburdened with the health related tasks assigned to them from the Block health departments which make them to see this responsibility as the additional task. Though the AWW they themselves belong to the same place and could help the VHSCs with her valuable inputs, but was very difficult to ensure their full participation here due to petty information regarding roles and responsibility of each other and also by sharing the status of competitors in terms of community acceptance. Despite of working as a team the president seems to be the subordinate of the Sahiyya. So, the overall impression received from the government strategy of taking shortcuts to strengthen the VHSCs by only focusing on Sahiyyas due to over-dependency of the programme officials for tracing and the follow-up of fund utilization in the village. And ignoring the other valuable elements comprising the committee due to low trust or rely upon them supposedly due to their inefficiency without considering the problems or constrains of the other stakeholders in ensuring their full participation.

2.1. A.5 Sahiyyas empowerment in disguise.

Though mostly the Sahiyyas were found to be self-motivated to voluntarily work, but they were usually pressurized to take decision under the influence of Government officials sitting at the block level or PHC. Her essentialist positioning in the community as key person is disguise due to the fact that she is also struggling to create her identity on day-to-day basis within the tensions inherently exists in rural community. The contestation among the key members/other influential groups and Sahiyya within the rural community for power and acknowledgement is an ongoing and never ending process. Placing Sahiyya in the key role reduces the project to a women centric project that negates the idea of everybody's involvement, but supports empowerment issues and leadership of rural women.

2.2 Forms of Decentralization

Forms of Decentralization by understanding the degree of space in decision-making of the VHSC member at the local level.

2.2.1 Political Decentralization

After the advent or an introduction of statutory panchayati system throughout the state in the recent year in December 2010 throughout the state, seems to have weakened the traditional tribal councils at some places, but generally speaking these statutory bodies have adopted almost all the functions of the traditional tribal councils with the added responsibility of implementing development work too. But tension between traditional leaders and the PRI members consequently tampers with the functioning of the VHSC owing to various power equations forming around contesting domains and interest groups, the tension creates and recreates. Traditionally, the self-governance has been the driving force of the village life and decision and the tribal population predominantly inhabiting in these areas are yet to adjust and harmonize with the state guided PRI structures under PRI schemes of governance. Due to the PRIs in its primordial stage, their members are not acting upon their roles in full-fledged manner due to lack of orientation and instructions by the block officials. As they themselves are in their earlier phase and struggling to develop a stake among the village and in the community and thus seems to cause the low ownership and giving less importance to the VHSC as an important committees of their village.

2.2.2 Fiscal Decentralization Perceived as Just Another Source of Fund

Due to the perception as just another source of fund, it reduces the other important components designed in the principle of the VHSC. This is seen as a tool for spending the untied fund through the proper and traceable channels which able to give an impression of collectivist in the community decisions. The self-sufficiency of the VHSC in terms of having their funds besides disbursed untied fund is an element completely missing out in the programme design. This increases the dependency of the community on the Government apparatus and thus controlling of their decisions and prioritization by petty bureaucracy at block and Panchayat level government establishments. Such dependent relations consider as a part of this general rule and make it a puppet and medium to smoothly implement government schemes on health and not fulfilling communities own health well-being demands.

This is substantiating the fact that the fiscal decentralization is very low in the VHSCs as the untied fund is based on the principle of the flexible amount spent on the priority of the community rather in actual practice the VHSCs were given a activity list and asked to ensure that they spent on the particular activities. This indicates the non-flexibility and boundary to the VHSCs in spending of the funds negating the meaning of provisioning of 'untied fund' to meet the demands of the community.

2.2.3 Administrative Decentralization

Here, in the absence of the statutory body (PRI or Gram Sabha members) involvement in the VHSCs action, the Sahiyyas are confined with the roles and responsibilities of the VHSCs. Though she has the sole responsibility, but the space she gets in the decision-making seems to be very low and thus can be realized that at what extent the power have been devolved within the health committees to create a space for the control and the decision-making for the Sahiyya as community representative. So, it can be assumed that the government apparatus VHSCs in a disguise way of lending support, facilitation towards the delegation form of decentralization seen confined only to the transfer of the managerial responsibility for certain functions pertaining to health to the VHSCs.

2.3 Social Mobilization

2.3.1 Social Mobilization through Non-Governmental Organization

In the Intervention area of CINI (NGO) basically deals with the social mobilization process to strengthen at the local level through several strategies. They have Animators who are responsible for capacity-building and awareness generation at the VHSCs and in the community. The conflict in coordination between the Animators and the Sahiyyas are evident in this area. The identified reasons were the unwillingness of the Sahiyyas to be interfered by the animators and pretending her as an outsider who are accountable to the NGOs the other agency. The visible ego clash between them because of the comparison with the amount of work load and the remuneration rewarded against them which is considerably low income in case of Sahiyya. The basic sense of discomfort of the Sahiyyas with the animators is that they are not willing to take any responsibility of the VHSCs in their hands then why interfering in Sahiyyas work through raising question in a way of monitoring despite of solving their grievances and implementation issues which seem to be logical to a great extent. The extended fact is that the animators who otherwise represent NGOs have differential intentions to intervene at different levels which is often in conflict with the practical roles of the Sahiyyas to carry out her tasks or may be Sahiyyas have self-assumed themselves in the centre stage of VHSCs would not like to share their authority and power with the animators or dislike to fall puppet of these animators.

NGO claims *Nukkad Natak* (street play) to be the most effective tools for generating awareness, but it seems doubtful as they were arranged in the time when people almost away for their daily work and it was done as the task-based manner without ensuring and assuring that it touched the cords of local issues and problems at the village level or not. Organizing the Community Based Monitoring (CBM) by the Government officials and the developmental agencies slightly brings the difference in awareness level of the VHSCs members and the villagers. But in the real sense it is unable to achieve the expected advantages, and thus provides very low opportunity and space to put forth their complaints and opinion regarding their needs of health services. This results in a low participation of the community in the analysis, planning and implementation for their entitlements. And the VHSCs contribution in terms of labour and kind still is not so much evident and to be said as a long way to go.

The question arises here is that to what extent the mobilization process of the NGOs are effective in knowledge dissemination, sensitization, and motivation and awareness generation from the point of view of the community.

2.3.2 Government Initiatives in Social Mobilization

Here, strengthening is done through the structured support system. There are several constraints in the developing of the support systems lacking basically the intangible motivational part among components of the systems. The contractual positions and the managerial orientation of the district and the block level officials complementing with low prioritization by the CMOs and MOs, focusing basically on the national level health programme with the overburdened work schedules leads towards the demotivation among the health officials though they are keen to focus on the VHSCs. There is a proper need to acquaint directly responsible for the strengthening of the VHSCs through their capacity and knowledge building regarding the need of such health committees apart from the managerial task based orientations.

2.3.2A. Capacity builders from the community: Their familiarity in the community, approachability, trustworthiness and first hand contact ability to the VHSCs members helps in bringing out an evident change at the execution level.

2.3.2B. Narrowness of the Training Contents: mostly based on the objective of fund utilization and the SOE preparation, despite of giving a clear orientation on the need and the roles and responsibilities of the VHSCs as a whole.

2.3.2C. Low sustenance of the training output: with lot of transmit losses at the execution or at the practice level is points towards the low quality of the training due to time and financial constraints faced by the officials.

In practicality the approach unable to translate in a well manner as lacking their prime purpose to make VHSC itself into a social mobilizers who creates awareness in the village about available services and their entitlements and most importantly evident in their executions. Heavy fund and time is invested towards the social mobilization process including the involvement of both government and non-governmental agencies, but the outputs in terms of capable VHSCs with the raised awareness and demands for a particular programme in terms of services delivery of resources and services and sustainability of community participation and self-reliance is yet a distant dream.

2.4 Major Issues Emerged in Communitization Process

2.4.1 *Fatigue Syndrome:* Due to disrupted fund flow the VHSCs members seem very less enthusiastic in up-taking the health related activities and meeting irregularities, no role clarity and very less space to practice innovations at the village level spreading poor presentation of the committees.

2.4.2 *Iterative Training Programme:* contents of the training programme are very iterative resulting in the degradation of the interest.

2.4.3 *No innovative activity:* same activities such as infrastructural shortcomings and sanitation drives for the fund utilization.

2.4.4 *Women empowerment in disguise:* though the 91 per cent of the VHSCs composition is comprised of women folk and headed by the women representatives, but still they are dependent on the male folk for any kind of concrete decisions such as to the Village Headman, religious leaders and influential male of the villages.

They lack support from the male part as the health activities are purely perceived as a women related activities (nursing and care giving) and due to this perception somehow clashing their male egos they hardly show interest in taking-up and supporting VHSCs members in their activities.

Overall the local people have very low expectations from VHSC in the progress of their village except confined or approach the Sahiyya for the institutional delivery purposes.

2.5 Outcome of the Communitization Process

The accessibility of the VHSCs in the Gram Sabha is very minimal. Because the Gram Sabha themselves are struggling between the two systems of the local governance body namely traditional institutions and the Panchayati Raj system, making them unable to undertake initiatives to incorporate each and every village level committees in the development process. Due to this VHSCs is definitely missing a reliable platform trusted by the community for bringing or discussing on the health needs. It was evident that the tribal community struggle with the abrupt shift from the traditional institutions to the alien concepts of elected representatives as a result there is very low participation from the tribal community leading towards the underutilization of the institutions. By overlooking the inevitable shift of indigenous laws and institutions that accompanies the imposition of non-native system of governance (Kurup, 2008). For instance the Manki-Munda system in the study area compete with the state laws enacted to impose PESA because the tribes prefer their traditional law's emphasis on collective and consensual making.

The absence of VHP (Village Health Plan) and Panchayat level Plans to support the district level development plans. It seems that the degree of community participation is in between co-option refers to the token involvement of local people with the selection of the representatives, but with no real input or power and compliance level which refers with the glimpse of incentive based tasks assignments where outsiders decides agenda and direct the process giving an impression of very low degree of community ownership and sustainability. This leads towards the non-participatory way of involvement in the implementation and execution process confined to the few sections of people. This only ensures the completion of tasks prescribed by the government with the fund utilization an ultimate objective by narrowing the broad objectives of the communitization process and deviating from the prime objectives of the VHSCs model.

The VHSCs in the study area is at its primordial stage and there is much scope for being communitized. But fact cannot be denied that its foundation is not so strong enough to support the communitization process. Community participation ideally should be based on the 'community involvement approach' or 'bottom-up approach' through 'conscientisation' with the organization and mobilization of the masses so that their consciousness could be translated into a change by supporting the empowerment model that believing in enabling the community through giving education or information and through involving and experiencing them. This further leads to gaining access and control of health care resources. Instead of 'top-down approach' where planners decided the objectives and then try to convince people to accept them with an effort on the part of government or donors to use local resources to offset the cost of services provision more efficiently, effectively or cheaply by collaborating people voluntarily or as a result of some persuasions or incentives in turns of some expected resources.

2.6 Communitization Supports the Devolution Form of Decentralization

In the study area the devolution form of decentralization is very rare and the delegation form is been practicing with the transfer of the authority and responsibility delegated from the central agencies to the organizations such as local organization not directly under the control of those agencies. But the underlying question is that whether there is an appropriate mix of central control and local management or else there is much control of the central actors. The ultimate goal or output of the decentralization is yet to be achieved due to the limitation by weak institutional base and dearth of efficient local level institutions compounded by the confusion on the concept and practice of decentralization due to lack of clarity for all the levels including those who gets benefits out of it. To create the healthy relationship to ensure more communitization the institutions (government) respect the intrinsic worth of the community, accept the idea of indigenous for the sustainable development with the cultural roots and native genius for avoiding the impositions of the foreign model supporting to the consideration of the counter rationality of the community (such as much importance to the needs according to the geography and epidemiology of the area instead of the government's own perspectives and objectives of the intervention for the programmes focusing on the few vertical programmes).

2.7 Grounded Suggestion

2.7.1 Stakeholders

This brings out the expectations of the community and the VHSCs stakeholders from the health committee. Came out from the VHSCs members are for ensuring the meeting regularity of the committees with full and active participation of all the members including the Gram

Pradhan, other CBOs, PRI and the health extension workers such as ANM and AWW. Urge for ensuring the male folk participation in the VHSCs activities undertaken in the villages and to erase the build-in perception of VHSCs as a female based affair conducted by the women folk considering only their health problems. They brought the aspect of lacking the male folk participation in the health related activities that have been undertaken under the health programmes, due to the basic tendency and the perception prevailed in the society that the activities related to the care giving and sanitations works are the domains of women and it could be the reasons for lacking interest of men folk in participating in the committees that specifically deals with promotive health activities. Ensuring the active involvement of the PRI members in the health related activities through discussing the health related matters and unanimous decision-making, in the Gram Sabha as no such instance has been taken yet. VHSCs members suggested that there is a need of streamlining the discussion on the health related issues at the village centre level, i.e. in the Gram Sabha and must be given the similar importance to the other developmental issues and programmes in the village. There must be the regular fund flow as it is one of the greatest motivation among the committee to uptake the activities by regularizing their meetings and it creates an enthusiasm among the members as well as among the community for ensuring the funds related planning and its activities implementations. There must be the regular payments of sahiyyas on time as its works as an extrinsic motivations for them to work enthusiastically on the field.

2.7.2 VHSCs other Stakeholders

The block and the district level working as the support systems such as to the BTT, Sahiyya Sathi and also the STT seems to the closest link to the community and belongs to the same locales. And they are seen as the better linkage in redressing the problems and hindrance of the field workers at the field level, and also the direct linkage with the Government officials for transmitting the valuable information. Ensuring the remuneration in a regular basis can be able to ensure the sustenance of these support systems. Enhancement in the fund allocation by the government for the training purpose for improving the logistics and accommodations facility which affects the training quality directly: this is important for retaining the quality and lessening the transmission loss for the betterment of the quality of trainings.

Encouragement for the VHP: instead of influenced plans by the health officials with the underlying intensions of planning for target fulfilments of the VHP. Community must come up with their developmental ideas for their village which later lead them to bid for it.

Giving an impression that community is not numb about the dysfunctions of the VHSCs in fact they are facing some of the structural constraints and wanted to figure out soon with the proper initiatives and supports from the government and the people themselves.

Summary

Many instances at the implementation level depicting towards the failure of the communitization process. The unsuccessful communitization process could be the consequences of the top-down approach of the decentralization adopted in the implementation as well as in its substantive content disguised in it. In terms of decentralization theory an essence of Communitization hardly is considered devolved authority because even though there has been a transfer of some degree of responsibility for regulating, the activities of the committees are not considerably outside the direct control of the Central authorities. It has become subject to simple administrative measures and decisions made by higher authorities. Second with the counter rationality that keeping away the community from its real need and the context overshadowed by the Centre's health objectives. Then the dubiousness related to the sustainability of the participation strongly arises here.

The question arises that how the communitization is possible only in the health sectors ignoring the other developmental activities and conflicts taking place around leading to the distrust towards the government by the community. So, is it possible to achieve without solving the other constraints prevailing in the society especially in scheduled area for gaining trust of the community for the real partnership.

Question that are anticipated to be answered: Is the VHSCs a model of communitization is only the medium of government programme conducted from the Central and the other way of controlling mechanism for the tribal community or is it really seen as a democratic way of ensuring people's programme from the grassroots considering the needs of the community and ensure it endogenously.

References

Abraham, C.T. (2000) "*Communitizing Education through National Service Scheme*", Published Ph.D. Thesis—Mahatma Gandhi University; School of Gandhian thought and development studies, Kottayam: Mahatma Gandhi University.

Agrawal A. and Ribot J.C. (1999) "Accountability in Decentralization—A Framework with South Asian and West African Cases", *The Journal of Developing Areas,* Volume 33, pp. 473-502.

Baru, R.V. and Gopal, M. (2006) "Decentralization and Disease Control Programmes: The Case of Filariasis" *Local Governance in India, Decentralization and Beyond*; Chapter-6, Oxford University Press, pp. 145-161.

Banerji, D. (July-September, 2005) "Politics of Rural Health in India", *Indian Journal of Public Health,* XXXXIX(3), pp. 113-122.

Chen, L.C. (1988) "Ten Years after Alma-Ata: Balancing different primary health care strategies" *Tropical and Geographical Medicine*, Vol. 40 (3); pp. S22-S29.

CINI (August 4, 2011) '*Annual Report 2010-11*', pp-3-8 (online); Available at: http://www.cini-india.org/cini.pdf.[Accessed on: Dec. 3, 2011].

Dasgupta, R. and Qadeer, I. (July-August, 2005) "The National Rural Health Mission (NRHM): A Critical Overview", *Indian Journal of Public Health,* XXXXIX(3), pp. 138-140.

Dekadt, E. (1982) "Community Participation for Health: A Case of Latin America", *World Development,* 10(7), pp. 573 584.

Duggal, R. (January, 2005) "Reveiw of Health Care in India: Historical Review of Health Policy Making", *Cehat,* pp. 21-40.

Gill, K. (March 2009) "*Primary Evaluation of Service Delivery under National Rural Health Mission (NRHM): Findings from a Study in Andhra Pradesh, Uttar Pradesh, Bihar and Rajasthan*", New Delhi: Planning Commission of India.

Government of Nagaland (2008) "*State Programme Implementation Plan 2008-09*", Draft V.3, NRHM, Nagaland: State Health Society.

GoI-UNDP Project (2011) "*Communitizationand Health—The Nagaland Experience: A Thematic Report-2009*", Department of Planning and Coordination, Kohima: Government of Nagaland.

GoJ-NRHM: "Gaon ka Swasthya Sabka Sath: Gram Swasthya Samiti-1", pp. 1-53.

Hadenius, A. (2004) "Social Capital and Democracy Institutional and Social Preconditions", in Prakash S. and Selle P. (eds.) *Investigating Social Capital-Comparative Perspective on Civil Society, Partciaption and Governance*, Sage Publication India Pvt. Ltd., Chapter–2, p. 15.

Hasnain, N. (2007) "Administration, Welfare and Development", in N. Vaid (eds.). *Tribal India.* Delhi: Palaka Prakashan, pp. 337-445.

Husain, Z. (2011) "Health of the NRHM", *Economic & Political Weekly,* XLVI(4), pp. S3-60.

Hota, P.K. and Dobe, M. (July-September, 2005) "National Rural Health Mission", *Indian Journal of Public Health,* XXXXIX(3), pp. 107-110.

Hutchinson, P.L. and LaFond, A.K. (2004) *Monitoring and Evaluation of Decentralization Reforms in Developing Country Health Sectors,* Partners for Health Reform Plus (PHR plus) USAID.

International Institute for Population Sciences (IIPS) (2011) '*Concurrent Evaluation of National Rural Health Mission (NRHM), Nagaland, 2009*', Mumbai: IIPS.

Jharkhand: An Overview (Online: Web) Accessed on September 13, 2011, URL:http://jharkhand.gov.in/new_depts/pland/Jharkhand%20Overview.pdf

Kim, IE. BAE. (2006) '*Communication strategy ananlysis of community-initiated social mobilization against a Road Dike Project in Tagrig, Metro Manila, Phillipins*', Malaysia: Asian Media Information & Communication Centre (AMIC).

Kurup, A. (2008) "Tribal Law in India: How Decentralized Administration is Extinguishing Tribal Rights and Why Autonomous Tribal Governments are better". *Indigenous Law Journal*, Vol. 7 (1), pp. 89-125.

Lesley, M., *et al.* (2004) "Comprehensive Versus Selective Primary Health Care: Lessons for Global Health Policy", *Health Affairs*, Vol. 23(3), pp. 167-176.

Mills, A., *et al.* (1990) "Health System Decentralization—Concepts, Issues and Country Experience" *World Health Organization,* Volume Part-1, pp. 21-42.

Morgan, L. (2001) "Community Participation in Health: Perpetual Allure, Persistent Challenge" *Health Policy and Planning,* 16(3), pp. 221-230.

Manikutty, S. (1998) "Community Participation: Lessons from Experiences in Five Water and Sanitation Projects in India" *Development Policy Review*, Vol. 16, Blackwell Publishers, pp. 373-404.

MoHFW (2011) *Fifth Common Review Mission Report,* New Delhi: Government of India.

MoHFW (2007) "*First Common Review Mission Report-2007*", New Delhi: NRHM (NHSRC), GoI.

MoHFW (2006) "*National Rural Health Mission—Meeting people's health needs in rural areas*: *Framework for Implmentation 2005-12*", New Delhi: GoI.

MoHFW (2006) "*Guidelines for Village Health and Sanitation Committees, Sub-Centres, PHCs and CHCs: Guidelines Regarding Constitution of Village Health and Sanitation Committee and Utilization of Untied Grants to These Committees*", New Delhi: GoI.

Map of Gumla District-Jharkhand (Online: Web) Accessed on February 8, 2012, URL: www.mapsofindia.com

Map of Khunti District-Jharkhand (Online: Web) Accessed on February 8, 2012, URL: www.indiamapatlas.com

NABARD Consultancy Service (Jharkhand Regional Office), District Agriculture

Plan—2008-09 to 2011-12 (Online: Web) Accessed on February 9, 2012, URL: http://www.sameti.org/RKVY/SAP/Agri%20Plan_Khunti.pdf.

NRHM Community Action (2008) "*Community Based Monitoring of Health Services under NRHM Jharkhand: A Pilot Initiatives—A Report; 2007-08*" (online), Available at: http://www.nrhmcommunityaction.org/media/reports/JH/CBM_Jharkhand_report%5B1%5D.pdf. [Accessed on Sep. 3, 2011]

Obergon, R. and Waisbord, S. (2010) "The Complexity of Social Mobilization in Health Communication: Top-Down and Bottom-Up experiences in Polio Eradication", *Journal of Health Communication,* Volume 15:S1, pp. 25-47.

Pandav, C.S., *et al.* (2005) "National Rural Health Mission: From Idea to Action", *Indian Journal of Public Health*, Vol. XXXXIX, No. 3, pp. 111-112.

Public Health Resource Network (2008) "*An Assessment of the Status of Village Health and Sanitation Committees in Bihar, Chhattisgarh, Jharkhand and Odisha*" as on March 2008, pp-1-130 (online); Available at: http://www.phrnindia.org/Village_Health%20and%20Sanitation%20Committee.pdf. [Accessed on: Aug 2, 2011]

Pandey, R.S.; Yhome, K. (2010) "*Communitization: The Third Way of Governance*", Downloaded from www. cdj.oxfordjournals.org at Jawaharlal Nehru University on Sep. 13, 2011.

Population Census of India (Online: Web) Accessed on: November 20, 2011, URL: http://www.census2011.co.in/

Population Census of India (Online: Web) Accessed on: Nov. 20, 2011, URL: http://www.census2001.co.in/

Rikfin, S. (1996) "Paradigm Lost: Towards a new understanding of community participation in health programme", *Elsevier Science B.A.,* Volume 61, pp. 79-92.

Singh, S.K. (2006) "*Inside Jharkhand*", 2nd Edition, Ranchi: Crown Publication, pp. 193-266; 280-299.

Shoultz, J. and Hatcher, P.A. (1997) "Looking Beyond Primary Care to PHC: An Approach to Community Based Action", *Nurse Outlook,* 45(1), pp. 23-26.

Smith, B.C. (1997) "The decentralization of health care in developing countries: Organizational options", *Public Administration and Development*, Vol. 17, pp. 399-412.

Shah, A. (1998) *Balance, Accountability and Responsiveness: Lesson about Decentralization.* Washington D.C.: Research at the World Bank.

Sandham, O.J. (5th January, 2009) "Unique Experiment of Communitization in Nagaland", *Kangla Online Your Gateway....* [Online] Available at: www.Classic.Kanglaonline.com, [Accessed on 3 September 2011]

Sinha, A. (2008) "*Role of Civil Society Groups in Supporting District Health System*", Regional Conference on "Revitalizing Primary Health Care", Indonesia: WHO.

Sahiyya Movement, Jharkhand (Online: Web) Accessed on March 6, 2012, URL: www.hsprodindia.nic.in/retopt2.asp?SD=25&SI=5&ROT=4

Taneja, D. (July-August 2005) "National Rural Health Mission—A Critical Overview", *Indian Journal of Public Health,* XXXXIX(3), pp. 152-155.

USAID (2003) "*Community Particpation and Mobilization: Participation's Handbook for Higher and Lower Local Governments*", Kampala: Ministry of Local Government.

Venkatesan, V. (2002) "*Institutionalizing Panchayati Raj in India*", Institute of Social Science, New Delhi: Concept Publishing Company.

Village Heath and Sanitation Committees (Online: Web) Accessed on: September 1, 2011, URL: http://www.nrhmassam.in/pdf/guideline/guideline_vhsc.pdf.

Welschhoff, A. (2006) '*Community Participation and Primary Health Care in India', Dissertation*, Unpublished, submitted to Ludwig-Maximilians-Universität München.

WHO (1978) *Primary Health Care: Report of International Conference on Primary Health Care.* Geneva: WHO.

WHO (2002) "*Global Programme to Eliminate Lymphatic Filariasis—Annal Report on Lymphatic Filariasis 2002*", Geneva: WHO.

World Bank (2007) "*Jharkhand: Addressing the Challenges of Inclusive Development*", Poverty Reduction and Economic Management; Washington D.C.: India Country Management Unit, South Asia.

WHO (2007) "Health Sector Reform in India—Initiatives from State", Vol. II, Nagaland: WHO-India.

Index